Praise for *Voice in the Wild*

"Everybody has experiences of things that aren't supposed to be able to happen, and suspicions of truths to be found in folklore and mythology, as well as in the many stories from around the globe about animals. Laurie Sarkadi dares to tackle such events, stories and intuitions, speaking of them from her own considerable experience as a wife, mother and journalist living for twenty years 'off-the-grid' in the Northwest Territories, as well as from her early life as a young world traveler. From the mountain gorillas of Rwanda to the bears of Canada's North, Laurie Sarkadi has gathered lore and applied it to her own experiences. Readers will be surprised and fascinated by this unusual, truth-telling, often funny and beautifully rendered memoir."

–Sharon Butala, author of *Wild Rose* and *The Perfection of the Morning*

Praise for Laurie Sarkadi's "The Bear Within," from the anthology *Dropped Threads 3: Beyond the Small Circle*

"While few would be surprised to learn that Margaret Atwood's entry 'Polonia'—which like all stories here, focuses on issues of wisdom—is a delight, readers will be taken aback by the unexpected elegance of Laurie Sarkadi's 'The Bear Within,' which traces the connection between motherhood and nature..."

–*Amazon.com*

"Writer Laurie Sarkadi, mothering in the isolation of the Far North in the company of black bears, slips easily between telling her own story and that of the bears that shadow her days. There is a sense of holy in this piece, of the mysterious and deep connection between the human world and the natural world."

–*Edmonton Journal*

"The high points included... the startlingly spare but elegant prose of Laurie Sarkadi's 'The Bear Within.'"

–*Toronto Star*

VOICE IN THE WILD

a memoir

LAURIE SARKADI

VOICE IN THE WILD

a memoir

Verge Communications Ltd.
Yellowknife, NT

Cover photo by Angela Gzowski copyright © 2016
Cover and book design by Pamela Schoeman, Laurie Sarkadi copyright © 2016
Illustrations by Jessica Gowling copyright © 2016

Excerpt from *The Perfection of the Morning* © 1994, 1995, 2005, 2012 by Sharon Butala. Published by HarperCollins Publishers Ltd. All rights reserved.

Excerpt from *Dropped Threads*, "Seeing." Copyright 2001 Sharon Butala, published by Vintage Canada, a division of Penguin Random House Canada Limited, reprinted with permission of author.

Excerpted from *Cloud of Bones* by Bernice Morgan. Copyright 2007 Bernice Morgan. Reprinted by permission of Alfred A. Knopf Canada, a division of Penguin Random House Canada Limited.

Excerpts from *Medicine Cards*, by Jamie Sams and David Carson, published by St. Martin's Press are reprinted with permission of the Authors. Copyright 1988 and 1999.

Excerpt from *Women Who Run with the Wolves*, by Clarissa Pinkola Estés, is reprinted with permission of Penguin Random House LLC. Copyright 1992, 1995.

"Bear: Awakening the Unconscious" previously appeared as "The Bear Within" in *Dropped Threads 3, Beyond the Small Circle* (Random House Canada); portions of "Caribou: Abundant Giving" appeared in *Canadian Geographic* (Canada); "Seagull: Subtleties of Communication" was excerpted in *Room* (Canada).

Canadian Cataloguing in Publication Data

Sarkadi, Laurie, 1962 –
Voice in the Wild
ISBN 978-0-9949132-4-1
1. Animals 2. Spirituality 3. Women 4. Nature 5. Sexual Abuse 6. Travel
7. Memoir 8. Arctic 9. Northwest Territories I. Title II. Sarkadi, Laurie

The author wishes to thank the NWT Arts Council for financial assistance with this work.

Printed and bound in Canada

To my mother, Janet Ilene (Chato) Taylor [1940-2008], and my grandmother, Jolayne (Kovrig-Chato) Novak [1917-2005].

And to the survivors of residential schools who were taken from their mothers and grandmothers.

We are in an age that has severed itself from Nature and Magic. Our fellow creatures, the animals, exhibit habit patterns that will relay messages of healing to anyone astute enough to observe their lessons on how to live... The lessons taught are eternal and they are forthcoming. If the learning is over, so is the magic and the life.

- *Authors Jamie Sams/David Carson*

Contents

Note to Readers...xi

Preface..xiii

1 GORILLA: Mutual Caring...1

2 BEAR: Awakening the Unconscious...19

3 CARIBOU: Abundant Giving..29

4 CRAB: Leave Your Shell...47

5 DEER: Gentleness and Loving..63

6 RAVEN: Magical Darkness...81

7 DRAGONFLY: Unexpected Change...95

8 BEE: Power of Cooperation..111

9 PRAYING MANTIS: The Prophet...125

10 SEAGULL: Subtleties of Communication...............................145

11 SWAN: A State of Grace...163

12 WOLF: Teach Me...187

Sources...207

Acknowledgments..211

Note to Readers

I have just used first names, and in a few cases, pseudonyms, to protect the privacy of people with delicate stories.

All italicized paragraphs are compilations of paraphrased information from sources referenced at the end of the book. Every effort has been made to track all sources over the years. My apologies for any inadvertent omissions.

Preface

It's rare for a young mother of three sons, including twins, to spend her days listening to the huff of a black bear or the howl of a wolf while gazing over a lake where she can dip a cup and drink. Rarer still—she's doing this from a two-storey home in the woods of *Denendeh*, the Subarctic Northwest Territories, completely independent of power or water lines, untethered from the rest of civilization. This was my life more than twenty years ago when I began this book about the synchronicities and confluences I experience with creatures of the wild. There were other things happening back then, legal events that shook me to my core and left me feeling isolated and needing solace. I discovered that solace in my connection with nature, and in my writing about that discovery, experience by experience. While the children are now grown, and the stress in my professional life has eased, I still live in the same house, in the same way. It continues to feed me.

I moved to Yellowknife, Northwest Territories, as a journalist in the summer of 1989. My plans to move to Africa and write overland travel books had just gone down in flames—inextricably linked as they were to a romance that started in Tanzania and ended when he suffered an acute case of cold feet. I believed my new job criss-crossing the Arctic as northern bureau chief for the *Edmonton Journal* would be a satisfying replacement for being in Africa—and I was right. Both places teem with animals large and small in thick migrations, exotic birds, dizzying swarms of insects, majestic landscapes void of human-made scars, and Indigenous people who still believe their heartbeats are an equal part of this giant symphony, no more or less significant than any other instrument in the orchestra.

In between my travels chronicling the changing worlds of Inuit and

Dene, I married and moved to our house by a lake in the boreal forest, a part of Akaitcho Dene traditional territory. Foxes, loons, ravens, bears, lynx, wolves, mosquitos—all share this diverse, wilderness neighbourhood anchored solidly on Precambrian rock. This close connection to nature, where I'm literally walking on the earth's crust, opens me to its lessons. That's a good thing, for I have much to learn.

I seem preternaturally inclined towards controversy, or it to me. As a young journalist, then as a mother, I sparked two legal uproars in the North over sexual abuse and the rights of women and children. The first episode led to a disciplinary inquiry into a territorial court judge over comments he made to me in two interviews about his views on why sexual assault sentences in the North were more lenient than in southern Canada. The second entanglement involved a defamation suit against me after I spoke out about the school district's mishandling of allegations a principal was sexually abusing adolescent girls at a public school.

Both of these events nearly paralysed me with stress and fear. I felt I was speaking up for the legions of abused women and children whose voices were not being heard. But in the process, I too was silenced by a cumbersome legal system.

At the apex of this upheaval, fractured and fragile, I underwent a profound transformation, one I can only describe as an awakening to a heightened consciousness. Like Leonard Cohen says, it's as if I had to *crack* a little, in order to *let the light in*. As I gradually put myself back together, I realized the cracks had become windows allowing more and more light in. Through serendipitous encounters with people near and far, I became aware of powerful forces that could protect and guide me and were intrinsically linked to nature. As I sought to better understand this relationship, I came to look upon animals, birds and insects as messengers providing clues to a deeper and more meaningful way to interpret my life and redirect my energies.

Most of my creature encounters have been in the flesh: the mountain gorillas of Rwanda, waves of migrating caribou on our frozen lake, dragonflies landing on my outstretched arms when summoned. Others came to me in archetypal dreams. I read voraciously to interpret these visitations, seeking meaning in myth, symbolism, biology. And I sought teachings from the Dene, Inuit and other First Peoples.

A colleague at CBC Yellowknife—where I worked for sixteen years producing northern television and radio after leaving the *Edmonton Journal* —told me, "Once you start thinking this way, your whole world changes. You can no longer watch an ant walk by without wondering 'what is it trying to tell me?'" He was born under a lean-to of branches in the Mackenzie Mountains near the Yukon-Northwest Territories border and spent his first eight years travelling with his small clan of *Shuhtoatine*, the Mountain Dene, by moosehide boat and dog teams. They spoke their own language and lived in harmony with their formidable northern environment using skills and knowledge passed down through the ages from their ancestors. He was unaware other people existed until he was stripped from his family and forced to live under the harsh rule of church-run, federal residential schools. While assimilation into Christian, Euro-Canadian ways and systemic abuse persisted under this system for more than a century (the last residential school closed in 1996), it's remarkable to me that within my lifetime, at age 54, there are still Indigenous Canadians who began their lives wholly immersed in nature. Such exquisite experience. Such important knowledge. He said some Dene can see a physical manifestation of their animal spirit guides and are able to talk with them in times of need, such as when trying to decide which directions to take in the bush.

Many Indigenous peoples accept that a psycho-physical nature exists as part of "reality," that a sixth sense allows us to "know" or interact with matter or energy beyond our physical realm. Some scientists don't acknowledge this belief as credible, mainly because it's difficult to prove through experiments, but as the French playwright Victor Hugo once said: "Science has the first word on everything and the last word on nothing." While I'm not religious, and hold in the highest esteem the genius of physicists who've dedicated their lives to understanding the world and the universe, there's still a considerable amount we don't know about both. According to NASA, the visible universe—everything on earth, the solar system, other galaxies and all that can be observed through instruments—adds up to less than 5 percent. The rest is an invisible substance called dark matter, and a force that repels gravity known as dark energy. Yet their properties are unknown. Ninety-five percent of our continuously expanding universe remains a mystery.

Within that context, science is still working towards fully understanding gravity, light and time, questions of such considerable heft it only seems prudent to keep an open mind when pondering the ultimate nature of things. With the modern focus on technology and large migrations to cities, many people feel estranged from the animal kingdom, but evolutionary biologists, such as E.O. Wilson, believe our *desires* to connect, to have deep and intimate association with the natural world and its creatures, is something built into our DNA—a biological need handed down from the earliest hunter-gatherer times. Wilson defines this connection humans seek with the rest of life as "biophilia," our hereditary dependence on nature for everything from sustenance to spiritual satisfaction. Although many of us now respond more to our digital devices than the call of the wild, our time in machine-regulated, artificial environments represents only a tiny speck (1 percent) on our evolutionary scale. So, Wilson argues, we're still instinctively and genetically rooted in nature. In the book *The Biophilia Hypothesis*, which he co-edited, Wilson says this is why zoos attract more people in Canada and the United States than all major professional sports combined, and why people in cities continue to dream about snakes for reasons they can't explain.

For me, lessons from the natural world are weekly, if not daily, occurrences: black bears roam my dreams, as well as my deck, teaching introspection; wolves inspire me to persevere. As my worldview aligned more towards primal thought, I discovered my own spirituality and, to my surprise, it has a voice that sings. I began to believe that our material reality has some transcendental underpinning, in fact was given my own proof of it. My answer to the existential question, "Is this all there is?" became a heartening, "No."

I did not want this book to be a journalistic "he said, she said" attempt to set the record straight on my experiences with the legal system (tempting as that may be), mostly because revisiting them in such detail would feel, and read, like the bitterness of a court battle. And to what end? Justice can take many forms, over many years, perhaps many lifetimes. I wanted, instead, to write of the magic and wonder that unfolded for me during that time of tumult. I wanted to pay reverence to nature's majesty and reach out with healing thoughts, particularly to those who suffered abuse as children and still carry a Great Hurt.

That reverence and those healing thoughts are wedded in each chapter to a particular animal, bird or insect that was pushing its way into my physical world—and my psyche—at that time. It was easy to recognize the creatures most linked to a significant challenge or event. More painstaking was the research into all aspects of its being: its physiology, mythology and mating habits; how it rears its young, and how it is portrayed in folklore, religions and popular media. All that to find clues about the lessons I could learn from them. More challenging still is now alchemizing that knowledge into wisdom, the kind that directs the path towards a higher self, and the steps I believe I'm meant to take as I walk this earth.

Part of discovering that path includes wrestling with what Jung termed, "the shadow," our alter ego, the "dark side" of our personality. I tell you this because it's often the creatures (or people) we fear or dislike most that hold the key to unlocking the shadows of our consciousness. According to Jungian psychology, none of us can be fully whole until we access this darkness, listen to it, perhaps wrestle with it, then integrate it into our identities. I would not be surprised if this book prompts some re-evaluation of the thorny relationship you may have with the squirrel helping itself to your birdseed, or the spider cascading towards the kitchen sink on a dangerous mission to sip from a single droplet of water pooled on the drain. A friend who was sorting through a difficult life passage once took time to watch a spider in this very scenario. When it had satisfied its thirst, successfully negotiated the concave, stainless steel ascent, and survived the brightly lit, naked exposure of its silk-road trek back to its web on the ceiling, my friend felt renewed, inspired by the spider's daring and tenacity.

Even in the most urban settings, Mother Nature's rhythms form the backdrop of our lives: the wax and wane of the moon, the traversing migrations of the songbird, earthworms emerging after a rain—then slinking out of view. By consciously relating these events to our own lives, by acknowledging our shared world and interdependency, we grow in respect for nature and, in turn, for ourselves. I hope this book will grow your appreciation for all creatures, large and small, that inhabit our earthly collective. If you find these stories at times a bit fanciful, good. I can assure you, I've aimed for truth in every word.

GORILLA
mutual caring

1

November 1987

A percussive sound like no other—primal and urgent—pierces the thin mountain air; a rapid *POK-POK-POK-POK*... so near it steals my breath and rattles the empty space in my lungs. I look in anticipation to the Rwandan leading us up the steep slopes of this misted volcano, a high point amongst central Africa's towering Virunga Massif. *Yes,* he nods, mock-beating his chest with cupped hands. His *panga* slices the thick curtain of vines and nettled foliage before him, all that separates us now from a family of mountain gorillas. We crouch through the leafy portal, like time travellers stepping back seven million years for a visit with ancient kin.

After chimpanzees, gorillas are the next closest living relatives to humans—sharing 98.4 percent DNA.

A phalanx of two-dozen shaggy black bodies barely registers our arrival. A few cast furtive glances, but most continue grooming or lolling on their backs or pulling choice shoots of bamboo and wild celery from a carpet of jungle greens. Their trampled quarters smell earthy and reassuring, like a well-kept barn. I want to pile in with them a-la Dian Fossey, feel their elongated arms drape across my back, their leathery hands explore my long woolly hair—but I am restricted to one hour of voyeurism at a polite distance.

The gorillas' habituation to people in part explains their calm, but an enormous male, easily the weight of three men, has much more to do with their sense of security. He surveys his anthropoid clan like a sentry, making rounds on curled knuckles and the soles of surprisingly petite, human-like feet. A saddle of silver fur across his muscled back demarcates him as leader. He lies down casually on his stomach, propping himself up on his elbows and the feathered fur of his forearms—like a child playing cards—and stares at me. It is his job to protect the females and his progeny from predators.

The first recorded gorilla sighting was around 500 BCE by the explorer Hanno who described capturing women with "hairy bodies" who "bit and scratched... and would not follow us. So we killed them and flayed them, and brought their skins to Carthage," a city state in what is now Tunisia.

Sadly, Ian isn't here with me. He stayed at our base camp just outside the boundary to Rwanda's Parc National Des Volcans. Last I saw him, he was greasing the ball joints on our itinerant home, a 9-tonne Bedford army truck retrofitted as a bus, which he drives through Tanzania and Rwanda with adventure-addicted tourists, of which I am one. I took an extended leave from my job as a newspaper reporter in Alberta to travel Africa, a dream I've had since the first intoxicating images of its wild kingdoms held me spellbound to the television as a young child. I came here by myself for a six-week tour, along with nineteen other international adventurers. In that sense, it hasn't been the most intimate of settings for my burgeoning love affair with Ian, but the backdrop has been stirring and romantic: the warm embrace of the Indian Ocean, teeming migrations on the Serengeti, elephants and pink flamingos in Ngorongoro Crater.

My relationship with Ian has complicated the dynamics of a group with high expectations of its leader. From the first day when he ordered us into the sweltering markets to buy provisions, to our unintended overnight stay in Maasai territory—the truck sinking ominously into mud as the red-ochered faces of young warriors watched in bemusement—we have all depended on him for everything.

The male silverback gorilla is the centre of the troop's attention, making all the decisions, mediating conflicts, determining the movements of the group, leading the others to feeding sites and taking responsibility for the safety and well-being of his followers.

Resistance was futile. I could no more stop myself from loving Ian, than I could stop loving Africa. Stepping out of the Dar es Salaam airport, my first breaths of coastal Tanzania—a steamy mix of chlorophyll, salt water and sweat—rushed straight to the limbic system of my brain, that emotion-processing home to our "pleasure centres," the place where, when fired up, euphoria lives. The high-definition colour and vibrancy of the plants, birds, people and animals, that low hum of energy (perhaps the sound of heat) that so boldly distinguishes equatorial Africa from northern Canada, infused me like a garden hose to parched soil. I became my own Eden.

Ian was wearing that most seductive of male uniforms—faded jeans, a soft cotton T-shirt and a weathered Akubra hat from his Australian homeland—when I first met him walking along Kunduchi Beach at the run-down Rungwe Oceanic Hotel, the starting and end point for the many overland trips his employer offered through Africa. I wasn't initially signed up for the gorilla trek, but listening to those who had just returned from one piqued my interest. I arranged a switch through Ian. He had been scheduled to lead my original trip, but at the last minute was reassigned to the gorilla trek when its driver took ill. From the outset, our union showed signs of destiny.

A mechanical engineer and machinist by trade, Ian was a logical thinker with sturdy hands and a wiry body. I watched him maneuver our aging vehicle through Africa's crumbling infrastructure, all the while catering, with relentless good humour and teasing, to the demands of his international passengers. He rarely shaved, but his dark scruff never matured into a full beard and his eyes sparkled underneath the thick leather brim of his outback hat and boyish curls. He wielded both a playful immaturity and the self-assured charms and resolve of a man who loves his life. I wanted in.

We did the anticipatory dance of two people attracted to one another but still unsure of the other's intentions—those electrifying accidental brushes of skin, moments caught staring for no reason—until he sat beside me one night at a local watering hole in Rwanda's capital of Kigali. As Bob Marley's *Stir it Up* pulsed through the speaker, the Mitzig quarts of beer flowed freely and we were close enough that the sides of our limbs touched, often. Then, in some strange flashback to Grade 8, *Stairway to Heaven* floated out as the last song and we got up to slow-dance it together, our arms draped across each other's backs, his hands exploring my unruly, thick and tangled tresses of brown curls. Both of us laughing.

The next night we set up one tent instead of two.

It is the female gorilla's responsibility to initiate mating with the dominant, silverback male.

~

My first trip to see the gorillas had been a gruelling, three-hour ascent up the Visoke volcano, past women hoeing tiny plots of fertile soil, along steep ruts formed by the pound of elephant feet and buffalo hooves, into a rainforest where George Schaller once observed ancient Hagenia trees exhale their wisdom through beards of lichen and gallium vines. In contrast, my second visit is a low-altitude walk in the park, with Ian by my side. Our tracker easily locates the gorillas and in less than an hour, I am once again camera ready and revelling in the company of these gentle giants.

This prolific group reminds me of my childhood gatherings with my mother's large extended family, my doting Hungarian aunts awash in babies and toddlers while the older children somersault across the living room; the sheen off my glorious grandmother—most likely working in the kitchen—reflecting in all of us. Here, fuzzy black apes the size of dolls are wrapped in their mothers' arms. Slightly larger gorillas pick their way curiously through food stocks or tumble over one another. I am kneeling down, beading in on one with my telephoto lens, when I feel a strong tug on my camera strap.

I expect it to be Ian, but instead I look down into the glassy round eyes of a tiny baby gorilla. It is staring at me, childlike, as if imploring a chance to peer through my camera. To see what I see. I experience a split-second of rapture before a scream, too shrill and powerful to be human, accompanied by a thunderous charge through the trees, fills me with terror.

An older female gorilla with wrinkled, sagging breasts has been spying on us from behind a bamboo thicket, and does not like what she sees. She is coming fast towards me beating her chest and I want to turn and flee but remember I am to move back slowly and look away. The little one has bolted like lightning, leaving me staring at the ground with a pounding heart.

The mountain gorilla's fierceness has been seen protecting its young from illegal animal traffickers intent on capturing baby gorillas. For every mountain gorilla baby that is found in the marketplace, an entire family of gorillas has died trying to protect it.

I hear low grunts. The trees are still. Slowly I look up to see the grandmother halted at the edge of the clearing, our guide communicating a collective apology through his twenty-some learned gorilla vocalizations. His body language is submissive. She is appeased, but continues to watch me with distrust.

I would never, ever, do anything to harm the young ones, I convey silently as I step backwards, my head down in deference. *I would help protect them.*

∼

Ian and I are sitting cross-legged on the open deck of a ferry, traversing Lake Victoria's Mwanza Gulf, plotting our future together. We are in a rare moment of oneness with Tanzania's punishing midday sun, made tolerable by a breeze that wicks the sweat from our skin and fans us with swirling, invisible droplets of evaporation. A plan combining our two vocations—journalism and expedition guiding—pours out effortlessly. Ian will drive us through every country in Africa, and I will write and take photographs along the way for a series of overland travel guidebooks. It is everything I've ever dreamed of—a writing career combining perpetual motion in the natural world, with a mate who shares my animal instincts. We'd been together ten days.

There is a definite chemistry to falling in love, something psychiatrist Norman Doidge calls *globalization*, an enthusiastic state filled with so much optimism there is no room in the brain to feel, or even consider, anything averse in the world. The Africa-Ian combo had me completely globalized. Doidge explains that lovers in the throes of early romance experience an effect similar to that caused by cocaine: they have so much dopamine impairing their judgment that they think *everything* is good, and, like an addict, they want more.

I wanted more of Ian just at a time when he had begun feeling pressure to distance himself from me, and he went out of his way to encourage me to perform extra work duties to appease those group members who disapproved of my *de facto* elevated status.

Female mountain gorillas can spend as much as 50 percent of their resting time and approximately 20 percent of their feeding time within five metres of the silverback male. Females appear to be more responsible than males for maintaining social proximity with the group leader.

Part of Ian's strategy was to encourage me to go off on my own. At his insistence, I climbed Africa's highest peak, Mount Kilimanjaro, without him, although I made sure to carry his walking stick with me to the summit. And, also at his insistence, I remained an extra week in Tanzania at the end of the trip so we could at last experience some time alone together. We booked into an airy, marble-floored hotel along the Indian Ocean with a spectacular Arabic dome and rounded archways—everything white—in a lobby and mezzanine permanently open to the heavens. We sailed a catamaran to a deserted island and watched distant fishermen in their dugout dories while we gorged on thick, juicy mangoes, shared Marlboro cigarettes and made love in the ocean when we thought no one was watching.

I left for Canada at Christmas with a detailed expedition To Do list: contact Toyota about possible Land Cruiser sponsorship, establish freelance connections, investigate solar chargeable computers, mosquito nets...

Ian wanted to complete a few more expeditions with his company in Africa and perhaps the Middle East before joining me in Canada. "We'll be together soon, Mate, don't you worry," he told me, wiping away my tears.

~

LAURIE: DO NOT OPEN UNTIL YOU ARE ON THE PLANE
The words stare up at me from Ashley's envelope. It is April, and I am leaving Los Angeles on the second leg of a marathon journey to Australia to meet up with Ian again, when I remember to open the card she had given me back home in Alberta. We haven't known each other long, but had formed the quick bond of two single women new to town, with time on their hands outside of work to share meals, hikes and discuss with edito-

rial veracity the steady stream of social injustices that form the backbone of a journalist's workday.

A bald and hapless Ziggy character wishes me, "Have a wonderful time," as he waves at a red airplane. Inside, Ashley writes: "Give Ian a big Canadian hug, eh! Phone me as soon as you're back in town." Oh Ashley. Such a sweetheart. She's like a puppy, albeit a drinking, smoking puppy, full of energy, easy to love, a little scrappy. A bit of a homebody—I don't think she'd ever been on a plane herself—she, more than any of my friends, has been vicariously caught up in the excitement that keeps building in my life like a giant wave carrying me on the crest of its swell.

Shortly after I returned home from Africa at Christmas, Ian wrote to ask if his younger sister Jill—who was on a student exchange in South America—could stay with me while she visited Calgary for the 1988 Winter Olympics. When, instead of Jill, Ian walked through the airport arrivals gate wearing his Akubra hat, an oilskin slicker and a smile as wide as Australia, I felt as if I'd been struck by lightning and infused with a high-voltage happiness almost too bright to bear.

Two days into our reunion, while strolling past an *Edmonton Journal* newspaper stand, I stopped, yanked Ian's hand and we both stood there slack-jawed. Above the banner was a photo of the silverback male gorilla that had so captivated me, the gorilla on his stomach "playing cards." My photo. Inside: more of my photos and there, gracing the front of the science section, a full-page article I'd written about gorillas. I'd sent this freelance effort out to several papers, including my own, but this was the first response I'd seen. It was "a sign" that our Africa plans were on track, we marvelled. I would be able to write and sell our story.

Our cross-continental courtship took a detour to Banff for a weekend of skiing in the Rockies and planning our next moves: Ian was to resume his work in Africa (just a few more trips there... and an attempt to cross Iran... and maybe one or two trips in South America... then he should be in Canada by September). While in Banff we decided I would meet him in Australia for his brother's wedding in April, and spend some time snorkelling. My supportive bosses granted me yet another leave, I scraped together the airfare, and here I am, counting down each second until I land in *Oz* and can breathe him in again.

"It's just completely undemocratic, a farce really," I spew to Ian as I slam my notebook down on the dining room table. Conservative Prime Minister Brian Mulroney is in Edmonton campaigning for his fall re-election, and I covered the event for the Canadian Press. I got a job with the wire service shortly after my three weeks in Australia and moved into a rental house near downtown Edmonton. Ian finally joined me there at the end of the summer. While he hasn't yet found work, my career is taking off, and that bodes well for expanding my contacts and laying the foundations for our Africa books.

"There's this giant protest against Mulroney with hundreds of people backing the Lubicon Cree who want a treaty but are getting royally screwed out of their ancestral lands by oil and gas and logging companies. But the national press just blindly follows Mulroney into this gymnasium where all these card-carrying Tories are cheering and a completely staged speech takes place. All the other people there, including me, were forced to watch the event from a television in another gym. Canadians won't even get a chance to *see* the protest!"

Ian is listening, but he looks pale.

"Are you alright?" I ask him.

"Mate, there's something I have to tell you."

And so it began. That giant wave I had been riding for almost a year slammed me with cold indifference into a break wall. Ian had been in Edmonton less than two months, but he missed his expeditions and felt he could not endure the time it would take to raise the funds and prepare for our return to Africa. He just couldn't do a Prairie winter working at an under-the-table restaurant job, not when the entire world was already his oyster.

In the wild, gorillas like to sing after a fierce thunderstorm has ended and the sky has cleared. They do not sing in captivity as a rule. No mountain gorilla has ever survived in a zoo.

Reminiscent of the Blue Rodeo song climbing the charts at the time, I was a casualty of *Bad Timing*. I met Ian a year-and-a-half after he'd made the painful decision to leave Australia—and a fiancée there—to pursue a job with a London-based overland tour company, a career that couldn't have been more tailor-made for him. He'd paid a big emotional price for his brief, exhilarating independence. His former fiancée still loved him, I know, because she'd continued to write him until he explained his new circumstances to her when we were in Australia. But he did carry her letters in a bag, along with correspondence from other women he'd met in his travels, including a voluminous amount of passionate mail from me.

Gorillas live in harems, generally with one dominant male and several females.

He loved me. This I'm sure. How else to explain his presence, however fleeting? Or his tenderness, or gentle, romantic notions, such as his response to my suggestion that I cut my thick mane of hair for practical reasons before we reach Africa.

"Oh no Mate, don't do that."

"But how will I stay cool?"

"I will braid it for you every morning."

While bonding is the main function of grooming in primates—being groomed prompts a release of beta-endorphins that cause pleasure and relaxation—it also serves a hygienic purpose.

The ensuing days before his departure, as he arranged flights and was readily welcomed back to England by his employer, we lived in love purgatory. While I ached to spend every last minute with him, intuitively, a sense of self-preservation kicked in. I banished him to the guest room where my dog Abby, a German-shepherd cross, took up residence. In her concern for the pack, I'm sure she sensed Ian was even more alone than I was. I told him we were to have no contact once he left—I would not put my life on hold awaiting a reunion that might never come, while he answered his calling. There would be no phone calls, no hopeful letters to carry around in the bag. If he was moving forever out of reach, the sooner I reconciled myself to that the better.

To this end, on the cold December morning before he left, we stood facing one another in the drab kitchen of my inner-city Edmonton house, every ounce of African sunshine drained from our weary, tortured beings.

"Well, I'm going to be late for work," I said with forced steeliness.

"Mate, can I hug you, please, to say goodbye. I am so sorry. Please."

I knew if I let him put his arms around me in that moment, my heart, swollen with the heaviness of sorrow and lost dreams of a future, would burst on the spot, hemorrhaging all of my love for him and Africa in an unstoppable flow. "Goodbye, Ian," I said, then turned and walked out the door.

Koko, the female gorilla born at the San Francisco Zoo in 1971 who was taught extensive sign language, has watched the movie Tea *with Mussolini several times. When it comes to a sad part where the boy is leaving on the train and waving good-bye to all his relatives, Koko turns away from the TV with watery eyes, signing, 'frown, sad, cry, bad, trouble, mother, love." She cannot bear to watch.*

~

These harrowing winter storms along Alberta's Highway 2 are legendary. For all the heartache it's come to symbolize, I'm grateful tonight for my used four-wheel-drive Toyota Land Cruiser. I'd bought it to surprise Ian after we checked it out in Edmonton and he said it would be ideal for our venture. While he slept, I drove it home and put a big "Africa or Bust" sign on the windshield. The fact he blanched at the sight of it, instead of jumping for joy, was the first presentiment that he was having second thoughts. He offered to sell it for me before he left, but I'd sold my Nissan Micra to pay for it, so I needed a vehicle. I pull into a highway truck stop to get some diesel.

I'm too lazy to throw on my winter coat, and a hat would ruin my hairdo, so I let the sleet lash my face and dress clothes, still too numb to feel much of anything anyway. The worsted wool men's suit I'm wearing was bought at the Salvation Army in Lethbridge years before. It still had its original price tags from England—never been worn—and was such fine cloth I had the jacket custom fitted and the slacks tailored into pencil pants. My friend Roger, an author, has invited me to a splashy Christmas party with literary types. Roger is the only person who predicted my "Great White Hunter"—as he'd unapologetically called Ian—would not go the distance with me. Poor, cynical Roger, I'd thought at the time.

A drip of diesel lands on my boot, then a tear, as I remove the nozzle. I am able to hold myself together for eight-hour stints of newsgathering, but outside of work, I cry most of the time. It's the loneliness. Working alone on night shifts has done little to promote my social life, and I know no one in Edmonton. I call Ashley almost every day looking for sympathy, and she gives it. She drives in once to visit me, and it's as if I've been released from an isolation cell, so comforting is the sound of another person in my home.

The only time a gorilla is solitary is when it is emigrating from one group to join another. Usually it is leaving its natal group.

My house is a museum exhibit of painful memories. Before Ian arrived I'd sold my living room furniture to frame the African art, photographs and maps we'd acquired on our travels, including an enlargement of my photo of the poker-faced silverback gorilla staring at me through two blades of grass, the one Ian and I had once taken as a sign our future was bright. Now I stare back at that gorilla and wonder if it's been trying to tell me something else all along.

Among some creatures—the dog, wolf, rhesus monkey, gorilla and man—a direct, unwavering stare is a form of threat.

I take a few seconds to dry my face and re-pin the hair that's blown out of my up-do, before firing up the diesel engine and returning into the dizzying black and white eddies of the highway. This is the only party I have marked on my otherwise blank social calendar, the one event—with its promise of stimulating, writerly conversations—that forced me to crawl out of the doldrums and add a veneer of shine to my sad and dreary self. I'd arranged to stay overnight at Ashley's after the party. Finally, some company.

∼

Unbelievable. I've reached the party but every door is locked. No lights are on. Clearly, this venue is closed. Maybe I'm at the wrong place. I drive to Roger's townhouse.

"Come in," he responds to my knock.

I open the door. He's lying on the couch wearing sweatpants and a T-shirt, watching hockey on TV.

"What the...? What are you doing here?" he asks, putting down his bag of chips. "And dressed like *that*?"

"I came for the Christmas party."

"It was *last* weekend."

This news doesn't shock me. Disappoints me, yes. But my life is so disjointed, so out of my control that no matter how much authority I try to exercise over it, not getting what I want, what I crave, is beginning to feel the norm.

Roger laughs and invites me in. We talk books most of the night and true to his nature, he says, "I told you so," about the Great White Hunter, although he was most interested in hearing about our snorkelling experiences along Australia's Great Barrier Reef. I leave in better spirits.

Ashley isn't home when I get to her house. On her kitchen table she has left a note.

LAURIE,

I'M AT THE HOSPITAL. NEED A CONTROLLER. CALL NURSE SUE AT THE PSYCH WARD IF YOU WANT.

I quickly dial the number.

Ashley had arrived by taxi twenty minutes previously, I'm told. She's waiting to see a doctor to get a sedative, her "controller." She seems calmer now, but she'd been talking of suicide.

I get back into the Land Cruiser and drive to the hospital. Ashley's pacing back and forth under the unholy, blue-bright glow of the emergency ward's florescent lights. I call her name and she looks at me with such frightful wildness that I think she's going to bolt. It takes a few seconds for her to register it's me.

"I don't want to wait any longer for a doctor," she says, resuming her pacing. "I want to go home."

I smell alcohol on her breath and ask if she's taken any pills.

"No. No pills."

I speak with the psychiatric nurse who says if I think I can handle the situation, we can leave. This isn't the first time Ashley has sought some type of sedative at the hospital. Not the first time she's not trusted herself to be alone.

"I'd like to take her home, maybe go for a walk, then I'll make her a cup of tea," I say. "Let's try this way for a change. She usually doesn't have anyone around when this happens."

She's never told me all the details, but I know that somewhere in Ashley's childhood, she was sexually violated. Otherwise hearty and accomplished, she's had vital pieces of herself stolen by this horror so that, as an adult, she's never been quite whole, never been able to stare down the demons alone when the darkness of her past lurches from the shadows. Alcohol and drugs are her emotional anesthetics, as is the way for so many victims of child abuse, and when those can't numb the pain, she contemplates what she thinks will be a more permanent release.

We don't go for a walk, but back in her kitchen I pour out the beer she's started on and replace it with a cup of tea with honey, which she declares she "doesn't fucking want," but drinks two cups anyway.

"I couldn't believe it when I saw you at the hospital," she tells me, "dressed in that black suit, with your hair all up and those silver rhinestone earrings. It was like you were some knight in shining armour coming to save me." She yawns and I convince her to go to bed.

"I'll wake you up in the morning with a good breakfast," I promise her.

We are finding our way, Ashley and I, like lone gorillas excised from the troop. That night I feel like a silverback, regulating her movement, her food and drink, protecting her from the chill of loneliness when the sun sets, just as she'd done for me.

I know with the right help, Ashley can bring back to life what was stolen from her so many years ago: the part of her that could have the courage and strength to bark back—without booze or drugs—when the black dogs of the past scratch at her door. I realize I, too, have to find a way to beat back the demons of my own mounting depression, write a new adventure for myself. Rise from the ashes.

∾

I'm standing at the receptionist's desk at the *Edmonton Journal* showing her my engagement ring, a nineteenth-century family ring purchased at an antique store. It's been just over a year since Ian left. I work for the Journal now, but I live in Yellowknife, Northwest Territories, where I am northern bureau chief for the newspaper. I'm just passing through on my way back north after having met my family and future in-laws in Ontario for Christmas. The receptionist excuses herself to answer a call.

"Yes, yes she does. Yes, in Yellowknife. But the strange thing is, she's working here today, she's standing right in front of me. Would you like to speak to her? Okay. Hold the line, please." She pushes a button and looks at me.

"Laurie, there's a call for you from Australia, a man named Ian." I ask her to transfer him to my desk.

∾

When I was working for Canadian Press in Edmonton, desperate for adventure and distraction from the shadowy demands of my broken heart, I was assigned to follow up the *Globe and Mail's* story about the surprising discovery of Persistent Organic Pollutants, or POPS, in the Arctic. With virtually no industrialization in the region, the Arctic was thought to be one of the world's most pristine environments. PCBs, DDT and other contaminants from countries around the globe were being drawn north on air currents, then working their way up the food chain: fish, caribou, seal, polar bears, and the Inuit who depended on those food sources, all tested positive for the pollutants. I begged my bosses to fly me to Baffin Island for a series of articles on how POPs were affecting the people of Qikiqtarjuaq (then Broughton Island), where the studies had taken place. They agreed. Soon I was travelling by dog team on the frozen Davis Strait with esteemed hunter Pauloosie Koonelusie, checking seal nets in minus forty-two degrees, garbed in caribou-skin pants and a parka I'd borrowed from the RCMP.

When I motioned to him that my feet were cold, despite the waterproof comforts of my handmade sealskin *kamiks*, he took off his *kamiks*—which had long, burnished red fur—and traded them for mine.

"Husky. Best warm," was all the English he could muster. As the saying goes, I walked a mile in Pauloosie's moccasins that day; I felt the haunting richness of the natural world all around me, the austere, animal-dependent landscapes of the Arctic and its people. And, like my first breaths of Africa, I wanted more.

I applied to become the Journal's northern correspondent, nearly camping out on the managing editor's doorstep until I got the job. In the summer of 1989, I moved to Yellowknife with my dog Abby as a record-breaking heat wave was taking hold. For weeks on end, temperatures surpassed those in California, and the beaches were far less crowded, too. A manic sun that would not rest until fall guided midnight canoe trips across clean, drinkable lakes and rivers. I set up the bureau in a small house, on an island facing west across Back Bay, where sunset hues of pink, and gold, and mauve, and orange lingered behind corrugated clouds. The summer heat was nice, but it was the autumn cold I responded to most. The frigid, dry air seemed barely to contain oxygen, forcing me to breathe deeply, maybe zapping my heart with a little bit of freezing, until gradually my grief no longer poured out in great gushes each time I wondered what Ian was feeling, but instead trickled out like a partially healed wound; forgotten until it's knocked or scraped, and bleeds anew.

On Thanksgiving weekend I went to dinner at a chef's home, which he'd converted into a mini version of the dining room of the large hotel where he worked. A handsome man chose to sit across from me. He extended his hand with explosive enthusiasm, knocking over my glass so red wine ran spilled across the white tablecloth towards me like a river of blood on a frozen pond.

Replacing the linen wasn't an option, it was heavily weighted down with utensils and people had begun sitting with heaped plates and salivary anticipation.

He opened his napkin and softly laid it over the damage, like a covering of fresh snow, so it was no longer a distraction.

"There," he said, flashing a charming smile. "Let's start again. I'm Francois."

He extended his hand with undiminished enthusiasm.

I'd heard about this Francois from a lawyer friend. He's intriguing, she'd said, and very attractive, but a bit of a lone wolf. He won't let anyone get close.

He was forthcoming enough with me, sharing that he was born in South Africa and moved to Canada when he was ten, which explained his glimmer of a slightly twisted British accent. He'd wandered north with a friend, looking for work after studying forestry in college and landed a job with the territorial government. We talked a lot about South Africa, apartheid, Zimbabwe (where his mother was born). The entire evening rolled out with such beguilement, our common love affair with Africa sizzling and popping like a campfire that begs to be stoked and tended, I completely lost track of time.

"Oh, I have to get going," I told him. "My dog's waiting for some company."

"Mine too," he said.

I didn't think about him again until I was standing downtown a week later with my back towards Franklin Avenue, in conversation with the same lawyer friend, who interrupted me by exclaiming, "Look, there's

Francois!"

I turned around with incredible speed and blurted out, "Where?" in an urgent, breathy voice that took even me by surprise.

His vehicle had passed, and I missed the opportunity to catch a glimpse of him, but clearly my instincts were telling me I'd caught the scent of something worth pursuing.

I met Francois again on Halloween. I was a witch, dancing by myself, when someone dressed in white, wearing a bowler hat and a large black star painted on his check—a droog from the movie *A Clockwork Orange*—began circling me on the dance floor. Eventually, I figured out who it was and in between dances, we talked. He told me he'd seen me driving around town and liked my Land Cruiser. Since his house was on the way to mine, we ended up there. A fairly weathered and unassuming trailer from the outside, inside was a cozy brown lair of cedar-panelled walls with a crackling wood stove. We put the Scrabble board sitting on the table to use, he made me a cup of tea, and as the bewitching hours drew to a close, he covered me with his duvet on the daybed and retired to his room.

The next morning, he made a wicked batch of scrambled eggs, the consistency and fluffiness of whipped cream just before it starts to peak, on toasted rye bread with a hint of butter. I learned quickly he was a consummate epicurean. Obsessed with every aspect of food, from procurement and preparation, to presentation and ingestion, he reminded me of a wild animal on constant high alert for its next meal. He could hunt, butcher, cook and serve, and shared the fruits of his labour with grand generosity.

I left his trailer with no exchange of phone numbers, no promise of a next meeting. We'd spoken at breakfast of wolves. "I have a book at my house," I'd told him, "filled with amazing photographs and text by Candace Savage." I'd scooped it from the review collection at the Journal before I left, and had just started to read it. The author lived in Yellowknife and much of her research had been conducted in the Northwest Territories with the help of people in Francois' department.

I was holding onto that book the next day, thinking I might drop it by his trailer later on, when the phone rang.

"I saw the phone number for the *Edmonton Journal* in the book and then the next thing I knew, I had the phone in my hand and I was dialling it," Francois told me.

"Well, I was just thinking I'd like to come by tonight with that wolf book to show you."

The first few encounters with Francois, I couldn't look him in the eyes. It was not that he threatened me in any way. Far from it. He just shone too brightly. There was a strong, effervescent energy inside him, the kind of vitality that can only emanate from a fiery core, which made looking into his eyes—those "gateways to the soul," as Shakespeare called them—feel a bit like staring at the sun. Best to just sit in the radiant heat until things cooled down some. Plus, he had a beauty that surely would have rivalled Paris' when Hera, Athena and Aphrodite were seeking out the world's most handsome mortal. I didn't want to be caught staring.

One day, as we warmed ourselves by his woodstove after a long hike in the bush with our dogs, I told him I'm most happy when I'm outside. "I can't believe this place, I truly love it here," I told him, to which he stopped and said: "I can't believe you exist."

On the tenth day of our courtship, he set the salad bowl in front of me on his small, wooden table and as he turned to fetch the rest of the meal, casually asked: "So, when are you going to marry me?"

Marriage hadn't been something I'd allowed myself to think about since Ian had rejected my suggestion we marry to facilitate his ability to work in Canada. He'd reassured me in so many phone calls and letters that we would be together forever that it seemed, to me, little more than an administrative detail. Obviously, he felt differently. Francois' question seemed to knock the wind out of me, like a hard landing after days of jumping for joy.

"You know, you can't joke about that," I told him. "I'm still feeling pretty fragile."

"I'm not joking," he said.

"Well then, whenever you want, I guess."

And with that, we wolfed down dinner, perfectly seared steaks he'd managed to barbecue in the Arctic cold.

When I gave Ian the "do not contact me" decree before he left, I invoked a total and immediate blackout to our relationship, creating a void so deep it felt as if he'd died. But I'd left the door open a crack as well. I told him that if someday, it didn't matter when—five years, ten years, two months—he was absolutely certain he wanted to come back to me, he could telephone. He had to be sure, and it had to be a phone call. We could reassess our situations at that time. I had not heard from him, until now.

"Hello," I say.

"Hello Mate, how are you? It's good to hear your voice."

"It's good to hear your voice too, Ian," I tell him, amidst a heavy drone of traffic noises in the background. "It sounds really busy where you are."

"Yah, I'm at a phone booth along the highway. I was driving, and I just had to talk to you."

"Why Ian? Why are you calling? Do you want me back?" I've never been good at small talk and sense this is not the time to start.

"I'm heading back to Africa, Mate, and I thought maybe I could stop in Yellowknife and visit you."

"It's hardly on the way Ian. And you don't want to stay, right?"

"No, I can't stay. I have to get back to Africa. I just really want to see you."

For all the hurt Ian caused, I always understood the powerful forces that pulled him back to the open road and continue to hold his allegiance. They pull me, too. He was not a vagabond. He had a job that paid him to wander exotic places with interesting people. And now I did, too.

"I don't think it would be a good idea to come, Ian. I just got engaged three days ago."

"Oh Mate, congratulations. That's wonderful. I'm really hap... " CLICK
The line goes dead. In the few minutes before the receptionist alerts me that I have another call from Australia, I take stock of how clear and resolute I am about my future, how unflustered I am by his call, which only a few months ago would have left me shaky and weeping.

"I'm sorry Mate, my money ran out," says Ian, a bit breathless. "I had to go get some more coins. I just didn't want you to think that I hung up on you because of what you said. I'm happy for you."

"I know you wouldn't do that, Ian. Thanks for calling back."

"Well, I don't have much time left. The phone is going to... CLICK

In groups containing only one silverback male, females disperse and find new social groups after the death of the silverback.

2

BEAR
awakening the unconscious

A mother black bear is visiting our house. I've awaited her return for four years. Her young ones are with her: two. My three sons, and Francois, are with me.

We watch through the big square window in our kitchen. She sniffs the air before rising onto her hind feet to walk towards me. For a moment we stand face to face, staring through the glass into one another's eyes. I know I've been given a powerful message, the breadth of which I will decipher later. But one thing feels certain. I am safe again.

The Pawnee of the American midwest believe when a bear stands on its hind legs and lifts its paws towards the sun, it is receiving its healing powers.

The decision to move to a property alongside a small lake outside of Yellowknife, beyond the reach of city services, such as water, electricity or cable, had an air of newlywed rashness, but wasn't without impetus. The owner of the quaint bungalow in Old Town where I'd set up the newspaper bureau (the same one, coincidentally, Elizabeth Hay lived in when she worked at the CBC in the seventies and later wrote about in her Giller-prize winning novel, *Late Nights on Air*) gave notice she planned to retire there, so, just a few months after Francois and I were married, we had to shop for a home.

We first stepped foot on the property in the frozen depths of winter, when everything but the long-vacant house and the spindly spruce and pine of the boreal forest was hidden beneath snow. I walked up to a wood-pecker hammering on a jack pine tree, close enough to feel its reverber-ations in my chest, and immediately decided this was where I wanted to live. The bird made no attempt to distance itself from me. I felt welcomed, as if I too belonged. Later, we toured the shag-carpeted interior at night with flashlights because the realtor didn't know how to start the diesel generator. Upstairs, the commanding view of the frozen lake reflecting sparkling glints of blue and silver from a full moon's gaze drew gasps when we pulled back the dusty curtains. Sold!

In April 1991, we began "to live deliberately," as Thoreau once said of the rigors of rural solitude. With no utilities, we are completely left to our own devices to acquire water, power and heat. Even in the minus forty degree jags of winter, we augur a hole in the frozen lake, unfurl a long canvas fire hose down to it, and pump water up to a thousand-gallon hold-ing tank inside the mud room. Once the tank's filled, we quickly recoil the hose lest it freeze pencil stiff. When there is sun, solar panels charge the large batteries that funnel 12-volt power into an inverter, which flips it to AC, so we can watch TV, turn on lights and listen to music. When it's dark, or we need to power up energy-sucking items like the wash-er-dryer, we start the generator. For the seven months of the year that we require continuous heat, the heart of our home is in the kitchen—a boxy, flat-topped wood stove pulsing its fiery radiance into the main arteries of the house. Wood-hauling features prominently in our lives.

This wasn't perpetual motion in the natural world, with a mate who shares my animal instincts, in the way I'd imagined my life with Ian. I'd never envisioned myself a homeowner, or a mother. But there was an organic flow to our movements as Francois and I planted roots in the thin layer of topsoil that nurtures so much life atop the bedrock foundations of Akaitcho Dene territory. Perhaps on some level, I knew I would travel in different ways here.

In this Subarctic frontier, unburdened by the technological crush of civilization, I am able to feel the ancient ways of knowing that guided the Dene. This is where my odyssey of motherhood begins: alone in the woods, save for the babes at my breast, the ravens outside my window and the unspoken mysteries beyond. The more I seek to unravel those mysteries, the more I see of the bear.

~

Francois and I discover the bloated, fetid bodies of some three thousand whitefish, northern pike and suckers floating beside our new home in June 1991. The lake's giant ecological belch, later deemed a natural phenomenon caused by algae dying and robbing the water of oxygen, is a wonderful way to meet the new neighbours, who mind not a whiff that the place stinks. Gulls and ravens gorge on the death, yielding only to the authoritative swagger of a half-dozen bald eagles. Three black bears appear at the farthest point of our bay, eating their way closer to us each day. When they finally reach our driveway, Francois yells, "Go away bears." And they do.

We conceive our first son in July after a spicy hot sauna and naked dip in the lake.

July is a time of estrus for female bears and promiscuity for both sexes.

The first thing I do after confirming my pregnancy is cycle ten kilometres, rationalizing that childbirth will require the ultimate fitness and stamina. My mind brims with thoughts of the new life inside me, of how I will do everything within my power to ensure it grows into a healthy baby. As I near the steep hill that always defeats me, I look to my left and see a bear running beside me. We travel at exactly the same speed, glancing at each other, straight ahead, then back at each other. A surge of adrenaline wells from my abdomen, from the embryo itself as I imagine this fledgling being ripped from inside me. "Not now," I say to the bear. "Not with my new baby." The big hill fast approaches.

As I begin my ascent, so does the bear. My thighs feel detached from my upper body, now rigid from my death grip on the handlebars. I reach halfway, the point where my legs and lungs normally scream in agony, without being winded. The bear veers left into the thick brush. I cycle home as if two lives depend upon it.

In time, I conclude the bear was a test. My instinctual reaction to protect my unborn child had been correct. As for physical fitness, what further proof did I need that my body is capable of feats I cannot yet imagine? Like the bear, I am strong and protective, fit for motherhood. My prize comes the following April. A son.

Bear cubs and their mothers emerge from their womb-like dens together in April, a time of rebirth and new beginnings.

I nurse Max day and night for nearly two years. I am mesmerized by his beauty, and both ferociously protective of, and exhausted by him. During this period, no bears visit my house. I see bears along the highway, but always far from my home range.

Most male black bears avoid the territories of lactating females, preferring those in heat. Mother bears generally move out of another bear's territory, rather than risk a turf war.

Each day I anticipate hiking through the wilderness with Max on my back. One morning, I cross-country ski under a canopy of bent willow and spruce laden in hoarfrost. We're showered in sparkling light as the sun refracts off the icy branches like diamond confetti on a snowy bridal path. "Nice," a little voice from behind whispers. It's only the second word I've heard Max speak. So calming, so invigorating are these enchanted woods compared to housework and its nagging drudgery, I never give a thought to any possible harm. The forest casts a benevolent spell over us.

∼

I'm pregnant again. This baby is due in November, the same time tiny blastocysts in a pregnant black bear have to decide whether to attach themselves to her uterine wall.

The fertilized eggs in a bear sow float freely in her womb for five months until she is ready to den. If she does not have the fat reserves necessary to bear and nurse her cubs through winter, the blastocysts dissolve, sparing her the agony of starvation.

I miscarry at eleven weeks.

Sympathies pour in, but I revel in relief. The disquieting depression that accompanied this pregnancy has been a bad hormonal trip. I drink beer and paint Zulu and Haida designs on the kitchen and garage doors, unable to discern if I'm being driven crazy—or kept sane—by my environment.

My dog Abby is barking maniacally at a raven as it taunts her from the roof. Max toddles out and conciliates the dispute by speaking to the bird *in* Raven. Then I watch all three of them walk side-by-side down a path, Max in the middle, the raven hopping awkwardly, struggling to keep up. In that moment, I realize there's greatness and beauty and magic in my life, if not adult conversation and paycheques.

Come winter, I crave another baby, mating dutifully on all optimum days for conception. My pregnancy is quickly apparent. At three months, I look six months along. I cup my swollen belly, musing that this cannot be just one baby. It isn't. Like a faulty gumball machine that drops more than one goodie at a time, I have doubled ovulated.

Copulation induces ovulation in a female black bear shortly after each encounter.

As my September due date looms large, so do the pressures of toting my enormous girth. My pointy, rock-hard abdomen juts out like the conical nose of a twin-otter airplane, skin stretched so taut it's bordering on see-through. I turn forgetfully and whack it on things, nearly passing out from the pain. My stomach prevents my arms from reaching the kitchen sink to do dishes, and I am grateful when my mother comes to look after me. I insist she and Francois help me into the forest—easing me down on my side, so I can pick cranberries. Other than that, I'm too slow and foggy to do much except wait.

As bears prepare for denning, they can spend virtually the entire day resting. This is known as "walking hibernation."

At term, I deliver my strapping twin boys, naturally. Both Calvin and Levi wriggle determinedly for sustenance at my breast, latching on hourly after that with a tenacity that leaves my nipples chafed and bleeding and fuels record-breaking weight gains within their first month.

Mother black bears nursing multiple cubs have been known to splay themselves belly down to stave off relentless feeding efforts.

The twins are in baby swings on the deck watching Max tour in his push-pedal car. I'm doing dishes. Two cubs play in a tree at the back of our house while their mother grazes below. When Francois spots them, he tells them to go home. The mother gathers her young and walks away.

August 19, 2002, a healthy black bear in the resort town of Fallsburg, New York, knocks five-month-old Esther Schwimmer out of her stroller and carries her into nearby woods where she dies of head and neck injuries. A wildlife pathologist says the bear may have been attracted to Esther's milky odour.

Sleep is but a fantasy. By October, when bears crawl into their dens, I wear my fatigue like a disease. Each day becomes darker and drearier, heightening my desire to curl up and tune out. Occasionally, all three boys fall asleep with me in bed after nursing in our den of flannelette and down. The heavenly gift of sleep, the four of us enveloped in darkness. For all the times I miss the work world, this isn't one.

By November, the mother black bear's metabolism slows to half its summer rate. She continues to slumber while her cubs are born in January or February, blind and nearly hairless. They are about eight inches long and weigh less than a pound. The mother begins an external pregnancy, or second womb-time. Even in this suspended state, she is able to respond to her cubs' cries and needs, maintaining a level of sub-conscious caregiving.

The bears are out in force the next summer, all around our house. Our first encounter is a mother with two cubs no bigger than teddy bears, and a much larger third, shambling across the road. She manages only a glazed stare of forced interest in the direction of our van. Her ribs show through her dull-and-matted fur. *They're sucking the life right out of you, aren't they, I commiserate.*

It's a plentiful season for raspberries. We pick at a nearby patch we call Raspberry Heaven. At just eleven months old, Levi rips whole branches off, stuffs them in his mouth, then spits out the unwanted bits. Calvin wants the berries from my hand or basket. I lead them to the richest bushes then try to pick elsewhere, but they follow me. Eventually I just stay and turn the laden branches upside down for them.

Do you do the same for yours? I wonder of the mother bear, sensing her nearby.

Black bears can articulate the claw tips of their forefront paws to grip branches when feeding on berries. But most often they grasp the morsel behind the incisors and pluck it with a pull of the head.

As so often happens, Max responds to my private thoughts.

"I'll use my knife, if we see a bear, Mom," he says, proudly displaying the old fish scaler we'd dulled on a rock then given to him.

I smile. "We'll just go home if we see a bear, Max."

I pack the twins into the pouch of my *amautiq,* an Inuit coat designed for carrying children on your back. Walking home along the highway, a man in a pickup truck pulls up beside us.

"Ma'am, you better get out of here quickly. There's a mother bear and three cubs just up the way."

We're very close to our house, I say, thanking him, and stifling the urge to add, "I know." I step up my stride, and my focus, until we're safely home.

By late summer, the mother bear looks magnificent. Her fur is thick and shiny. She's put on weight and seems more alert. The same can be said of all three cubs. I'm happy for her, and I'm feeling better myself these days. On the eve of his first birthday, Calvin weaned himself, leaving me only the occasional feeding for Levi. Without the demands of nursing, my body becomes more selfish of the calories I take in. Increasingly, I have five or more consecutive hours of sleep. My heavy stupor lifts.

Daily hikes are still integral to my happiness, but when the twins get too big to carry in my *amautiq*, I push them along the highway in a double stroller. One day in September, a cold, snowy rain pelts down the back of an icy wind. I put off the walk until I can no longer stand the anxieties that accumulate after a day cooped inside. The twins howl in protest as I strap them into the stroller, while a raven stares down at our spectacle from a tree. "I hope I get an especially good reward for this," I say to the bird.

We manage the equivalent of a city block when the dog bolts across the road and begins chasing a bear, towards us. I turn the stroller around and order Max to head home. "Don't run!"

Fleeing-prey behaviour can trigger a bear's predatory pursuit instincts. In July 2000, Canadian Olympic biathlete Mary Beth Miller of Yellowknife is killed by a black bear while jogging outside of Quebec City.

When the galloping bear is right beside us, it glances at me, then veers in the opposite direction.

∼

Max is five. We take him on a fishing trip to a pristine lake accessible only by a gruelling trek through five kilometres of swampy, mosquito-infested portages. The night before the trip, I dream I'm standing with the children on a concrete platform of stairs surrounded by lake and woods. Francois is canoeing towards us when a male bear, snarling and frothing at the mouth, appears in the water behind him. When Francois tries to climb onto the concrete, the bear claws and eats his arm and back. I clang on a pot with a wooden spoon. The bear rears on its hind legs, twists its head towards the sound...

I awake so tired and hazy, I forget to tell Francois the dream.

Five minutes after launching the canoe, we see a bear on a flat outcrop of rock ahead of us. It paces back and forth, then sits complacently on its haunches, content to watch us drift silently past.

The summer is hot and dry, fraught with forest fires and long spells of single parenting as Francois' job is to help mobilize the government's fire-fighting response. I grow ambivalent about an ambitious home renovation—telling the workers to go home—when a nearby fire closes our road to traffic and ash rains down on the skeletal frame of the new playroom. My most immediate concern is keeping my three energetic boys from slipping unannounced into the blackness of the lake, or dismembering themselves with power tools. A cousin arrives in the midst of this mayhem with her three-month-old son, whose tiny lungs cannot handle the black smoke outdoors, or the choking drywall dust inside. I feel trapped and personally responsible for everyone. Daily, I consider fleeing my home range.

Mature mother bears may spend 75 percent of their time in the company of their offspring, compared to males, who remain solitary except when breeding or when congregated at plentiful food sources.

The fire dies before it reaches our house. The workers, and Francois, return.

~

I'm driving in our truck with Levi to pick up bookshelves. When we return, the other two boys and my neighbour Jeanette are playing on the driveway. Levi's asleep in his car seat, so I open both truck doors wide to keep him cool and load myself up with wooden shelving. A few strides past the truck, I hear the loud *crack* of a branch snapping under enormous weight. I turn to stare directly into the black-rimmed eyes of an adolescent bear. An unsavoury list of options flashes before me. I choose to run, lumber in hand, up to the house, yelling at the others to get inside. I retrieve a pot and spoon from the kitchen, race back outside, then freeze.

I don't want to confront this bear.

I don't want it to maul *me*.

I *have* to rescue Levi—I know I *will*—but I don't want to.

These fleeting, unmotherly thoughts make me feel selfish and ashamed.

Clanging the pot and bleating strange noises, I leap up and down to make myself appear large and foreign as I head blindly toward the bear, unaware that Jeanette has already scared it away by rustling gravel in a metal dog dish. She's standing near Levi as he awakes. I walk over, draw him close and breathe him in deeply.

My relationship with the bear changes that day. I'm afraid to go camping, afraid to pick berries, afraid to fish. Bears disappear entirely from my natural landscape, and I struggle to understand why. Have I offended the mother bear's protective spirit? Am I being punished for having put my own safety before my son's? These questions can't be answered until I see one again. I need to feel a response in my belly to know whether symbiosis will ever be possible again.

∼

I'm painting the deck when I hear on the radio that a black bear has killed a camper about two kilometres from my house. Helicopters swoop overhead with infrared scanners, and SWAT teams and wildlife crews assemble to hunt the marauding killer. June 2, 2001, eighteen-year-old Kyle Harry becomes the first recorded person fatally attacked by an American black bear in the Northwest Territories, suffering more than two hundred severe puncture wounds from teeth and claws over most of his body. His left arm and lower back are eaten. The bear is shot, but only wounded, by an RCMP officer. Search crews scour the region. Parks close. Roadblocks and traps go up. I'm oddly calm. My anxieties having borne fruit, Kyle's tragic death feels sadly conclusive.

Wildlife officers shoot and kill the wrong bear before eventually gunning down a second, which has matching bullet fragments from the gun of the RCMP officer in his body. This emaciated animal has other puncture wounds, including a large hole through his sinus that probably blinded his right eye. Experts say he was likely attacked by another bear, perhaps a week before Kyle's death. I'm relieved to learn the killer may have been going mad.

It's still another year before the bears make their return to my kitchen window. I safely observe them from inside; my gut instinct is one of relief and joy.

Perhaps I wasn't being punished. Perhaps the mother bear's spirit was guiding me all along, instilling fear to protect the children and me. For all I know, the young bear I encountered that fateful day with Levi was the same adult male that later killed Kyle Harry. A medicine woman I consult tells me punishment is never part of an animal's psyche, or part of our own higher selves or the divine, that imagining it only creates fear. You either live in love, or you live in fear, with all its manifestations. She suggests I created the fear because I felt I needed to punish myself.

For what though?

For harbouring ideas of abandoning my relentless responsibilities? From the entropy of housework, the daily hand-to-hand combat with human excrement, the unsexiness of fatigue, the stress of keeping everyone alive, the longing to resume my career? All true. But ultimately love, beauty and magic have a greater hold than any of this.

When the bears come back to me, it feels counterintuitive to shoo them away. I can't hide my true feelings from one I see on the escarpment behind our house.

Oh, all right, I do love you, I confess in exasperation. But twenty-seven people will be camping here tomorrow for a family reunion. It's best if you stay away. It appeared to listen, then lumbered up the hill.

Two days later, at 4:45 a.m., the dog is barking. Francois gets out of bed and eventually spots a bear heading away from the house. My sister-in-law later notices the clock stopped at 4:50. She changes the batteries, but it never works again. Jung calls these meaningful coincidences, "synchronicity." The Dene call them, "medicine."

For me, it's subtle communication with the otherwise intangible forces of nature. Magic.

3

CARIBOU
abundant giving

Max is still a babe in arms when the caribou arrive unhurried and unannounced on our frozen lake. First in small groups, then swelling into hundreds, then thousands, their leggy, silver-brown bodies move like puffs of campfire smoke in the morning fog; their sharp-edged hooves dig into ice like teeth into a snow cone.

Perhaps it's the caribou's giving nature, perhaps they don't know to distrust us, but as we stand awestruck amongst them, they soldier past with minimal wariness, unfazed as well by the steady crack of nearby gunfire.

Some Aboriginal people credit their very existence to the abundant charity of the herd.

It's an unprecedented slaughter. Never before have the caribou made themselves so accessible to nearly twenty thousand people in the territorial capital. Just a thirty-minute drive outside of Yellowknife, Dene and non-Aboriginal hunters turn the snowy white landscape into a bloodied killing field. With wanton disregard, some hack off only choice parts of meat, leaving near-whole carcasses to waste and rot.

Before there were high-powered rifles and pickup trucks, when circumpolar peoples followed the herds by canoe and dog-team into the Barrenlands to survive, it was believed caribou offered their entire beings for food, shelter and clothing in return for respect and good behaviour.

Clearly today, that agreement is being breached.

The Bathurst herd is an estimated three hundred fifty thousand-strong on October 26, 1992. While I had witnessed the teeming migration of wildebeest and impala along the Serengeti plains of Africa, like most Canadians, I'd scarcely been aware North America still had spectacular, and indeed larger, movements of wild animals. We'd killed off the buffalo of the Great Plains, but the sheer cold and rigours of Arctic terrain had so far shielded the caribou from a similar plight.

The caribou's annual migration from the tundra to their wintering grounds on the north shore of Great Slave Lake—earlier, and farther south and west than usual—alerts me to their journey and in some ways awakens me to mine. As a new mother, I'm shedding parts of my old self, pulsing with new blood and expanded awareness, like the budding antlers that crown the caribou each year, never growing to maturity in the same way twice.

Caribou are unique amongst deer in that females have antlers. Female antlers develop from June to September and are retained throughout winter to defend cratered feeding spots in the snow from older males, who drop their antlers after the fall rut. This provides a survival advantage for the female and her calf.

The herd largely disperses over the winter, but occasionally, some make stirring appearances, like the lone female that stands outside my house the day my friend Jeanette's mother died.

For ten years, Jeanette had lived alone in her A-frame log cabin a few kilometres past our house, but at the time of her mother's death, she lived with her roommate France, one lake down the highway from us. I met them both at a gathering of ecologically minded people in a room filled with baked goods and talk of good deeds that need doing. My herd of friends was changing, branching out from mostly media types. Jeanette was a psychiatric nurse who worked as an addictions counsellor for youth. She also had no hip joints.

It feels blasphemous to introduce Jeanette by her handicap, given the depths of her strength and fortitude, not to mention her wholesome, short-haired attractiveness, all of which made much more lasting impressions on me during the years of our friendship than the click of her cane and her lopsided gait, the result of a genetic bone condition that precipitated two failed hip replacements and robbed her at age twelve of the chance to defend her title of fastest girl in school. This could also explain why I think of Jeanette as being tall, with her long limbs and big feet and hands, when in fact she's not.

Caribou have slender "deer-type" legs but much broader and flexible feet to facilitate walking on snow and ice. The feet make a clicking sound while walking—a noise produced by a tendon slipping over the sesamoid bone in the foot.

And yet Jeanette's physical challenges are significant given the rugged lifestyle she's chosen, living alone in the bush without a continuous power source or flush toilet; heating her log cabin by wood that she chops and carries herself; hauling her water from town in big heavy jugs—all testimony to her strong will and deep affinity for nature.

On January 7, 1993, Jeanette awoke to a temperature of minus forty-five degrees after receiving a phone call the night before that her mother wasn't expected to live through the night. The diesel generator that powered the house she shared with France wouldn't turn over, which meant there was no power to plug in her car to heat its battery and engine. The battery bank that provided alternative power sat dead in the extreme chill of their front entrance—which meant there was no power for the phone. France's car was in their garage and sputtered to life. They rode to town together so Jeanette could be updated on her mother's condition.

Her mother died later that morning, alone in a faraway hospital. France picked Jeanette up to bring her back home, only to learn the house problems hadn't yet been rectified. So in those numbing first few hours of reconciling her motherless existence, Jeanette arrived at my door. I didn't know her well then and didn't feel qualified to deal with her grief, which manifested in quiet contemplation, likely shock, instead of tears. There was the requisite tea and soft-spoken inquiries, then a call from France saying the house was repaired and Jeanette could now work the phones from home.

I went to the garage to start my car, only to realize Francois had taken it to work because his truck had also frozen. I suggested to Jeanette that I put Max in my *amautiq* and accompany her on the twenty-minute, mostly downhill, walk to her house. Perhaps because I didn't think of her as handicapped, I didn't fully appreciate the difficulties this could entail for her. We bundled up and stepped outside.

Everywhere was white light. The sun ricocheted off fresh snow that coated the landscape like a jug of spilled milk. Glassy hoarfrost wrapped itself around every needle and branch of the forest. Our entire surroundings—highway, lake, rock and trees—glittered as if a giant disco ball spun above us in the crisp blue sky. We took a few steps then simultaneously stopped to drink in the view a bit longer. The stillness was electrifying; nothing moved except the Arctic cold that circled our breath, turning each exhale into puffs of vapour. That's when I noticed her, the lone caribou staring plaintively at us, just a few metres away in the direction we were heading.

Some Inuit believe when a caribou comes very close to a community, it is a relative coming to visit and it should not be harvested.

This timely visit boosted our spirits and heightened our senses, although years later when I discuss that day with Jeanette she has little recollection of the caribou, but remembers how the bracing cold and the migration to her house had grounded her and how Max's soft brown eyes watched her from the back of my coat. She does, however, recall a dream she had some time afterward in which she was moving down our road and a large caribou jumped in front of her face. She awoke with a start knowing instantly the caribou had been her mother—the one and only time she ever felt her mom's presence after she died. We'd picked our way carefully, and very slowly, over the icy highway on that day, me with my precious cargo, Jeanette with her heavy heart.

According to Inuit Qaujimajatuqangit *(What has always been known), when people cut themselves, they would use the dried up outer covering of the caribou heart as a bandage because it does not leak.*

∾

Jeanette marvelled at my three boys. Nothing about them intimidated her—putrid diapers, shrivelling umbilical cords, illness. With typical aplomb, she was a fearless and consummate occasional caregiver. She didn't drink or smoke and rarely swore, although once she was watching Max and told us through tears of laughter that he'd insisted she watch "the fuckin' hound," which she eventually discerned was Disney's *The Fox and Hound.*

Francois was travelling a lot for work and many times when I thought the domestic workload would subsume me, Jeanette's little green pickup truck would appear in our driveway. She had to drive directly past our house every day and would often stop to bounce a baby on her knee or drop off cookies or muffins. Every new mother should have a Jeanette. That I should have one, given the remoteness of my home in addition to the thousands of kilometres that separated me from my family's helping hands, felt like a gift from angels.

Caribou are gregarious, often travelling in small bands of particular composition such as cows and calves. About the only solitary activity is calving when females usually give birth alone, but soon after rejoin "nursery bands" comprised of other cows and calves.

Once when Max was sick I watched Jeanette hold her hands a few inches above his head, sweep them down his body and past his toes then flick both hands towards the ground while rapidly fluttering her fingers, as if trying to loosen something sticky. She had the longest fingers I've ever seen, almost as if they had extra joints, and her face was a study in concentration. I asked what she was doing. She called it therapeutic touch, a rebalancing of the body's energy fields. She said she was scanning Max's body, feeling for spots where energy might be blocked.

"And why do you flick your hands down like that at the end?" I asked.

"Oh, you don't want that stuff floating around, heh," she replied with a smile. "I tell it to go back into the earth."

My eyebrows raised, but Max looked visibly more relaxed.

Jeanette told me she also dowses and is able to detect water sources beneath the earth's surface by holding a branch and watching for its subtle vibrations. Therapeutic touch became a natural extension to her intuitive gifts. The updated version of the ancient healing practice of laying on of hands was developed in 1972 by clairvoyant healer Dora Kunz and her long-time student and colleague, nursing professor Dolores Krieger. According to their website, since childhood, Dora had been highly sensitive to unseen human energy fields and had spent her lifetime studying how they work and how they relate to attitudes and emotions. Physicians began referring patients with difficult diagnoses to her. Eventually, the two women developed a program in New York State for teaching the procedures and attitudes necessary to practice 'TT,' now taught worldwide in universities and nursing schools as a widely accepted alternative therapy, but one that still has its sceptics.

Despite my own initial scepticism, I welcomed therapeutic touch for the children. The twins contracted a serious respiratory illness, likely in the hospital at the time of their birth. Whenever Jeanette hovered her healing hands above their little bodies, their barking, convulsive coughs would settle. After persistent requests by Jeanette to try therapeutic touch on me, I reluctantly acquiesced. Receptivity and openness being key, not surprisingly I felt little difference, although sometimes I detected a heaviness that wasn't there before, a combination of fatigue and relaxation.

As is so often the way on the learning path, Jeanette's introduction to this form of healing led me to discover that several other acquaintances were practitioners, including France, who was a master at it, and my family doctor, who was Western trained, but also attuned to the medicine traditions of her Inuvialuit heritage. At a visit to her office once, she placed her unusually hot hand on a particularly aching part of my neck, a pain I hadn't mentioned. "I just feel compelled to do this," she said. Her touch deposited a shock of heat and revitalizing energy into my body that relieved the pain and caused a persistent flush to my face, prompting several people, even hours later, to ask me if I'd been jogging.

~

Jeanette is in my kitchen and doesn't look well. She's just come from some sort of counselling session. I know she's in therapy for childhood horrors, but we'd never discussed them. In the sparest of details, I learn she suffered the most heinous betrayal as a child by her father. Again, I don't know what to do other than make tea and just sit with her. She doesn't want to be alone. She looks fragile, vulnerable; her face is ashen. She doesn't seem as tall as before, and I wonder where the strong, determined woman I knew has gone. Eventually, she coaxes her twisted torso up, leans on her cane and assures me she's ready to go home to her cabin and, in that moment, I realize the brave woman I'm searching for is right in front of me.

Shortly after this, as I prepare Max for his first day in kindergarten, a friend shares some disturbing news. The former principal at his school had been accused of pawing adolescent girls, groping them at a basket-ball game. The school counsellor reported the girls' claims—as the law required—but in return she was reprimanded by the school district. Her name is Linda and I talk to her. She tells me she's been told in writing she must consult with the district before making any future reports of abuse allegations, a directive which she calls "screening," and illegal. Confused and unwilling to break the law, she took sick leave. While away, she was informed by letter from the principal that the locks on her confidential client files had been drilled to aid her replacement. When she returned, she says the reports of the students' disclosures of abuse against the principal were gone. Her replacement, a neighbour of mine, tells me he never asked for anything from her files.

An RCMP investigation into the girls' claims began with police interviews at the school. Despite being told to stay away, the principal returned to escort children to the swimming pool. While police were speaking to the girls, he was in plain view. Police concluded no charges should be laid. A week later, some teachers and students were upset when the principal came to school on pyjama day wearing a T-shirt, robe, socks and shoes. Linda says she saw him in the mezzanine surrounded by a small group of students, showing his legs and inferring he had nothing on underneath. Eventually, a male teacher convinced him to put his pants on. The princi-pal's contract was not renewed. He moved south, yet the entire incident had left a chill on the staff.

School will be Max's first foray into new territory without me. I need to know that he—and all the other innocents—will be protected by adults willing and able to sound danger alarms.

Caribou bunch as a herd and move nimbly together for protection against attacks by predators.

I try to raise my concerns with the school board, but they tell me, on the advice of their solicitor, they won't meet me. I persist. Other parents join me in a chorus of support for the counsellor. We ask hard questions. We get no answers. A local radio reporter directs his microphone at me and asks what's happening. I tell him there is a protocol, developed with input from the counsellor in question and backed by territorial law, which anyone who suspects child sexual abuse is required to follow. Linda followed it. She shouldn't be asked to have her reports screened. As parents, we're concerned about that.

~

As soon as Max points to caribou off in the distance on our lake, they beckon me. In the five years since the herd flocked our way, caribou sightings have become increasingly rare. Max is learning to cross-country ski, so I suggest we ski closer for a better look. It's just before Christmas. Snowflakes perforate a still, grey sky; falling like icing sugar sifting over a white cake. Max is intuitively quiet as he makes slow, steady progress towards the camouflaged shapes. He will be a good hunter someday. I'm acutely aware of how privileged I am to be here with him, sharing our habitat with the animals that have sustained the North's Indigenous peoples and continue to feed our family. The sharp edges of my life melt away, allowing me to be wholly present in this hushed glide towards the animals, all my senses saturated in a type of holy oneness with my environment.

The mysterious, migrational movements of Barrenland caribou herds is said to be directed by a language, or song, they speak to one another over vast distances, a language which the Dene and Inuit have long understood, spoken on the margins of human consciousness.

"Mom! Where are you going?" Max asks in a loud whisper, breaking me from my reverie. I turn to look behind. He's pointing to a nearby caribou, its oversized head frozen in a penetrating gaze towards me. I'd been so focussed on the two others off in the distance that I hadn't seen the one to the side. Blindsided, I suppose.

~

On December 18, 1997, there's no reason to fear the man who walks into my office, but the receptionist walking two steps behind him wears a look of apprehension. I've taken a job with the territorial Department of Aboriginal Affairs, helping negotiate a formal return of powers to the Dene and Inuvialuit, who had governed themselves for millennia before the arrival of Europeans. Max is in school; the twins are with the young nanny we've hired. The man introduces himself as the sheriff then serves me papers indicating I'm being sued for defamation over comments I made in a radio report. The man suing me, a senior public school administrator, is backed by the school district. Unless I retract those comments and apologize, I could face fifty-five thousand dollars in damages.

My gut wrenches, twisting into a nervous knot that takes up residency inside me. I couldn't know then, but the slow, grinding machinations of our legal system would keep that knot vexing me for years, like a bad tenant who refuses to leave. I'd said nothing untrue, had ample, written verifications, and was still waiting for answers from the school trustees, into whose care I was entrusting my children for seven hours each day. I will not retract or apologize. This means there will be no avoiding lawyers. I have a disheartening sense of déjà vu. It'd been eight years, but I'd learned about the dangers of a woman drawing attention to an injustice of power.

In 1989, a story I wrote for the *Edmonton Journal* included a judge's comments on why sentencing for rape in the North was more lenient than in southern Canada, a longstanding question that had been raised in the Northwest Territories legislature. In an interview, the judge told me there was essentially less violence, less trauma in the North: "The majority of rapes in the Northwest Territories occur when the woman is drunk and passed out. A man comes along and sees a pair of hips and helps himself." He'd contrasted that to rapes on a southern university campus, where a dainty co-ed gets jumped from behind, suffering vaginal tears and psychological trauma related to sex for years to come.

Political debate around the issue had been reignited by the judge's sentence of five days in jail for a male MLA who confessed to repeatedly putting his hands under a pubescent girl's clothes and rubbing her. The MLA was having marital problems, the judge told me, and needed to redirect his feelings: "So rightly or wrongly, he cuddled (the girl) and touched her breasts and fondled her genitals." (The term "inappropriate cuddling" had been used by a Yellowknife psychiatrist to describe the sexual assaults in a pre-sentencing report. The same male psychiatrist was later reprimanded by a Northwest Territories board of inquiry after a female patient filed a complaint of sexual harassment. Four subsequent verbal complaints were made against him from patients. Prior to this, he'd been under investigation by the Alberta College of Physicians and Surgeons, but that investigation ended when he erased his standing with the college and moved to Yellowknife, where he worked until 2010.)

The story appeared less than two weeks after the massacre in Montreal of seventeen female engineering students. It was an intensely emotional time. Women in Yellowknife were outraged, taking to the streets to protest. The territorial justice minister made a fiery speech about rape and called a disciplinary inquiry into the judge, which was supposed to last four days, but dragged on for four months—thanks in large part to the flashy, theatrical oratory of the Alberta criminal lawyer the judge hired, who turned much of the attention on me.

Mature male caribou are very active in the fall—rushing about, thrashing bushes with their antlers, sparring with other bulls, and pursuing females.

Other lawyers started showing up just to watch his performance. With calculated precision, he shifted the focus onto my competence as a journalist. Under inquiry rules, I initially had no standing, no means to cross-examine or defend myself; something that my newspaper fought to change, but by then it was too late. The attacks against me in the witness chair were relentless. One time the judge's lawyer appeared to be trying to dupe me into perjury at the exhausting end of the day by presenting false "facts" from a story I'd written and asking me to confirm them. I ultimately didn't, but he was so convincing, and I was so tired and confused, that I was tempted to agree, my head hung in shame. The next day he opened the proceedings by correcting his error, "for the record," but the reporters had already filed their stories, including the falsehoods. It was frustrating and humiliating, yet I kept it in perspective. I imagined a woman being subjected to this same type of character assassination, a re-victimizing, after having been raped. It is no wonder so many women choose not to seek redress through our justice system. The adversarial courtroom can be a highly dishonourable place.

In the end, the female inquiry judge ruled that while those comments made by the judge in the story were inappropriate, careless... even crude, he was not biased or unfit for the bench. My article contained inaccuracies and unsupported innuendo, she said. The tragedy in Montreal, the justice minister's comments, and a general feeling of discontent among northerners regarding sentencing of sexual offenders, all contributed to people venting their frustrations out on the judge. He went back to work. The Journal stood behind the story, and me, and I went back to work too. The inquiry did prompt a government study on the treatment of women in the justice system in the Northwest Territories. In 1992, Katherine

Peterson, special advisor on gender equality to the minister of justice, made several recommendations, including reforming the judiciary so it was more representative of the population.

∼

It's fall. In one week I'm supposed to testify at something called an Examination for Discovery. It will determine whether the defamation claim filed against me in December will make it to court. I welcome the chance to defend my right as a mother to raise these concerns, but I'm frightened and I have lost my voice from an intensely painful throat and sinus infection.

Nostril flies deposit dozens of larvae in the nostril of caribou and these maggots crawl through the nasal passages until they reach the entrance of the throat where they remain all winter. In such concentrations they make breathing difficult for the caribou, especially when it has to run.

My lawyer assures me it is routine to reschedule, then is surprised when the other side balks, demanding medical proof of my illness. The examination begins instead with the radio reporter, but in opening remarks my lawyer tells me I am painted as a raging feminist who revels in taking down men in positions of high power. Like judges.

As the November date for my rescheduled court examination draws nigh, Max has a debilitating case of chickenpox and I'm single parenting while Francois travels for work. Jeanette, my saviour, agrees to assume my role as nurse-mother. To ease the flow of her day, I awake before sunrise to split wood, fill the kitchen wood box and stuff the wood stove. I light the propane heater in the generator shack, so the diesel engine will warm sufficiently to fire up. And I prepare two meals. I'm filled with worry about the pending legal grilling when Jeanette arrives at 8 a.m., just moments before I have to leave.

"Thank you so much for doing this Jeanette," I say as I'm donning my coat. "I'm really scared. Do you have any words of advice?"

"Do you know about summoning the white lights?" she asks.

"The what? No. What are you talking about?"

"Get yourself grounded then ask for white lights to surround you. You'll see them. Put them around anything you want to protect, like yourself," she explains. "And go someplace quiet and ask the Great Spirit to speak for you... lose your ego."

"Ask who?" I begin, but I'm running late and the answers to my questions will have to wait. I give Jeanette a quick hug and dash to my car.

I arrive at the law office with just minutes to spare before the proceedings begin. I hastily greet everyone and hand the radio station owner a bouquet of roses to thank her for airing the story. Then I excuse myself to the washroom, where I make a quick look around to assure I am alone. Standing by myself I close my eyes and take a few deep breaths, then, somewhat embarrassingly, say, "Great Spirit, please guide my words today."

A tingling wave—like tiny electric shocks—travels from the back of my feet, up my spine, over the top of my head and back down to my feet in a rush so powerful I lurch forward and give my body a shake, before looking behind me.

Sometimes when a caribou is extremely nervous or frightened it will rise up on its hind legs and bound forward, a rare movement called an "excitation jump," which deposits a scent from its back hooves that alerts other caribou to possible danger.

I'm escorted into an office where we sit around a table—my lawyer and I on one side, the man suing me and his lawyer on the other, the court reporter at the end. Every word spoken, every sound uttered, will be transcribed. I put both feet firmly on the ground. As the lawyers begin exchanging formalities I try to conjure up white lights. It is difficult to draw upon this level of fanciful concentration for a concept that I could not have imagined just an hour before.

But there they are.

Hundreds of vertical white lights, like geometric diamond stakes with sparkling tops, slimming to a point at the bottom. They undulate clockwise, like the aurora. I picture them surrounding the table, hold them up in my mind's eye between my adversary and myself— innervate them. When the questions begin, I split my concentration between the lights and my answers, often taking laboriously long times to respond, but each sentence perfectly reflects the information I wish to convey. The transcripts show not a single "um" or "uh."

After the first day, I'm as exhausted as if I'd run a marathon.

The wolf is the major predator of caribou, and will often spend time test-

ing the herd through chase to expose the unfit, the weak or the careless.

Jeanette promises to return the next morning, and I feed the children and put them to bed. Then I call a woman who's been a strong supporter. She'd known Linda, the school counsellor at the centre of my legal storm, as a caring professional who'd made tremendous strides with one of her own children. She'd also started a petition to demand accountability from the school board as to why it was using tax dollars to finance a private civil suit against me, a parent. I tell her about my day, starting with the electrifying shiver that ran up my back.

"Wow, you've got it quite strongly," she says.

"What is 'it'?" I ask, but there's only a long, silent pause in response.

Then I tell her about the white lights and how I kept envisioning them surrounding the table, making a wall between me and the plaintiff during the proceedings, which made her laugh uproariously.

"You don't have to see them the whole time," she says. "Just summon them once and they stay with you a good long while. No wonder you're exhausted."

And she points out I hadn't surrounded myself with protection, but rather the table.

"Tomorrow, just put them around you and your lawyer," she advises.

I heed the advice, narrowing my white-light circle of protection to just my lawyer and myself, and make it through day two, although the mental sparring again takes a physical toll.

The clacking crash of antlers can be heard for three weeks as male caribou butt heads in the fall rut until they are drained of all strength in their jockey for dominance over who will sow the seeds of future offspring.

I phone my neighbour France and ask if she could do some therapeutic touch. Maybe ground me a bit. She arrives and works her hands over my head and down my body as I sit silently in a chair, eyes closed. I feel two separate shoots of pain in my head, like momentary blasts of a migraine. At the end she's on her knees with her hands placed on the tops of my feet and for the first time in weeks, I feel my body's energy move down there too.

"You're definitely 'in your head'," she says when she's finished. "I felt two really sharp electric shocks around there. It kind of hurt, so I moved my hands up higher."

I keep having imaginary legal arguments in my mind. I ask pertinent questions, as opposed to the minutia I'd been subjected to over the weekend, and give cutting rejoinders outlining what's at stake when children are violated: their humanity, their ability to trust, the very social foundations upon which they'll build the rest of their lives. Instead, they learn bewildering shame, humiliation and fear. Many seek temporary relief in drugs and alcohol, some choose suicide. "Life-robbers" is how my elderly neighbour Thelma, a longtime counsellor, once described child sexual abusers to me.

I vividly recall the heaviness of visiting my teenage friend in a hospital in Guelph, Ontario after she'd been raped at knifepoint in her home and later attempted suicide. "Why didn't you tell me?" I asked her. She said she was going to, but I arrived at her house that night with a friend and the opportunity was lost. She told me the hospital was trying to help her recover her self-esteem.

I ask the woman who started the petition in my support for advice on how to stop the dialogue of arguing in my head?

"Well, try saying something else instead," she says. "Every time the chatter starts up, maybe replace it with, 'I choose peace, love and joy.'" I try this when I'm outside building snowmen with the boys and it works, but will require practice to maintain.

Some of that negative chatter also includes discrepancies I'm experiencing in my work with the Department of Aboriginal Affairs. My allegiances at the self-government negotiating tables feel misaligned. I agree with the Indigenous peoples' arguments, and in particular, their insistence that they be in charge of child protection services with the ability to create their own culturally appropriate social services. My experience with the current system has shown it to be heavily flawed. When I had taken all of my documentation regarding the abuse allegations at the school, including the illegal, written directive issued to Linda, to the government's senior child protection officials, they took no action. They told me I was right, told me the letter was an offence under the Child Welfare Act (which they were paid well to oversee), and encouraged me to keep pursuing the matter. But they personally did nothing, not even take a copy of the letter as I held it out to them. How could I, in good conscience, insist that this system—with all its supposed checks and balances—be mirrored by new Aboriginal governments?

When our nanny announces she's leaving, it's the final push for me to quit my job as well. I start freelance work at the CBC. I'm not looking forward to going back to the station, as ongoing news reports about my lawsuit will surely drown out my new mantra. As if on cue, the twins contract Max's chicken pox, one at a time, buying me two full loving weeks at home devoted to their wellness. I receive a phone call saying I've won a dozen red roses. Unknowingly, my name went into a draw when I bought the flowers for the radio station owner. Jeanette picks them up for me, and we share the bouquet. I stop to smell the roses, surrounded by peace, love, joy.

Jeanette administers her therapeutic touch on all of us. I've begun to crave it, but so far haven't heeded her pleas for me to learn the healing effects my hands could have on my children, or the centring skills I could acquire to navigate this minefield of a lawsuit. Jeanette had worked with Linda professionally and had great respect for her. I couldn't have found a more understanding or sympathetic person to help see me through this ordeal. As needy as I was for Jeanette's healing company, I had to remind myself that she'd suffered—and was still recovering from—a far more acute violation within this same cruel sphere of transgressions. I should be shouldering *her* with strength.

When her personal well is no longer deep enough to deal with the problems of addicted teens, Jeanette quits her job as a counsellor and acquires less taxing work. Then a protracted infection related to her hips puts her in and out of hospital, forcing her to convalesce in town at a friend's home. When she breaks the news she's selling her beloved A-frame for want of an easier lifestyle and moving to be closer to siblings, I'm crestfallen, but wholly supportive. She lives in the Yukon for a while, before moving to various places in British Columbia. Her hand-written letters sealed with floral stickers arrive faithfully on each of our birthdays, always filled with lively descriptions of the beauty of the mountain vistas and the flowers that seemed to flourish in her presence. She visits me once after that.

By 2007, seven of the twelve dwindling caribou populations in the northern reaches of the continent are either threatened, endangered, or of special concern.

Her feet are mysteriously swollen and walking is difficult, but she smiles the entire time. With the children more independent, I'm able to lavish my whole attention on her comfort and pleasure, and she appears to revel in every moment.

~

I'm writing this story about Jeanette on January 8, 2008, when France calls to tell me she was found dead, alone in her apartment that morning, likely from a brain aneurysm. If she passed before midnight, her death comes fifteen years to the day after her mother died alone in hospital and we made that long, frigid trek down the hill to her house.

The average lifespan of a caribou in the wild is fifteen years.

The Cree believe the soul takes three days to find its way after death—the Three Day Road—and I pray Jeanette is making steady progress on her spiritual journey. I'm also making travel plans to see my gravely ill mother, Janet (so-named because her Hungarian father did not know how to spell Jeanette).

My heart is filled with grief and worry and sorrow, but somehow I carry on with the sundry details of the household. Three days later, I even manage something spectacular—to assist a friend in hospital with the safe and speedy delivery of her baby. A girl.

The Alaskan Inupiat have a legend that says when a caribou gets caught and dies, its head severs from its body and its living being leaves to go with the other caribou. Because the other caribou know of this death, they surround this living being and clothe it, making it a caribou once more. This leaves the first body for food for the people.

I think of Jeanette often. I see her every day in the healthy outlooks of my children, whenever a brilliant yellow or orange wild poppy catches my eye, or when caribou come to mind. She helped open me to new ways of knowing, awakened me to subtle vibrations that I could not only detect, but harness when I needed support. In a way, she "thrummed," a term biologist Karsten Heuer uses in his book *Being Caribou*, to describe a discrete, oscillating humming noise and vibration he could detect coming from the caribou during the months he and his wife followed the Porcupine Herd on foot. He described it as uncovering "that hidden realm of consciousness," an innate, but forgotten, wisdom that flowed into him when he began to see and hear directly, instead of sifting every feeling through his rational and scientifically trained mind. Before setting off on his epic journey, Heuer listened in disbelief when a Gwich'in man told him there was a time when people could talk to caribou and caribou could talk to people. He no longer disbelieves this.

Jeanette's brother tells me they've as yet been unable to lay her ashes at her chosen resting place, the Telkwa Mountain Range of northern British Columbia. He's unsure why she chose that spot, but thinks she might have hiked there as a child before her hip problems, possibly even with her friend Margaret who'd often go there on horseback. But it's difficult to reach now.

All motorized access into the region is banned—the rugged plateaus and grassy meadows only open to hikers for a brief window during late summer so as not to disturb the rehabilitation of the Telkwa Caribou herd. The herd declined to about a dozen animals in the mid-1990s, then thirty-two caribou were relocated there. Since then, the isolated herd has been making a slow, but steady comeback.

The Bathurst herd has waned as well, to as few as sixteen thousand animals (a devastating decline of 96 percent since the mid-'80s). Unstable migration routes and increased insect harassment from climate change, industrialization, including diamond mines, oil and gas and mining exploration and over-hunting are to blame. Their historical abundance had lulled me into believing they would always be here, that I could always rely on them to nourish my body, mind and spirit. As my lawsuit heats up, it would be nice to be surrounded by the safety of the herd, to have the caribou near once more.

CRAB
leave your shell

At the behest of my new friend, Shauna, I'm standing outside the dilapidated Las Terrenas jailhouse in the Dominican Republic, notebook and pen in hand, 'feigning' that I'm a Canadian newspaper reporter. Shauna has told the guards that I'm following the story of Lindo, a twenty-year-old street kid detained for stealing a motorbike. I'm not really, but she hopes the presence of a foreign journalist will temper their thuggish tendencies and improve Lindo's chances of release. Lindo has been given a scythe and told by the pot-bellied warden that if he cuts a small patch of grass within ten minutes—before the bus for Samaná arrives—he won't be locked up in Fort Alesa, a squalid, medium-security prison where his *de facto* guardian Shauna says he's sure to die in obscurity.

Lindo moves without the slightest hint of urgency, as slowly as a ninety-year-old man bending to pick up his dropped cane. He wouldn't move at all were it not for Shauna's low, steady urgings in Spanish. When he stands up lazily after ten seconds of cutting, wipes a brow that shows not a drop of perspiration and stares defiantly into the warden's eyes, I can't help but feel a sense of panic for him. "Get cutting Lindo!" I screech. "Cut it! Cut it!"

This is my family vacation. I'm running away from my infamy in Yellowknife, where the defamation lawsuit against me is making headlines—infuriatingly one-sided reports as a result of my lawyer's advice not to comment. The more I try to shield myself from the controversy, the more it screams out at me—like the day I walked into work at the CBC as my name was ringing through the halls on a morning newscast. Later, managers rescinded an offer to do on-air radio work, citing my legal entanglement as the reason. I'm hoping the turquoise waters of this sultry Caribbean island will wash away my bitterness. This is a familiar pattern.

Nine years prior, national and local media had closely followed the aftermath of my story on the territorial court judge whose comments on sexual assault sentencing led to a judicial inquiry. I couldn't turn on the TV or radio, pick up a newspaper or walk down the street without being reminded I was swirling in the eye of a storm. The only person who could truly appreciate the strain of all that turbulence was the judge himself, who shared the spotlight with me under our small-town microscope. I coped by escaping down the Yellowknife River with Francois every night in our aluminum fishing boat, taking refuge in quiet shoreline dinners around open fires.

There is welcome anonymity in the Dominican Republic, but it's not without its own challenges. Our pasty bodies were slow-moving—still reconciling to a sixty-degree temperature change and the exhausting demands of flying pre-schoolers and a six-year-old from the Subarctic to the tropics—when we made our first stumbling venture onto the beach in Sosúa. In contrast, the children's pent-up energy sparked an explosive dash to the ocean, a full-speed hurtle directly into the flight path of the largest wave I've ever witnessed. Bowled over like a three-pin spare, they disappeared in a sea of angry white foam before Francois and I could register what was happening. Their mewling bodies resurfaced face down in the sand, rolling like Coke bottles in and out of the ocean while we chased and fumbled to retrieve them. No one on the beach offered to help, even though we could have, obviously, used another set of hands. We left that day in search of calmer waters, feeling our way to the island's north-eastern Samaná Peninsula where we settled amidst the white sand beaches and tangled mangroves of Las Terrenas, spending much of our time in the company of crabs.

I hadn't given crabs much thought before that. As a child growing up in landlocked southwestern Ontario, they were not part of my natural landscape, although we occasionally caught crayfish when my parents rented a cottage further north. On the rare occasion that crabs made their way to my dinner plate, they were headless shells of their former selves—all legs and claws—requiring heavy tools and much smashing and wrenching to reach their sweet meat. Even in death they seemed hard and defiant. Occasionally in my adult travels I have glanced them on beaches, always in a hurry to hide. Not here. Here, they command my attention in ways too brazen to ignore.

Our first encounter with the sidewinding crustaceans is during a paddle through a red mangrove on borrowed plastic kayaks. The twisted trees are amphibious, with roots that snake through land and sea like snarled skeins of yarn, able to adapt themselves to salty tides and river inlets alike. Crabs swarm these roots like insects, their hard shells clattering against one another in a defensive scramble for cover. I'm in completely foreign territory, within arm's length of hundreds of creatures with bobbing eyes perched on stalks sticking out from their shells, and small pairs of feelers in between them. Unlike the lifeless crabs awaiting the smash of my mallet to crack them open, these alien-like beings are on the move and on the ready, with claws able to inflict much pain should we accidentally make contact.

All crabs when threatened keep both claws expanded. If a predator clamps down on a crab's claw or limb, the crab may "self-amputate" so it can free itself. The claw can continue to squeeze with incredible force for nearly a minute. A new, slightly smaller claw will regrow in its place.

For those reasons, the crabs spook me on that first foray into the mangrove, but I find that exhilarating. My fright acts like tiny shock waves, bringing back to life facets of my personality that were starting to atrophy under the stagnation of routine. Part of my love of travel is that delicious realization that there's an infinite possibility of discovery to be had beyond the small circles of our cramped and domestic home lives. Crabs seemed foreign and scary because they're beyond that known circle. By the end of my time on the island, they'll have moved into my own sense of familiar, my sensitivities towards them will have expanded, and they'll no longer be as threatening.

I'm conscious not to project my own fears onto my children when they seem, even to me, a bit unfounded. Yet children are able to pick up on our emotions with incredible accuracy—a survival tactic we share with many other species. While my son is never able to articulate its origins, I wonder if my own anxieties that day, coupled with the haunting, dappled light strobing across their scuttling shells, are what spawn Calvin's persistent fear of crabs over the next few years, including recurring nightmares in which they nip at his toes.

In Greek mythology, a giant crab sent by the goddess Hera gets a claw-hold on the toe of the mighty hero Heracles as he battles the nine-headed water serpent Hydra. Heracles crushes the crab with his foot, but in honour of its fighting spirit, Hera places the image of the crab in the night sky, which becomes the constellation Cancer.

Despite the region's history as a slave trade port for the British in the early 1600s, there isn't much English spoken in Las Terrenas. The majority of the tourists are European, so when Levi, just three-and-a-half years old, stands on a chair in an outdoor restaurant and belts, "Jingle Bells, Santa smells, Robin laid an egg..." the Canadian kids on the other side of Diny's Restaurant take special note. Francois and I are surreptitiously sniffing the twins' backsides, trying to root out the source of a truly foul stench which we do trace—albeit too late to save the chair—to dog shit on Levi's running shoes, and inexplicably, on his face. "Ca ca?" he asks innocently, just as Shauna walks over to introduce herself. She's a social worker from British Columbia with her Dominican-born husband, Charo, and their two children: KC, nine, and Marisa, seven. From this inauspicious beginning, we forge a unique friendship that dramatically alters the course, if not the aspirations, of our month-long holiday.

Shauna is living with her children and working in a nearby village on a grant from CIDA, the Canadian International Development Agency, helping the people of Los Puentes set up a water-filtering system and vegetable gardens. Charo is an electrician at a resort a short bus ride from where we're staying. Obtaining her masters degree in social work and international community development, Shauna has spent years off and on in the Dominican Republic, first in the capital of Santo Domingo and more recently in this village alongside five hundred local women, children and men constructing a regional medical clinic. At the time we met, the clinic was in need of help with its solar power system. Given Francois' photovoltaic experience powering up our own off-grid house, he offered to give a hand. We agreed to meet the next day and travel together up the mountainside to Los Puentes.

Our boys couldn't believe their good fortune when they were instructed to clamber into the open back of a Nissan pickup truck and sit on a plywood ledge behind the cab with KC and Marissa—passengers pressed against them, warm trade winds whipping their hair—as we wound our way up the steep, lush heart of the Samaná Cordillera. The old "when in Rome..." adage had served me well throughout my globetrotting, but this *gua-gua* ride (to be rivalled only by the beeping *motoconchos* we occasionally took to a distant beach—with Levi, Calvin, a driver and me all squished, unhelmeted, onto a two-stroke trail bike) surely pushed the limits of acceptable parenting. Shauna looked at ease, a broad grin on her freckled face, her nut-brown ponytail flailing behind her like a cheerleader's pom-pom.

Past the coconut palms, rubber trees and honey-sweet wafts of coffee fields owned by wealthy foreigners, we came to the ragged village of Los Puentes. A small child sat at the side of the road with a knife almost as big as he was tucked into his underpants. Women wearing brightly coloured curlers hung laundry against a backdrop of sprawling, verdant hills. Within minutes, our children were sprinting down the dusty road chasing chickens, while Shauna lead us all to the medical clinic, which, from what I could decipher from its sign, was a gift from the non-profit group Pueblito Canada, Falconbridge mining company, and the United Church in Muskoka, Ontario.

Francois was introduced to the workers and before long he was sweating it out on the rooftop with Charo as interpreter, helping install solar panels to bring light to the clinic and a water catchment system to supply its water. Shauna and I took the children to her friend Azalea's house, where they joined other children, some naked, in a single-file march down a foot trail to a bamboo thicket and the village's water supply—a clear, shallow stream that served as both drinking water and bathing area. As heartening as it was to see how easily my boys connected with all living things in the village, fearlessly catching tree frogs and lizards, brazenly helping herd a donkey, I worried constantly about their safety and what dangers may be lurking beyond my motherly reach.

I came to know the people of the village thanks to Shauna's fluency in Spanish. Azalea, a stout, aproned woman with a shy smile, and her husband Andreas had six children and ran the store, which is where I met Lindo. For much of his twenty years, Lindo had been a part of their lives, as well, after following Shauna to the village—literally chasing after her car—when he was a young boy. Andreas's nephew Sangeye let him share his double bed, even though Lindo had been, and remained, a chronic bed-wetter.

"I met Lindo while I was volunteering in Santo Domingo, giving free lunches to street kids," Shauna tells me. "He was seven, but he was a really tiny guy, the size of a four-or-five-year old, and he was carting around this little puppy on a string."

Had Shauna not gradually filled in the blanks of Lindo's life for me, I would've left the island remembering him as curly-haired and handsome, perhaps a bit childish, but with a cocksure attitude he liked to play up for my camera. It's unlikely I would've felt compelled to rise early, enduring Francois' admonishments as I dressed ("This is supposed to be a holiday Laurie") to drive with Shauna and take part in her sketchy 'save Lindo from jail' scheme after he stole a motorbike and drove it home from a bar in Las Terrenas. Sangeye discovered it behind their house and told Shauna, who convinced Lindo to secretly return it, but somehow he was still arrested. Because we'd chosen to travel in a way that connected us to the people, not walled us off from them, my struggle had become entwined with Shauna and Lindo's. The boy's story of survival on the streets, as it came from Shauna, invoked a maternal sense of awe and pathos I couldn't ignore.

"I remember seeing him curled up in a street corner late one night, soaked in urine and obviously sad because his puppy was missing," Shauna says. "I took him home that night and I explained to him right away that I wasn't bringing him home to Canada, that this wasn't his dream come true. But in all these years he's never really given up that dream."

Lindo's mother gave him up eleven days after he was born. Locked in a small room and deemed mentally insane, she does favours for men to pay the rent. Lindo lived with his abusive, alcoholic father in a cardboard shack until he was thrown out on the streets at age three. I try to picture my three-year-old twins fending for themselves in the hurly burly of Santo Domingo. I see them holding hands and crying. Lindo survived by rinsing plastic garbage bags from the dump and reselling them, ten bags for a peso.

Shauna says the shoeshine boys introduced him to glue sniffing. *Cemento.* "That's how he got to sleep every night, that's how he got through those hungry days." Some of the scars on his face and shoulder are scalds from a pot that tipped over as he tried to steal soup from the market. Another facial scar is from lye, which Shauna believes he mistook for food.

As he grew older, Lindo acquired a much-coveted shoeshine kit himself, and then worked unloading beets and cabbages at the market where he slept at night. As a teenager, he had a construction job that allowed him to fulfill his dream of owning a pair of Nikes. Walking home one day, he was hit on the head with a hammer and his shoes were stolen. Some unknown benefactor, a passerby, paid to have him taken to hospital, where he stayed in a coma for three weeks, waking up only to despair the loss of his shoes. He still gets bad headaches.

Not being one to think through the consequences of his actions—a typical problem for children who suffer fetal alcohol syndrome or brain damage from solvent abuse—Lindo, at age seventeen, agreed to sit on a couch full of cocaine until the dealer arrived. The cops came first and arrested him, hanging him by his hands and beating him for five days.

Shauna says Lindo has never stolen anything from her or her friends. He still goes to visit his mother, who abandoned him, and his father, who beat him with electrical wire. He tells Shauna he wants to buy his mom a new dress someday and take her out for lunch. "I think because he knows about hard times and about hunger, he has a real soft spot," she tells me. "No matter how friggin' starving the guy is, he never finishes all his food. He always gives half away to an old lady or a kid or somebody. And if there isn't anyone around, he shares it with a dog."

It's telling that Lindo, who scrambled his brain with toxic chemicals as a means to cope with the extreme wilful neglect of his childhood, responds to the poverty and starvation of others with such empathy. In giving away half the food that could assuage his own hunger pains, he is, in effect, choosing to live always with some pain, to bear it in order to ease the burden of others, whether those "others" are two or four-legged. Maybe survival of the fittest is just a form of gluttony. Maybe some of the pain I bear from the lawsuit is helping ease the pain of others more directly affected. Lindo's capacity to keep giving in the face of such startling depravity is inspiring, and gives me a new perspective on my perception of the injustices against me, which pale by comparison.

～

I'm daydreaming, staring at a large tree that overhangs a shallow river where it empties into the ocean. Its thick, denuded trunk is the colour and shape of ginger root, bearing rounded nubs of branches from centuries past. The tree dates back 750-1,200 years, to ancient times when the matrilineal Taíno fished at this idyllic confluence and worshiped Atabey, their goddess of fresh waters and fertility, and her son Yúcahu, the god of the yucca plant. Upon first encountering the Taíno in nearby Bahamas in 1492, Christopher Columbus wrote, "They traded with us and gave us everything they had, with good will. They took great delight in pleasing us... They are very gentle and without knowledge of what is evil; nor do they murder or steal. Your highness may believe that in all the world there can be no better people." It's hard, then, to fathom the depth of heartless avarice that followed. On his second voyage to Hispaniola (now Dominican Republic and Haiti) Columbus demanded from each Taíno fourteen and older a "hawk's bell full of gold every three months," or twenty-five pounds of spun cotton, or else their hands were cut off and they were left to bleed to death.

A woman's gentle voice floats into my thoughts.

"It's a wishing tree," says Ricki, the young, Danish manager of the only restaurant on Playa Las Ballenas, a two-kilometre-long stretch of beach paradise we've come to love and visit daily. "You hold it and inhale and make your wish, but it can't be for something material," she tells us.

The children and I wade through the ankle-deep river channel and carefully tread barefoot up its black volcanic shoreline to the base of the Gumbo-limbo tree. Considered one of the most wind-tolerant and hurricane-resistant of all trees, it bends at nearly a right angle over the water, reaching out from its base like a T-Rex about to pounce. The boys straddle its girth and silently invoke their wishes. I think about what I want.

After the children scramble down and make their way towards Francois, I walk beside the tree, resting my face on its smooth bark and wrapping my arms around it. I breathe in and make two wishes. The first is that my family remains safe and healthy; the second is more personal. "I would like to understand why, when I speak out for what I think is right, I'm attacked in such a vicious, public way. If I could make some sense of this, I think I might become a lot happier person. Thank you."

My tree hugging's interrupted by an exuberant announcement from Max.

"Mom! Mom! We're going to go catch crabs off the bridge with Dad."

"Okay. Put your hat on," I yell across the river.

"This is about crabs, Mom, not wearing hats," Max declares, as he runs with purpose to the arched, wooden bridge that spans a deeper section of the river, where young Dominican boys wile away days dangling bread-baited string, hoping for a bite.

I walk back toward the restaurant and mindlessly flop into a chair at a table wedged into the sand. Holding the tree has made me feel heavy. It's not just the tree. Ever since I was served papers for my defamation suit, I've felt as if I'm locked inside myself, in some dark, hardened place where laughter isn't welcome. I yearn to bust loose. Feel softness and light.

Crabs cannot grow in a linear fashion like most animals because they have a hard outer shell, or exoskeleton, that won't grow. It protects them like armour, but must be shed to allow them to expand.

"Would you like a drink?"

Ricki startles me. I'd been so lost in thought, lulled by the azure hues of the ocean and salty breeze that I hadn't realized I am, in fact, the only one sitting at her outdoor restaurant.

"Or maybe a beer?" she offers.

"Oh, it's a bit early for that don't you think?"

"Perhaps, but it is hot and the beer is cold," she tempts.

I glance down the river at Francois and the boys who seem well ensconced in their crabbing mission, all wearing hats.

"You know, sure. I'll take a beer Ricki. Thank you."

A day before molting, the crab starts to absorb seawater and begins to swell up like a balloon. This helps expand the old shell and causes it to come apart at the seam that runs around the body, or carapace. The carapace then opens up like a lid.

Gradually, the tall, perspiring bottle empties and I'm filled with a boozy mixture of gratitude and self-pity. When Francois arrives with the boys for lunch, I burst into tears; the pressures of holding myself together throughout my legal ordeal have taken a toll and slowly, I'm releasing them.

Max arrives with a smile as wide as the island and so much unadulterated joy and enthusiasm that, for a moment, I long to be six.

"Mom! Mom! Look. We got crabs for dinner."

~

Shauna is visiting our place, an Italian-owned vacation condo we stumbled upon for a steal. A two-storey Haitian mural of women with impossibly elongated necks touting pineapples on their heads looks down from the living room over slate tile floors and thick pine railings. It would seem well-appointed even in Canada, but here, compared to the tin shed without electricity where Shauna stays in Los Puentes—almost daily refuting village elders' pleas she keep a gun under her pillow for safety—it feels like an embarrassment of riches. Shauna notes there is even a blender.

She speaks with the same calm, rhythmic cadence regardless of what she's talking about. When I ask if her husband was able to buy the building supplies for the medical clinic with the money we gave him the other day, she replies calmly that no, he never made it to the hardware store. She's not exactly sure what happened to the money, but believes Charo may have spent it at a bar. If this discomfits her, I don't detect it in her speech.

I'm angry the money didn't reach its intended destination. I know Charo's frustrated by the pitiful wage of the all-inclusive resort where he works and the racist attitudes that bar his daughter from riding the hotel bus or using its toilets because she is, in Shauna's words, half brown. He's tasted human and worker's rights under union protection in Canada, only to return to his homeland and be treated no better than his slave ancestors. And he's a man who wanted to escape his responsibilities by tying one on. I decide, for everyone's sake, not to make a big deal over thirty-five dollars.

Somewhere between cutting up mangoes and pausing for yet another examination of the small green lizards our children catch with pride, Shauna mentions, almost casually, that the village has been a bit hushed of late after the murder of a ten-year-old girl. She went missing and was discovered just days before our visit in an outhouse that I'd used. Beyond being shocked and dumbfounded, I need to know how Shauna can live like this—all of it. What is her story?

I learn her mother died when she was nine and she never knew her father. An uncle raised her until she was eighteen, after which she drifted to Belize, where she lived with a fisherman's family. She was much like an orphan, in some ways, like Lindo.

∼

Our boys don't want to eat the crabs. Fine. All the more for us. After devouring three, Francois and I join the children in the living room where, to our astonishment, we happen upon a satellite TV broadcast of the ceremony heralding the creation of Nunavut. It is April 1, 1999, and the Inuit land claim has woven a new territory into the Canadian fabric. Were I at home, I no doubt would've been covering this event. The Inuktitut language from the broadcast sounds even more foreign against the whir and hum of our ceiling fans pushing the humidity around. We watch as the new flag is unfurled; its one-legged stone emblem of a place-marking Inuksuk easily doubles as a crucifix. Its red and yellow colours look incredibly vibrant. And my hands seem to be growing.

I've always had long fingers, but my hands look really big. I look up. Those painted Haitian women on the wall peering down at me seem REALLY big, too. Wait... no, it's the room getting smaller. And the Inuktitut seems to be staying in my head longer now, like tiny echoes. My toes feel weird. I can't feel my legs attached to them.

"Francois?"

"Yes?"

"Do you feel kind of funny?"

"Yah, I do."

"Like how?"

"I don't know, I can't describe it. Like I'm expanding, maybe?"

"Me too. Why is this happening?"

"Maybe it was the crabs? Maybe it's food poisoning?"

"I don't feel nauseous or sick."

"Me either... it's not all that bad really," he says with a wry grin.

"No... unnerving though." I look at the boys, who are sun-tired and quiet.

"Hey guys, please go upstairs and get ready for bed. Dad and I will help you brush your teeth in a few minutes." They don't argue.

"The kids didn't eat any crab, right?" Francois asks me.

"No."

"Good."

"What should we do?" I ask.

"Well, let's just wait here and see where this goes."

We sit exploring our new dimensions—a stone like no other—until we no longer feel like we're puffing out or shrinking and feel confident we can go to bed and, like Nunavut, rise anew in the morning.

The crab extracts itself from its old shell by pushing and compressing all of its appendages repeatedly. First it backs out, then pulls out its hind legs, then its front legs, and finally its eyestalks, antennae and mouthparts. It leaves behind the esophagus, its entire stomach lining and some of its intestine. This moulting process takes about fifteen minutes.

When my eyes open the next morning I'm lucid, but in a more welcome kind of altered state. My first thoughts are that I'm happy to be alive, a refreshing change from the worrisome flood of accusatory legalese that's been the hallmark of my waking moments since the advent of the lawsuit. The tightness in my stomach, that nervous knot, has vanished. I wiggle my toes and stretch my arms above my head. Yes. Good. All limbs are in working order. And yet, I'm different. Transformed. After nearly a month on the island, I'm seeing the world through different eyes, with broader, less self-absorbed focus. Physically, whatever it was that took place last night has left me feeling a bit weak and vulnerable, but also relaxed, as if I've survived the gruelling punishment of a marathon and earned the right to slow down. Rest. I swing my legs sideways off the bed and take a few wobbly first steps into my day.

After moulting, the new shell is very soft at first, making the crab vulnerable to predators. Within a few days, the shell hardens up. It becomes very hard after a month.

From Shauna, we learn we'd suffered shellfish poisoning caused by a toxic type of plankton that gets eaten or filtered by the crab. We'd been lucky, ours was a relatively mild and short-lived neurotoxic poisoning, which explains our hallucinations, but other forms, such as paralytic shellfish poisoning, can cause paralysis, or death. When a local fisherman later shows up at our door with four juvenile crabs on offer, we politely decline.

∽

Shauna and I are sipping a cappuccino at an outdoor restaurant across the way from the Los Terrenas jailhouse. Lindo never did cut the grass. Yet, for reasons never made clear, he is allowed to go free. Perhaps by merely showing up with my notebook, by not looking the other way, I helped intimidate the gullible warden. The pen, then, *is* mightier than the sword.

As we wait for Lindo to gather his meagre belongings, I tell Shauna that Francois was not happy about my coming here this morning. I open up about the lawsuit for the first time. I tell her about defending Linda, a school counsellor who had exercised her duty to report allegations of child sexual abuse to social services, and how the school district subsequently disciplined her. I explain she'd actually been accused of making "too many" reports, and that while, yes, she did have the most reports in the region, every one of them had resulted in some intervention on behalf of a child who was being abused and needed a safe place. I end by declaring Linda was good at her job, the children trusted her, and yet she was forced out of the system.

There are striking similarities between Linda's circumstances and those Shauna then recounts. She tells me she'd been a paraprofessional at a high school in Kimberley, British Columbia, assisting students in the classroom. While she had a social work degree, she wasn't a counsellor, but students came to her with their problems—some serious enough she had to alert the authorities. One school counsellor felt she was being circumvented and a power struggle ensued. She ordered Shauna not to make any more calls to social services and to direct all students to her first.

"And I just said, 'no way.' I'd never turn a kid away, especially if the student took that huge first step to come and talk to someone."

Then a young girl in foster care asked Shauna to be at a hearing that would decide her future. The counsellor had social services bar Shauna from the meeting, but Shauna assured the girl she'd attend.

"I waited till the meeting was five minutes in, there were twelve people sitting around the table. I just pulled up a chair and sat very quietly beside the kid. I don't think I said two words," Shauna says.

"But I'm sure that was one of the last straws for me, doing the right thing for the kid in the face of the opposition from the school administrators. You don't get away with that too often."

After six years working at the school, her contract was not renewed. No explanation was given.

Apart from the uncanny parallels between Shauna's and Linda's experiences, I take note that during my four weeks in Dominican Republic, the only person I meet who speaks English is *this* woman, with *this* story. She reminds me in many ways of Linda. These women work in the trenches of child welfare. Dedicated foot soldiers saving lives. I'm just a messenger, albeit one who frequently gets shot at. My perspective has changed since coming to this island. I realize now I do my work from a privileged place, having friends and family who support me, a roof over my head, food in my belly, and the investigative and communicative skills to bring victims' stories to light. Like the crab with its hard-shelled armour, I'm well protected.

Despite our different roles, Shauna, Linda and I share a common goal: to clean up the dark, tainted underworld that allows child abuse to fester. And that requires digging deeper, poking holes in people's stories, moving sideways and behind—our antennae alert for anything we may have missed. We don't march in a straight line with blinders on and ears covered, avoiding dark, murky places. We tunnel through them. When mangrove crabs tunnel into the mud, they create a complex series of interconnected burrows that act as conduits for change. Water, nutrients and air follow them, altering the structure and chemistry of the sediments, breathing important new life into the ecosystem. This makes more refuge, shelter, and food for every species that lives there. It's a life-supporting process known as "bioturbation." The crabs are a kind of ecosystem engineer.

I like to think that Shauna, Linda and I are doing something similar, "shaking things up" so we can engineer safe and healthy habitats for children to grow. I'm so happy to have met Shauna, to have left my shell and ventured into her caring, albeit at times disturbing, world.

~

Shauna buys Lindo some soap and shampoo. He'd been detained in a small cage with a dozen other men and no toilet, the guards poking at all of them with broomsticks like they were circus animals. I understand better now why Lindo defied the warden. A lifetime of suffering had earned neither death nor authority his respect. Somehow he loses the toiletries by the time he reaches the village.

Shauna tells me she did seriously try to adopt Lindo when he was nine, getting all the way to the home inspection stage in Canada, but she didn't have the ten thousand dollars required to complete the process. Lindo still talked about taking an illegal refugee boat to Puerto Rico where he would make his way to New York City and "just ask someone where Shauna lives."

After my family leaves the Dominican, Lindo suffers another loss. His one true friend, Sangeye, is struck dead by lightning while working barefoot in a field with a machete. Lindo had stolen his shoes, which might have grounded the charge and spared Sangeye's life.

Two years after our Dominican trip, Shauna tells me Lindo had been contacting her weekly in Canada asking for fifty dollars with "a real urgency in his voice," so she sent him some money. At first, Lindo was trying to buy medicine for his father who'd been beaten in the same neighbourhood where Lindo had taken the hammer to his head. Then the requests just stopped. She suspects Lindo is dead, having met his fate in prison. She used all of her contacts and resources to try to find him, even calling Fort Alesa in Samaná, but it's particularly hard to track him down because he didn't go by his real name, Mariano Perez. Like many Dominicans, he used his nickname to prevent bad spells under *brujaeria*, a type of witchcraft, from being cast upon him. Almost every street boy in the Dominican is named Lindo—Spanish, for beautiful.

5

DEER
gentleness and loving

I'm at a five-day memoir-writing workshop in the Gulf Islands of British Columbia, sharing my cabin with Ruth and Nancy, women who were strangers to me until we converged here yesterday after I arrived. My bed sits kitty-corner to Ruth's, flush to a window overlooking the dark and dripping green forest of arbutus and juniper where we are told to be on the alert for cougars, but all I ever see are deer.

In Celtic mythology, deer appear as enticers into the Faery Realm, like the Greek mythological heroes who lure a person to new adventures and opportunities for wisdom. The adventures, however, come with inherent dangers and require some degree of caution.

The forest lays claim to Cortes Island, located in the rain shadow of Vancouver Island on the north end of the Strait of Georgia. It's home to the Klahoose and Coast Salish First Nations, who I'm sure have their own island place name, but the one on all the maps immortalizes the Spanish conqueror of Mexico, and was named so in 1793 by a Spanish mapmaker, just passing through.

Saskatchewan author Sharon Butala leads the workshop. Sharon's visionary memoirs about living in a remote region of endless prairie, extreme climate and isolation—separated from friends, family and career—have brought affirmation to my own struggles in the northern wilderness. Sharon comes to know that her landscape informs a new way of seeing. "In the purity of the morning," she writes, "I understand how much more there is to the world than meets the eye, I see that the world fails to dissolve at the edges into myth and dream, only because one wills it not to." I feel less alone when I read her books, as though she's validated my choice to live in the margins of society, but I am a fumbling novice by comparison.

More than simply marvelling at the beauty of my environs, I wish to truly *feel* them, to hear and see and smell with heightened awareness and sensitivity. Parts of me are splayed open and vulnerable, wild with craving. I crave the types of powerful dreams and visions that guide Sharon deeper towards her own spirituality, her "womanly soul," as she calls it. I'm venturing into that dark, uncharted territory and, admittedly, I could use a mapmaker.

Jeanette and France had started me down this path, awakening me to the idea of supportive forces or energies that could help me cope with the acrimony of my lawsuit. I'd begun to envision the possibility of a spirit world where guardian angels, gentle as deer, fawn over us with healing energy should we acknowledge them and ask for their help.

The Buddha, in a previous life, was believed to be a deer known as the Banyan King. He offered his own life after a pregnant doe pleaded to be spared from being hunted. His act was of such great compassion it led the human king to put an end to all animal killing.

But another part of me, the side of my brain trained by the empirical, scientific paradigm of "truth-proving" that predominates in our time, tells me to remain cautious and sceptical. I'm walking a philosophical tightrope, listing from side to side as the winds blow from all directions.

~

Ruth worked in corporate telecommunications before branching off on her own as a motivational life coach in Vancouver, where she also coaches breast cancer survivors on rowing dragon boats. Nancy put herself through law school while single parenting and has her own family law practice. The first day of our stay, she and Ruth invited me for a hike through the woods.

We'd barely left our room when Christa, a shy, elfin woman who's also in our class, joined us on the path. For no apparent reason, she flipped over on her ankle and wrenched it violently, leaving her hobbling. Ruth and Nancy immediately sacrificed our plans and tended to the injury, despite Christa's insistence she was fine and we should carry on. I wanted to venture into the forest, but my new friends were showing such selflessness, I quickly admonished myself and helped hoist the tiny Christa to our room to apply ice, heat and arnica to her ankle. En route I took a wistful glance down the path and saw a deer melt into the woods.

In shamanism, the deer is associated with gentleness, caring, sensitivity, graceful beauty, innocence and keen observation, teaching us to be kind and patient with other people.

Earlier that day, we read aloud a sample of our work. Christa's essay was about a fateful phone call telling her that her brother had jumped off San Francisco's Golden Gate Bridge and died. Ruth spoke to her later and learned he'd been a Hari Krishna for fifteen years and, having finally cut ties with the cult, could not bear the remorse over his lost years. Now, Christa confided that her husband of twenty years had just left her. Ruth listened intently, only taking her eyes off Christa's when it was time to wrap her ankle with a tensor bandage.

That night our class attended a public reading by Sharon. Christa and I were among a handful of other participants who also read. I am deathly afraid of public speaking—even giving a short introduction of myself the night I arrived caused my stomach to churn—but I'm determined to push my boundaries this trip. By volunteering to read, I confessed to the class I had purposefully invited terror into my life. The workshop participants were sympathetic, even encouraging me to practice aloud for them. An older American woman came up to me later and asked what my favourite colour was.

"Brown," I tell her.

"Well then darlin'," she drawls, "I'll wear brown tonight and sit right in front where you can see me." And she does. I'm anxious to the point of feeling like I could black out, but I make it through. Ruth played M.C., a daunting task given she only knew some of our first names. It isn't until we are back in our cabin about to crawl into bed, that Ruth informs me she sleepwalks. "But don't worry, if I start to walk around, just wake up Nancy. She knows what to do."

Deer are typically nocturnal, using the cover of darkness as protection against predators.

If Ruth hadn't felt it courteous to inform me she sleepwalks, I wouldn't have lain awake in anticipation, and I would not have heard her say, "Hi, I'm Tony Heywood, and I love football." She's in her bottom bunk in our wooden cabin, fast asleep, not walking. But her words are clear as day.

The next morning I tell Ruth she had been talking, not walking, in her sleep.

"You mentioned Tony Heywood," I say. "I think you must have been thinking about Christa, her last name is Heywood." Ruth looks at me in silence, a quiet calculation, before speaking. "I didn't know Christa's last name. I bet you Tony is the name of her brother who committed suicide. Sometimes people come to me at night, people who can't communicate otherwise." She continues on matter of factly. "It can get pretty crowded in my room. They're just comfortable with me. Christa's brother probably saw me talking to her about him. And then we helped her with her ankle, and that made him comfortable enough to come around."

The words hang in mid-air.

Come around? As in, a dead man comes into our sleeping area, somehow gets into Ruth's body and has her speak some testimonial on his behalf, as if confessing at an A.A. meeting, except, instead of declaring he's an alcoholic, Tony Heywood declares he loves football! I know I'm supposed to discount this information, file it alongside zombies and vampires in the realm of improbable ghost stories, but haven't I come here craving experiences that defy conventional, fact-bound logic? I'm fearful now of Ruth, the adrenaline fluttering through my stomach—my body's natural survival response to threat or danger—tells me so. Yet I stay with her. I'm determined to investigate, choosing neither flight, nor fight.

When Ruth locates Christa at breakfast, she first inquires about her ankle, then, satisfied it's on the healing track, gently asks what her lost brother's name was and if he liked sports.

Christa reports that his name was Phillip Anthony (Tony), and that he'd been keen on sports, but not great at playing them. He'd always dreamed of being a great footballer. Ruth explains to her the events of the evening and her theory on Phillip/Tony's spirit using her to communicate, encouraged in part by Ruth's kindness to her.

"I think he wants you to know that he's doing well now, maybe trying new things," says Ruth tenderly.

Christa smiles faintly for the first time, and nods her head. No shock, no disbelief. Those are my purviews, along with another surge of adrenaline. Fear, yes, but excitement too.

~

Privately, Ruth tells me more about her exceptional experiences. Just recently, the father of a family of five children, who were friends of hers, died. He was quadriplegic. On the eve of his funeral, Ruth was sleeping naked to battle the heat. She awoke when she felt someone staring at her. In the doorway, there stood the father, looking robust and healthy. He saluted her heartily and said, "Carry on." She tried to find some clothes and when she looked back, he was gone. Ruth told his children that their father was walking and raising his arms again, obviously wanting them to know he was doing fine. They all found comfort in this.

Her sleepwalking experiences began when she was a child and would try to climb out of her crib so that her mother had to fashion a roof over it to contain her. And then there was the time when she was sixteen and broke through a window to get into her neighbour's house. His wife was out of town and when the man and Ruth woke up side-by-side in his bed— Ruth bleeding from the glass cuts in her hand—they both screamed in horror at the sight of one another.

She goes on to say that when everything's going right for her, especially when she's in love, streetlights go out when she walks under them. After this happened several times, she decided to try to play with them and found that sometimes when she blows on them, she can make them flicker or go out.

"No way!" I finally say (of all her tales, I find this one most incredulous, and yet also most intriguing).

Ruth says she has more stories, but I don't want to hear them. It's eerie to think I'm sharing a cabin with a woman able to tap into some alternative universe, a spirit world where ghosts feel free to come knocking.

~

The second night, as soon as I lie down and close my eyes, I hear a low humming noise that seems to settle and reverberate in my lungs. *Go away*, I speak in my head. Something small falls off the wall, crashing onto the floor behind my headboard. Too dark to find it now, I think. Eventually, fatigue overcomes anxiety. I pull up the covers and drift into a restless sleep.

Deer sleep sporadically at night, hidden under foliage and on guard for potential dangers.

I awake to loud noises in the cabin, which I am certain is Ruth crashing about sleepwalking. I alert Nancy.

"Nancy. Nancy! Ruth is sleepwalking."

"Ruth?" Nancy says groggily.

"What?" replies Ruth.

"You in bed?"

"Of course I'm in bed!"

"Okay," concludes Nancy.

Then I think I see someone pass outside Nancy's window, someone wearing all white.

When a deer senses danger, it raises its tail to show a large white patch on its underside. This is known as "flagging," an alarm signal to other deer.

"It's just someone walking outside Laurie," says Nancy.

My heart is thumping. I can't go back to sleep.

Or do I?

Later I hear some bumping around. I think it must be someone in the room again, I try to yell out to Nancy, but no words come. I hear an inner sound, as if I have marbles stuffed in my mouth, but I know it's not audible in the room. I try to yell again and to sit up, but I can do neither. I try to thrash myself from side to side, using all my might. Nothing. I'm having difficulty breathing, completely locked within my body. I sense someone, some thing, watching me. I feel its silent derision.

Then, my eyes are open, yet all I see is a faint brown line. I am lucid, thinking this must be a dream, yet I have never felt more awake, more frightfully aware, in my life. *What do you want from me?* I ask in my head. *Leave me alone. Get out!* I am being toyed with, laughed at. I want to cry, to exorcise my terror, but there is no blinking, no tears, no release from this cement cast.

"NNNAAAAANCY!" I try...

Nothing.

Exhausted, I surrender.

I lie there, still, awaiting some fate. All that comes is sleep. As I drift off, my thoughts turn to Ruth, a feeling that she has somehow hosted this unwanted visitor, this presence.

~

I awake tired, a buzz of anger running through me. I want desperately to talk to Nancy alone, but that means I'll have to join her on her morning jog. Ruth yawns and stretches her long limbs and body. "How'd you sleep?" she asks, smiling.

"Not. Very. Well," I say, my voice spitting barbs.

Her face drops. She's stung. *Good.*

I tell Nancy I'd like to run with her.

"Sure," she says. Her blue eyes glance at Ruth. We begin uphill, finally, my first venture into the forest.

Rounding the first bend, I see a deer dart through the trees, the only wildlife we encounter.

Deer have acute sense of hearing and smell. Three sets of glands between and above the hooves serve to communicate the passage of a deer along a trail to others of its own kind.

Nancy's starting pace is equivalent to that of one of my sprints. Seeing as I've imposed myself on her daily ritual, I feel compelled to keep up, rather than ask her to gear down. Talking is out of the question until we reach the turnaround point and start our descent; then my account of the night's events spills out in one long uninterrupted sentence.

"Sleep paralysis," says Nancy, when I finish. "It happens to me too, and to my son; he told me that's what it's called."

This lawyer has just given me a clinical definition and is likely about to expound on some logical explanation for this terrifying phenomenon. Hallelujah! I'm easing back into familiar territory.

"So what is it?" I ask.

"I don't know really," she says. "But when it starts to happen to me sometimes I can leave my body and look down on myself being paralysed. And I've also learned to concentrate very hard on making my toes move and eventually that releases it."

I would come to learn that Nancy was right, the scientific explanation for hearing noises while lying supine, feeling completely awake but unable to move or speak while a shadowy figure looms or presses against you, is called sleep paralysis. According to the book *Sleep Paralysis, Nightmares, Nocebos, and the Mind-Body Connection*, by University of California professor Sherry Adler, sleep researchers believe it is a disturbance of the normal regulation of sleep, a waking awareness of the muscular paralysis that occurs during REM sleep, which is designed to keep us from acting out our dreams.

But Adler says that's only part of the explanation. She prefers to call the encounter a night-mare (different from a nightmare, or bad dream, and also not night terrors), which in its original sense meant "a nocturnal visit of an evil being that threatens to press the very life out of its terrified victim." *The Oxford English Dictionary* defines the creature as "a spirit or monster supposed to beset people... by night, settling upon them when they are asleep and producing a feeling of suffocation by its weight." These "nocturnal pressing spirits" have names, such as *Old Hag* to Newfoundlanders, *dab tsog* to Laotians and *Alpdruk* to Germans. Across cultures, most people relate their experiences as belonging to a spirit realm, albeit a demonic one. It certainly felt that way to me. Some cultures with a deeply ingrained belief in, and fear of, the pressing spirit, experience what Adler calls the nocebo effect (the opposite of the beneficial placebo effect) during a night-mare. There are even documented cases of nightmares causing death.

In her book, Adler quotes Austrian philosopher Rudolph Steiner as saying that besides waking and sleeping, there is a third state, "even more important for intercourse with the spirit world," and that's the brief time spent in the act of waking, or in the act of going to sleep. Adler says that's when the night-mare occurs, poised between the natural and supernatural worlds. Perhaps for Ruth, this threshold, this door, remains open longer than for most people.

Back at the cabin, the combination of exercise and talking about my experience with Nancy has softened me so I'm now able to speak to Ruth. I begin by telling her about the low humming noise. She nods her head in recollection, adding, "Did you also feel a slight shaking inside?" Yes, I did. Ruth listens as the rest of the tale unfolds, then, by way of explanation says only, "Sometimes higher learning comes when we reach a certain level of kindness." I want to ask her what she means, but we're late and rush inside to class.

~

That a shadow side might battle for my attention should I choose to believe in a spirit world had not occurred to me. Just as individuals need to understand, acknowledge and integrate the shadow aspects of their personalities in order to attain consciousness, according to Jung, it seemed probable that if I wanted to embrace a deeper understanding of my own spirituality, I'd have to acknowledge that the journey may not be all sweetness and light.

White circles on the reddish-brown coats of the fawn appear like shade and sunspots on the forest floor, making them masters of camouflage. Amerindian medicine teaches that, like the fawn's coat, to create gentleness, safety and thus peace, both the light and dark may be loved.

~

The earthy older woman who wears a gauzy brown tunic the night of my reading, says this week she's calling herself "Phairee." She has long silvery hair and tanned skin that reminds me of bark on a young tree. Her story is *The Silent Womb Screams*, bare-knuckle prose about the baby boy she bore at age sixteen after a date rape, and the shunning she received from her backwoods Tennessee community, including her heavy-handed preacher father and complicit mother. She held her baby for five minutes before he was whisked away. Her parents told her the birth was a dream.

I see her standing on a path staring dreamily into the woods, hauling on her hand-rolled cigarette. A doe stares back at her, until my presence startles them both. "I'm enjoying the deer here," she tells me, adding she's a sister of the deer and attuned back home to their many fine teachings. "I've always been drawn to them too," I say. Then she stubs her cigarette out and presses it back into her tin.

The Deer Woman is a mythological, shapeshifting figure known to American First Nations to appear as an old woman, a young maiden or a deer, with lessons regarding untamed sexuality.

Later, while I'm eating lunch, Phairee walks towards me carrying a large round Aboriginal drum and a drawstring bag. Apparently Ruth's spoken to her. Phairee is also a shaman.

"You shouldn't have any problems tonight," she says. She's been drumming and has just smudged my cabin with the lighting of dried, sacred herbs, such as sage. Phairee tells me that by smudging the room, she's purifying it, driving out negative energies.

An early Christian text states how deer would spit water into a crevice where a poisonous snake hid. When the creature was thus driven out of its hiding place the deer trampled it.

Phairee asks me if I live close to the earth. I tell her I live near a lake, right on the crust of the earth, the Precambrian rock, void of topsoil. She thinks living this close to nature enables a person to tune in to more subtle vibrations. She asks if I see wild animals? Yes, often, I tell her. Bears especially, but caribou, ravens, wolves, fox, fish, lynx, eagles... Her eyes grow wide.

She asks if I'd like her to conduct a ceremony to determine which of these animals are totems for me—my guides towards spiritual growth and protection. Deer guides her. The ceremony involves quiet, drumming and meditation. I decline. Much as it seems like a useful piece of personal growth information, I'm so full up with big new ways of thinking that the information has bottlenecked. I need time to dispel some of my old ways of knowing first.

Phairee understands. She pulls something from her drawstring bag, a small white deerskin pouch with a bone button and blue and red beading in the shape of a star. "I'd like you to have this," she says. "It was given to me by a very powerful woman when I was in the same place in my journey six years ago. It probably wouldn't hurt to wear it around your neck tonight. It will help give you strength." She tells me I'm to put anything I feel has "goodness and power" inside it—pictures of my children and whatever else makes me feel good.

By lifting her tail to show its white underside, the deer mother gives her fawn a mark to follow.

She's smiling and rubbing her hand in a circular motion across her stomach the way pregnant women do. She wants to share something with me. She'd chosen Paul as the name for the baby boy she gave up Sept. 6, 1958. She says she kissed her fingers and placed them on the middle of his forehead, which she called his "third eye," and told him she'd love him forever.

"Well, Paul is now Greg, and he's forty-one and had been looking for me too, and I saw him for the first time last week," she says. "I'm not talking about it much. I'm just savouring it all in here for a while, you know, in my belly."

I hug her long and hard, then I walk down to the ocean and find a small stick of driftwood I think Francois would appreciate, which I later use to pick up a small purple starfish that attaches itself to the stick, making an exquisite looking magic wand. I want to keep that starfish, but instead pry it off the wood and release it back to the ocean. As I walk to my cabin, a small deer appears in front of me. We both freeze in our tracks. It reaches down, pulls another mouthful of grass, then turns and flees up the path, past my cabin door and into the forest.

It's the closest I've been to a deer in the wild, perhaps a sign that I'm being accepted into their myth-steeped world.

That night, I envision white lights around me, clutch the deerskin bag next to my heart and drift into a peaceful sleep. With my fears under control, I'm able to open my heart more to Ruth. I learn that few people are aware of Ruth's paranormal proclivities, and that those close to her who are aware have chosen not to acknowledge them. Even her family would not discuss her sleepwalking. She acknowledges it's not always easy being Ruth, or Ruth's friend. She says having "razor-sharp psychic abilities" is a challenging power to hold. When she opens to all the energies that are available to come through her, she wants to share, but not everyone is ready for her insights. Like me. She sensed that even though I arrived craving an awakening to some of the higher mysteries, when that world began to open to me, ever so slightly, I became scared. She doesn't believe my "night-mare" was evil, or that there are alien energies waiting to attack us, only energies we bump into and are unable to immediately comprehend.

"We insert fear as part of the experience, for the mind needs to put words to those energies we don't yet understand," she tells me.

"All of this is an illusion. It may have felt nasty for you to be paralyzed, but it opened your heart and mind in a way that they'd never been before, and you'd been yearning for that and you needed the violent shock to shatter old paradigms and open yourself up to new ways of thinking."

I ask her what she'd meant when she'd said: "Sometimes higher learning comes when we reach a level of kindness."

"I said that?"

"Yes."

"I didn't make that comment. It came through me," she concludes. "I don't think that's coming out of my intellect pool. My sense is it's something you needed to hear in order to not be afraid—almost like you needed to find kindness for me too, so as to not push me away, to be open to the portal. Because higher learning's really great until you're asked to make a change, and move outside of your thought process or your way of operating. That can be really threatening because life as you know it shifts in the snap of your finger. The truth you've known forever is taken out from beneath you."

I connect with several people on this trip with whom I'm comfortable telling about my experiences, including the lawsuit and the paranormal activities of the night. None are surprised, and they in turn share with me other unconventional teachings. One of those is Sheree, the Oregon geologist who substituted energy work for anesthetic during thyroid treatment, and who draws strength from the playfulness of otters. It was Sheree who advised me not to deprive the ocean of a purple starfish, much as I coveted one. Then it was Sheree who later helped me peel a dead one from a creosote-soaked streetlight post, adding, "I think the message for you here is not to get stuck."

As the friendships among our group solidify throughout the week, we vow to meet again the next summer. And we will, on Idaho's Salmon River.

When I pack up my things to go, I find under my bed the silver necklace with the strange clover-like design on it that Francois had given me for Valentine's Day. It must've fallen off the nail that fateful night when I heard much bumping around, although its clasp is intact, and the nail is on a steep angle. There's no logical explanation for how it would suddenly fall while I lay still, but I fight temptation to attribute it to spirit energy.

Ruth and Nancy insist I drive with them and some others from our group to Nancy's cottage located on, of all places, Protection Island. En route, that bottlenecking of information I was experiencing seems to manifest itself physically. I contract sudden, and vehement respiratory problems. I have trouble breathing and begin to wheeze. My body aches in the onset of what I anticipate will be a wicked flu. When we arrive at Nancy's cottage, Miriam, a German doctoral student from our class, asks if she can perform Reiki on me—something taught to her by her aunt in Europe. It's very much like Jeanette's therapeutic touch. When she's done, the women leave me to rest while they take a walk. When they return, I've recovered and feel 100 percent. We go to a restaurant for dinner.

When I finally say goodbye to Ruth and the rest of my group of new friends, I'm ready for my days and nights to take on a semblance of their old normalcy. But this will not be the case. The learning continues on my journey home, only this time it unfolds more like the sacred lotus of Asian art and religion—in gentler, subtler ways.

My return trip includes a stop in Victoria, where I meet a niece and nephew for the first time. Niece Ayva, then nine, moves with a beauty and grace that would soon define her as a professional ballerina. On a walk with me near the ocean, she dances her way through an old growth forest, regaling me with heartfelt stories about the fairies who are everywhere in nature, pointing out the homes both the wicked and the wonderful would choose. One of her fairy friends, Bluebell, is pregnant, she tells me. Her due date is the same as Ayva's birthday, September 6—the same day that Phairee's son was born.

"There's a queen of the bad fairies," Ayva tells me. "She has a black dress with red flowers made of good fairies' blood to trick children into coming to her. She brings the children in by saying she's going to give them nice fairy treats. Then she puts them in a pretty flower room. With her magic, she then turns the room ugly and there are no doors for escape. The walls are magic, so they can't come open."

"So, are the children trapped forever?" I ask.

"The only way anyone can come out is with the help of a good fairy, or a child who believes in fairies. The good fairy or the child would have to use magic to get a whole group of older fairies and their power and then the children could escape and run away. When they're trapped, the children feel frightened and try to build up all their power to escape, but they're too young. It's only when they get older that they have enough. They yell and cry out, but nobody hears a single thing. It's like they're silent."

I tell her that I'd had a good fairy come to my rescue after I felt trapped this week: Phairee.

"Did she have long, silvery white hair?" she asks me.

"Yes, she did," I say. And her jaw drops.

Later that day, we visit Ayva's neighbour Charlie, a draft dodger from the Vietnam war who was arrested and imprisoned before becoming a labour activist and artist. Charlie is dying of multiple sclerosis and confined to a wheelchair. He shows me a large dark blue painting with a few faint shades of lighter blue within and says this is his rendition of what it would be like to be stuck in a dark, underground mine for six days, which is what happened to someone he knew. It looks reminiscent of what I saw during my night-mare, only my foreboding wall of colour was brown.

On the morning I'm leaving, Charlie summons me outside, where he tells me his wheelchair has a flat tire and he's completely stuck. The wheelchair company is coming to fix it, and his mother and brother are inside and able to help him, but he wants to tell me something before he's moved.

"I've been sitting here staring at the treetops, wondering what it would be like to be a tree and be stuck in one place all your life with the same view," he says, his gaze a permanent look upwards as a result of nerve and brain damage from his disease.

"That's an interesting thought, Charlie," I reply. "Well, it's been very nice to meet you." Then I hurry off to catch the ferry to the mainland. I marvel later when I open an Alice Munro book I'd bought at the Edmonton airport on my way to the writing workshop. I felt inexplicably compelled to have this book, but by buying it, I'd arrived at the departure lounge one person too late to make a standby connection, which caused a domino effect of travel headaches to get to Cortes Island—planes, taxis, hitchhiking and buses—that left me fatigued my entire stay, but also, perhaps more open, and susceptible, to just about everything. The book opened to a story called "Cortes Island" about a young woman tending to a man in a wheelchair, and how trapped they both felt. There was even a passage about the woman remembering being willingly trapped in her bed as a child, weary with illness and trapped as well by fever, contemplating an indecipherable message of the tree branches she sees through her window.

It was becoming quite clear to me that I wasn't to lose sight of my new way of seeing the world, not to let old ways trap me. Time to embrace the unknown and, as Ruth would say, trust that which could not be readily explained, "the place where nothing exists," in between those two ways of knowing.

One year later, in the 2001 national bestselling anthology *Dropped Threads*, Sharon Butala wrote of the propensity of midlife women "to have a more open conduit into what we call the supernatural," attributes which in previous centuries were considered witchcraft and led to burnings at the stake. She writes:

"It seems clear to me that my own unexplained experiences involve making contact with some power, or with the 'collective unconsciousness,' or, as I like to think of it, a manifestation of spirit that flows through the universe behind daily life and is available to all of us. Most of us who recognize the strengthening of our intuitive abilities, and who begin to have experiences of the unseen side of life on Planet Earth, have no desire to use such abilities for any reason except the improvement of our own emotional and spiritual life—that is, in the necessary pursuit and understanding of Self."

Sage advice.

My last stop in British Columbia before reuniting with my children is a visit with an aunt in Whiterock. While there, I have a powerful dream like none I've ever had. I open the front door of her house to see a large grey deer made of stone lying across her entire yard, facing out towards the ocean. I shut the door and call my three sons over to come see it. When I re-open the door, the stone animal has changed to a small deer and two beautiful young striped gazelles. They are very much alive, switching their tails playfully, staring at us and inviting us to come out and play. The boys and I look at each other with great anticipation, as if to say, "Let's go!" but just as we are about to bound out the door, an enormous ram head appears and blocks our way. It takes a few steps back as if preparing to ram us. I shut the door fearfully and wait. Nothing happens.

According to Jungians, deer in the dreams of women represent their own femininity in a primal, instinctive state—the Self, and its connectedness with one's surroundings.

I thought of the ram as an evil, masculine force, until I read a passage in Sharon's new book *Wild Stone Heart*. Once, while on a book tour in Missoula, Montana, she was recounting the story of how a full moon had enchanted her into walking towards her home during a dangerous flood, when a woman—possibly of Aboriginal descent—asked her if she knew the story of the boys who ran with the antelope. Sharon said she didn't. Then the woman told her the boys had been enchanted and had run with the deer until they were old men and had died. Her people have a story about following the moon to your death, she said. Be careful of the moon. I put the book down on my lap. It's one thing to be stuck in one mindset, quite another to run headfirst, without serious consideration, into another. The ram had been my protector.

By the time I reconnect with my own family in Calgary, I'm starting to feel like myself again—not the old me, but a positive, rested and more than half-full new me. I spend an evening with Francois visiting an old reporter friend of mine who lives in a small white house downtown. We sit on her front lawn, a tiny patch of green in a sea of encroaching grey office and retail development. The whole yard is framed in odd, yet exquisite small flowers—"odd," "exquisite," an apt description, as well, for the woman who planted them. I light-heartedly mention that fairies would like it here, then choose to tell the whole story of my week. When I get to the part about Ruth making streetlights go out, my friend says, "Oh, I do that too all the time." To which I reply, "That doesn't surprise me one bit." What a difference a week can make.

She bows out of going for drinks with us, but offers to drive us to Electric Avenue where the action is during Stampede week. Along the way, she notes that a streetlight went out when the car stopped under it. I hadn't noticed.

I choose an outdoor patio with a whitewashed façade because it reminds me of Greece and Francois and I can sit side-by-side at a table that faces the street. The bar across from us, my friend tells me, had been the scene of a drive-by shooting the week before. I didn't press her for details, and was saddened by this information, but Electric Avenue is buzzing with twenty-something revellers who've had too much to drink and are laughing and flirting and soon enough I'm caught up in their gaiety. I'm in love with the handsome man beside me, giddy to be footloose and free for the evening. It's one of the hottest, uncharacteristically humid nights on record.

Francois brings two gin and tonics. I'm thinking about streetlights.

"Wouldn't it be something if you could do that, just blow them out?" I say to him. "Like this one here." I point to the one just above where we are sitting.

"Oh, come on," he scoffs.

"Let's try. You go first."

He sighs, but looks at the light and gives it a quick blow to appease me. Nothing happens.

"Now I'll try," I say.

I look at the light for a moment and concentrate. I blow softly and picture my breath pushing through the humidity, timing to myself when I think it should reach the light bulb. At the exact moment I imagine my breath has arrived, the light goes out. And so do two other streetlights in front of the bar across the street.

We sit in silence, faces to the sky, neither of us moving. I'm grinning and grinning and so in love and filled with awe. The darkness doesn't elicit any "ooohs" or "aaahs" from the crowded street, everyone just carries on, although we can no longer clearly see who's walking in front of us. Francois says something, but I don't answer him. I don't want this moment to stop. I don't want to break the current of this circuit.

The lights reappear within minutes, and when they do, out of the shadows steps a cowboy.

He's dressed entirely in white, wearing a tall hat. He's thin, probably in his forties, with a weathered face that looks like it's seen its share of outdoors, and he carries a bucket of beautiful, long-stemmed red roses. He begins to politely explain that they're the symbol of love and generosity and kindness and that he's raising money for street children. Would we like to buy one? Francois asks how much they cost.

"Four dollars, sir," the cowboy replies.

Francois pulls out a ten-dollar bill. The cowboy tells me to pick out whichever rose I want. I choose one then Francois hands him the ten. He and the cowboy hold a silent exchange for several seconds, staring into each other's eyes.

"Do you want your change, sir?"

Francois slowly slides his head from side to side.

"Are you sure about that, sir?" the cowboy asks, still holding Francois' eyes.

Francois is sure.

"Why thank you, sir, thank you." He walks away.

I twirl the rose for a few seconds before asking Francois if he believes the man's story.

"I have to," he says. "What else is there to believe in?"

A man steps out of the darkness into the light with a message of love, generosity and kindness for children... yes, this is something I can believe in, too.

RAVEN
magical darkness

October 30, 2001
Dr. Richard Gerber
M.D. Livonia, Michigan

Dear Dr. Gerber
I hope this letter finds you well and safe during these tumultuous times. I want to thank you first for your most illuminating book, Vibrational Medicine. *It was brought to my attention by Bill Kompf of Edmonton, Alberta, a retired infantry officer and paratrooper. I recently interviewed him about his apparent ability to trigger streetlights to go on and off. My interest with this phenomenon started when I met a woman last summer who told me she had this same ability. I was incredulous at first, but have since experienced this phenomenon firsthand.*

To date I have spoken with our local utility company, to get a layperson's explanation of the mechanical workings of streetlights, as well as to an engineer with Southcon Technologies in South Carolina, a company that manufactures streetlights. I have also interviewed other people who claim to have this "power" to affect streetlights.

After reading Vibrational Medicine, particularly the chapter on frequency domains and human multi-dimensional anatomy, I wondered whether people who have reached what you term a higher quantity of consciousness and an accompanying frequency response may be interacting with the photocell mechanism on streetlights? According to the engineers, vibration can cause cycling within the ballast system of the lights, particularly if they are faulty to begin with. I have so many questions, and so few people to turn to for answers...

As this letter shows, I crave some explanation for my streetlight experience, refusing to believe that coincidence exacted such precise results. Even if wizards could transform things with the sweep of a magic wand and a vapour trail of stardust, at the exact point of change something physical must take place: energy moves from one form to another, atoms shift. So I turn to engineers and a physician for answers, despite—or perhaps in part because of—the bigger questions of the day. My investigation begins the week of the 9-11 terrorist attacks in New York, a week when ravens seem to be going out of their way to get my attention.

After the Tower of London was bombed during the Second World War, the ravens that had lived there for centuries, providing protection and prophecy to the kingdom, flew away.

Television is *never* part of our morning routine, but at 7 a.m. Mountain Time on September 11, 2001, Levi scaled down from his top bunk and walked into the living room where he turned on the TV and plunked his six-year-old self in front of a CBC special live broadcast. The North Tower of the World Trade Centre had been struck just minutes before. I heard the rumblings of the TV from my bed and got up to investigate, soon joined by the rest of the family. Standing stunned in front of the screen, we watched as a second jet, United Airlines flight 175, crashed into the South Tower three minutes later. Amid a sense of shock and disbelief, Francois and I managed to get the kids off to school. A new era had dawned.

One day before the attacks, in my quest to explain the phantasmagoria of my life, I speak at length by phone to a man named John Living. A retired professional engineer, John has worked for the City of Calgary's waterworks department. As a young officer in the British army, he was taught dowsing. It's a technique whereby a pointer, traditionally a forked stick, is observed for any changes in direction—supposedly in response to unseen influences—to divine the location of water veins, minerals, or anything invisible. Now John heads the Holistic Intuition Society and dowses as a means of directly connecting to what he calls energy bodies. He describes dowsing as the linking of the intuitive part of our heart-mind-brain team with the nervous-muscular system to give signals without interference from the logical thinking process. Tools, such as a stick, pendulum, or L-shaped rods are often used to magnify these signals.

I tell him what happened to me on Electric Avenue.

"As far as I can tell, it's orbs that are doing this," he says, intuiting my experience, as we speak, by dowsing with a copper coil pendulum.

"Orbs?" I ask.

"Yes, balls of light, not necessarily visible, sometimes they make things like crop circles. These are very high-energy beings, above the level of angels, let's put it like that. Probably retired gods."

John explains that energy beings—devas, angels, fairies, sprites, gods, whatever nomenclature you want to give them—are comprised of millions of caring, feeling, loving, electrons, each with a job to do. "And when you send them a message in a meaningful way, then they may well do what you ask. Perhaps your orb turned the streetlights off because you wanted proof it's possible."

Hmmm. Well, okay... I certainly hadn't anticipated this answer.

He says orbs are benevolent, having been promoted up the heavenly hierarchy through successive reincarnations, like the progressive cycle of a plant that grows, flowers and dies and then grows again. And *unlike* the lost souls of people who die suddenly, or violently, without a chance to reconcile their place in the spirit world.

Much like an exorcism, John tells me he was "clearing a person" and the force jumped right into him. "It took me over because I wasn't grounded first. I just asked that the force be taken into the light, to the right heaven, or family, or whatever, and become a force of good. And it did. It left me. Given the chance, everyone, even spirits, would rather be a force of good."

Because these ghostly musings came from a professional engineer who'd worked years for a large municipality, I was willing to give them more credence than had I been told the same information by a bejewelled crystal-ball gazer at the fairgrounds—who may very well be just as qualified to expound on such matters. But it was still just one person's interpretation, and I was determined to seek out other possible explanations in my quest for enlightenment.

John's words are fresh in my mind four days later as people around the globe paused at noon New York time to communally mourn those who died in the maelstrom of fire and twisted steel of September 11th. I choose to sit atop a sunny high point on a giant whaleback rock a short canoe paddle from my house, knees stacked directly over top of one another with my legs pointing behind me—the yoga pose of nobility. My two big dogs at that time, Shinto, a female wolf-Malamute cross; and Prince, a purebred Rough Collie male I adopted from the pound, lie panting and wet nearby, always insisting on swimming when I canoe. Facing east with my eyes closed to the still blue water and cirrus clouds that stretch before me, I concentrate on the souls of the victims, visualizing them as white figures rising up from darkness and asking that they be put to their best and highest good and find a safe place from which to do this work.

Blackflies buzz around my face. Eventually, I unravel my legs and walk into the forest. I briefly check around for cranberries, then notice Shinto looking up. There's a raven on top of a spruce. Despite the stillness and quiet, I haven't heard the usual *fhwoomp fhwoomp fhwoomp* of its powerful wings beating overhead. I turn my back to it and crouch down on the lichen-covered rock to relieve myself. But the raven flies right in front of me, lands on a nearby tree and starts "talking" to me.

It croaks, caws, gurgles, blips, bloops, coos, tut-tuts, screeches, wonk-wonks—a one-sided conversation that lasts several minutes. I remain still, listening intently. Eventually the raven flies back towards the spot where I'd been sitting. I follow. The bird's communication skills remind of a woman in Yellowknife who told me she kept answering her landline phone, only to hear a dial tone. She later discovered a raven outside her open office window had been imitating her phone's ring tone.

Ravens, like myna birds, are renowned for their astonishing array of vocalizations, including the ability to mimic. They are master tricksters.

I sit down and begin writing in my journal, but the raven once again flies directly in front of me, landing on a young birch just a few metres away. It leans in closer, as if wanting to share something particularly intimate and begins another lengthy dissertation. In all my years of living in the Arctic wilderness, I've never experienced a raven acting this way. I have a strong sense that the bird is somehow related to the worldwide prayer, and I'm shocked later that day when I consult Native American author Jamie Sams' book on animal medicine and read the following:

"Raven is the messenger that carries all energy flows of ceremonial magic between the ceremony itself and the intended destination. For instance, if a ceremony is being performed to send energy to a disaster area where people need courage and strength, Raven would be the courier for that energy flow. The intention could be to allow the people of the devastated area to feel the concern and support of the participants in the ceremony."

In Norse mythology, the God Odin had two ravens on his shoulders, Huginn (Thought) and Muninn (Memory) who flew about the world at dawn, delivering messages and gathering knowledge to report back to him. In Norse shamanic tradition, they were guides of the dead.

On my paddle home, the sun warms my back and lights the tiny curls of water moving across the lake like shards of shattered crystal. Both dogs swim ahead, hugging the shoreline. The raven follows, flying low in between us. When Prince swims into a marshy area and stirs a duck—briefly and unsuccessfully giving chase—I curse him out loud. However protective I am of wildlife's right to be in its native surroundings, free of harassment from my intruding domestic pets, I've not yet found a way to dissuade my dogs of their lupine instincts. As I shoot Prince a disapproving glare, the raven dive-bombs and pecks at him until he howls.

"The eye that mocks a father, that scorns obedience to a mother, will be pecked out by the ravens of the valley..." Proverbs 30:17 Old Testament.

Once we reach the house, I can hear the raven talking again, but I scour the roofs and treetops and can see no sign of it.

~

I spend an evening with two dear friends converting a bumper crop of wild cranberries into jams and chutney in the wake of the 9-11 attacks. The hard, deep-red berries tumble their way into large stainless steel pots where we stir and heat them with sugar and water until the whole concoction shines like liquid rubies. Our laughter mingles with the steam and the clacking of hot glass jars as conversation swirls around families, children and friendship, each of us cognizant of, and grateful for, our many blessings.

An overwhelming sense of well-being envelops me on my drive home, as if the love from that kitchen had followed me out the door and is glowing inside me. I start thinking about streetlights, about how I rarely look up. Alone on the highway, in the pitch of darkness, I take note of a string of cobra lamps coming up on my left, just before the legislative assembly, beading in on one in particular. "Like that one," I think, "wouldn't it be nice if that one right there were to suddenly go out as I drive past it."

Just as my vehicle approaches that streetlight, the light blinks. Twice. Off-on. Off-on. As if trying to speak to me.

~

If Allen Mueller thought me nutty, he did a great job of hiding it. Allen is the thoughtful, middle-aged, engineering-assistant-turned-customer-service rep who Northland Utilities Limited has delegated to answer my questions about Yellowknife streetlights. He tells me that, contrary to my childhood belief, there is not someone sitting at the ready with a giant switch deciding when to turn streetlights on, signaling an end to games of tag, statues and road hockey. The lights are all activated by the brilliance of the sun.

"Every streetlight we have operates on the same principle," Allen begins, as we head to the shop. "There's the bulb and it's connected to what we call a ballast and that's connected to a photocell, normally on top of the light or off to the side." In the morning, when the sun's brilliance inside the photocell measures a specified foot-candle value, it turns off, depriving energy to the ballast, which shuts off the streetlight. The photocell works in reverse at night. When it doesn't get *enough* brilliance, it switches on, which sends a current into the ballast that heats up the sodium gas to get the bulb working.

Smart ravens sit on the photocell, covering it so the device believes it is dark. This triggers the bulb to light up and give off heat energy, thereby warming the raven's feet on a cold day.

I tell Allen about the streetlight going off and on twice near the legislative building the other night.

"That sounds like a typical cycling," he says. "My personal feeling is there's something mechanically wrong with it. I would guess it's a loose connection or a ballast that may be malfunctioning."

Then I tell Allen about blowing the streetlights out in Calgary. He blinks. "Well, I'd be asking questions, too," he concedes.

He hypothesizes that one explanation for the Calgary experience could be that a large truck went by at that moment, or a wind, which caused a vibration strong enough to knock a faulty light out. The lights across the street could have been connected by some sort of relay system.

Yet he also says there have been reports from other Yellowknifers about streetlights going out when they pass by, but when the utility company checks out the lights, they're working fine.

"I think in a scientific mode, or a mechanical mode, so I find other reasons that the light might be going out," says Allen. "However, I've also been taught by my parents never to scoff at any possibility because I'm only in possession of a small amount of knowledge that may be out there in the world."

Ahhh. This explains your humble and cheerful demeanor, I think to myself. I thank Allen for his time, and his open-mindedness. I can immediately discount the big truck or wind theory, as there was neither that night in Calgary, but it's reassuring to know I am not the only curious person asking questions of the utility company about strange interactions with streetlights.

~

My lawyer asks if I can meet him for an update about the man who's suing me. It doesn't sound good. He tells me the statement of claim against me has been amended. A new allegation of defamation was added. "Did you talk to anyone about this?" he asks.

I think about it. I had been at a pub one Friday after work, joined by a group of women I knew well, except for one. A petition was circulating at that time, started by a mother who had deep respect for the school counsellor at the heart of my lawsuit. The petition was asking the school board to explain why it's funding a private civil lawsuit against a parent, using public education tax dollars. I asked people at the table if they would sign it. They all did, but the woman I didn't know well said she wanted more information. Fair enough. Then she told me she was a friend of the man suing me. Did she alert him as to where we'd been and what we'd discussed?

Raven: Magical Darkness

Ravens have been known to alert wolves to prey in order to help them with the kill.

Weeks later the same woman sees me again speaking with my lawyer. She interrupts us to tell me I have her full support, and she will sign the petition.

～

At Allen Mueller's suggestion, I phone the manufacturer of those street-light sun-sensing switches, the photocells, for more information on how they work. Richard Jones, an engineer with SouthConn Technologies in West Columbia, South Carolina is gracious and patient with my queries, first helping me re-establish the basics of the electromagnetic spectrum—Grade eleven physics having been a long time ago. The spectrum includes light waves in a continuous variety of sizes, frequencies and energies—ranging from the low energy, long wavelengths of radio and microwaves through to the higher energy, shorter wavelength X-ray and gamma rays. The only light waves humans can see, however, are the rainbow colours that combine to the white light. This visible light makes up only one-thousandth of a percent of the electromagnetic spectrum.

Richard explains that most streetlights come on when the photocell senses brilliance in the sun of only one to two foot-candles. By comparison, full sunlight is about 10,000 foot-candles. An overcast day would be one hundred. A person would have to be generating some form of energy in order to convince the photocell to switch off. "If the person is generating infrared heat, then you could conceivably do that, that's how some of these alarm sensors work and people do generate heat, which is infra-red on the spectrum," Richard tells me.

In a follow-up e-mail, he writes:

Laurie,

Some of the photocontrol sensors see not only what the human eye sees, but also into the infrared part of the spectrum. One could compare this to dogs hearing the same sounds you do, but in addition, they can hear higher frequency sounds, out of the human range. You could say that infrared is still light, it's just not in the part of the spectrum that your eye is sensitive to. It happens that some heat sources also generate heat in the infrared spectrum such that these particular sensors can "see" the source.

This is a fascinating subject, but it is one that my own understanding may fall a little short of giving you a good explanation.
Richard Jones
SouthConn Technologies Inc.

An interesting thought. But I know from Allen Mueller that street-lights are not heat sensitive; that would make them act on the wrong impulses. And infrared light waves will not travel through a car roof or windows. My search for a rational, scientific explanation as to how some-one could blow out streetlights remains elusive.

∾

Francois and I are waiting at a light on a busy downtown street corner, walking to the coffee shop and talking about the lawsuit. It's been two years since the last examination for discovery where I saw the man who's suing me. Against my lawyer's advice, after all lines of communication between me and the school board seemed closed and senior child pro-tection bureaucrats had chosen to ignore the matter, I'd written two ter-ritorial ministers and asked them to investigate. The minister of health and social services hired a local lawyer to conduct an independent inves-tigation. Her findings concurred with what the other mothers and Linda and I had been saying from the start: the written directive for Linda to alter the way she reports suspected cases of child abuse contravened the Child Welfare Act. Citing that and other reasons, the school board fired the man behind that directive, the man suing me, and he in turn sued the board for wrongful dismissal. He lost. He appealed. He lost again. He appealed some more. He sued the minister, the lawyer who wrote the report, the Northwest Territories commissioner, and two others. His energies directed elsewhere, my lawsuit was essentially abandoned.

Two ravens appear to be French kissing on the traffic light. When it turns green, Francois and I cross the road. A man in a shiny black trench coat cinched with a waist belt walks toward us. He looks familiar, but I can't place him until Francois whispers, "That's him," just as we pass one another. A bolt of fear nearly takes me down, striking my solar plexus and radiating into my extremities. It's the man suing me. Like thunder after a lightning flash, my body quakes a second time in response to the snarls and barks of large, angry dogs. I turn to look behind me. Two muscly German shepherds strain their reach from the back of a pickup truck ensnarled in the melee of pedestrians as it waits to make a right turn. The focus of the dog's angst appears to be the man in the black coat, but he walks past them, seemingly oblivious to the effect he's had on the dogs, or me.

~

A Eureka moment comes while I'm lying in bed with Francois, reading *Vibrational Medicine, New Choices for Healing Ourselves*, a dense, compelling textbook by Dr. Richard Gerber that attempts to bridge the schism between science and metaphysics. He presents an Einsteinian explanation of the workings of the human body, namely that if all matter is energy, the famous $E = mc2$ equation (energy equals mass times the speed of light squared), then *humans are beings of energy*. We are more than biological machines; we are animated by a primal, life-force energy, one that includes our consciousness.

"This is it! This explains it," I say, pushing the diagram titled "The Human Energy Field" before Francois' eyes. It illustrates an extended, energetic framework to our physical selves: in other words, there is the body we can touch, see, hear, smell and taste; then there are four other esoteric dimensions, auric fields, each with its own purpose and each vibrating with its own increasingly higher frequency. They are all part of our consciousness—not the "get hit on the head and go unconscious" kind of physical consciousness, but one that extends beyond the skull and skin. An *Energy* consciousness that gains experiences from interacting with its environment, evolving into its Higher Self, the fourth and highest esoteric body: the Causal.

Francois is listening politely, waiting for the point when it will be acceptable for him to exit from the 'discussion' and finish whatever *Globe and Mail* article he's reading. My streetlight experiences clearly do not hold the same fascination for him. I decide that I have to speak to the book's author, Dr. Richard Gerber. When I contact him, he agrees to a lengthy telephone interview from Michigan, where he practices internal medicine and teaches at Wayne State University School of Medicine in Detroit.

He tells me there's a name for people who interfere with streetlights in this way. SLIders. The SLI stands for Street Lamp Interference. There have been British studies, and media stories about them. His wife frequently experiences this phenomenon, and when he is in a high-energy state, he'll often turn on a light switch and *poof*, the light goes out. Or sometimes, a similar thing happens with his computer, or watch.

"I think there are different possibilities," he begins to explain. "The most obvious one is that there's a direct effect of consciousness on various physical systems. The old parapsychological term is psychokinesis, which is the ability to move or manipulate matter with the mind alone. There's actually been a significant amount of research that shows that consciousness can affect inanimate or inorganic systems that are outside the body," he says.

A second possibility is the different frequency domains of energy outside of the physical range. "On one level you have what's called the electromagnetic aura of the body, which is generated primarily by cellular activity. And that's actually something that's fairly well accepted. But then you have these other energy fields that would seem to be outside the electromagnetic spectrum as we understand it—energy systems associated with the physical body that we don't talk about in science. Things like the etheric body, the chakra systems, the acupuncture meridians—all part of an energy circuit pathway or biocircuitry system for life energy that the Chinese call ch'i.

"Each energy field has increasingly higher frequency rates. That's a relative term. If you ask a physicist, frequency is a certain rate of oscillation of cycles per second, but I think actually what we're dealing with when you get into the etheric and higher spectrum is a whole different type of energy that actually has very different properties than electromagnetic or gravitational energy; it doesn't follow the so-called inverse square law which is that the farther you go out from the source, the energy intensity decreases by a square of the distance." Dr. Gerber says this is where the discussion starts to lose the physicists, whose views follow conventional electromagnetism. "It's much easier dismissing an anomalous phenomenon that doesn't fit into everything you've been taught, than having to say, 'well, maybe everything I've learned isn't correct,' and then having to learn things over again."

"So is it possible my auric energy could be interacting with streetlights?" I ask him.

"It's very hard to quantify that energy right now, it's still in the realm of the theoretical because we don't have good measuring equipment for this kind of energy. The implication of your experience is it may not be just the energy field of your aura interacting with something, it's actually the effect of one's consciousness interacting, even at a distance."

In his book, Dr. Gerber describes consciousness as the "information-handling capacity of the nervous system." He says we increase our consciousness by gaining experiences through interaction with our environment. Those experiences extend beyond just day-to-day life; they're cumulative over all our past lives, as well. So, if I'm understanding his hypothesis right, he's suggesting that as I reach a higher consciousness, as I "evolve" into a better, kinder person (as Ruth pointed out), or move towards my higher self—"pure love" as John Living would put it—then my energy fields, and their frequencies and activities, expand.

This is a lovely concept that appeals to me, to think that beyond "growing up" physically into adults, we grow our personal consciousness and metaphysical selves throughout life by expanding our capacity for kindness and love.

Then, Dr. Gerber offers a third explanation for my streetlight phenomenon, but one which he says nobody really wants to hear about, and certainly not one a journalist would want to write about. It's remarkably similar to John Living's orb theory. He says if we accept the possibility that we are more than flesh and blood beings, that we have what he calls "subtle bodies"—an astral body, a mental body and a causal body—that exist on different planes of reality, then it's possible that these planes are inhabited by beings that people refer to as spirits. Supposedly everybody has spirit guides and sometimes these guides create phenomena around us to get our attention, and that often coincides with things we are thinking about... In my case, streetlights that undergo sudden power loss.

Ravens frequently plunge the City of Yellowknife into darkness after landing on power lines and becoming conductors for electricity to the ground, which causes a dead short.

"So," he concludes, "the third hypothesis is that when these unusual occurrences happen, it's not from what you're doing; it's being orchestrated by your spirit guides."

Spirit guides, orbs, how intriguing to hear a doctor and engineer espouse ideas so antithetical to the predominant Newtonian viewpoint of life, a viewpoint that sees the universe and the people in it as intricate machines. To suggest we live in a complex interface of energy fields and dimensions, to acknowledge spiritual elements are woven into our beings, our universe and beyond—the so-called "ghost in the machine"—has become almost heretical, "quackish," to the Western world. While I still don't profess to understand it, I am vibrating with excitement at the possibility that I'm vibrating in ways I cannot see, that my energy and awareness has shifted.

∼

It's dark outside as I make my way to our garage. Francois is out of town. I'm feeling for the garage door handle when something brushes against my face. Something firm yet silky, dangling against my nose and forehead. I shriek and step back, trying to focus on what's now swinging before me. It looks like... a dead raven? Hanging from a rope? I run to get a flashlight and confirm. Someone has tied a dead raven by the scaly ankles of its black, pencil-thin legs and hung the bird upside down from a nail above my garage door.

Now I confess, in the first few moments of this discovery, my mind searched for everyone I'd ever spoken ill of, for every person who might have a score to settle with me. (That I would even suspect someone of laying a bad omen at my doorstep as some sort of warning is indicative of the imbalance and fear within my life at that time.)

After a night's sleep, I decide that surely there must be a better explanation for this, and I inspect the bird more closely. For all the spooky lore that surrounds this intelligent creature, I have always been drawn to it. Even this upside-down dead one, with its ruff of long, beard-like feathers under its beak splayed out like an intricate black flower, seemed poised and in control. There was no damage that I could see. Its beak, the shape of a Swiss-army knife, was firmly closed with only a hint of menace at its sharp, curled end.

It turns out the raven was brought to our house by a wildlife officer. He knew Francois and knew that he had a collection of wild animal skulls and thought he might appreciate it. No one knows how the raven died. He hung it by the garage to keep it out of the reach of our dogs.

The bird remained hanging upside down on our property for years, first from the back of the house where it deterred woodpeckers and flickers from pecking into our wooden siding in search of flies and later from a tree. All this hanging around was supposed to facilitate its decay. Francois says he lifted it once and it was light, insects having quietly hollowed it out. But outwardly, its freeze-dried carcass, cloaked in feathers intended to withstand the most extreme weather conditions, showed little sign of deterioration. Its inky-black sheen was in turn reflecting blue, or purple or green, like a gasoline puddle toying with sunlight. According to Jamie Sams, it's this blue-black iridescence of the raven that speaks of the magic of darkness and a changeability of form and shape that brings an awakening, perhaps a higher consciousness, in the process.

This is what I think the raven could have been trying to convey to me that day I prayed for the souls of victims of September 11th. That prayer itself is a lifting of the universal consciousness, an energetic hum on which can ride love and forgiveness and healing, travelling through space and time, present in both darkness and light. The raven is legendary across the northern hemisphere as an intermediary, a messenger able to cross from this world to another. *Keep blowing into the darkness, keep searching, keep growing, keep praying,* it seemed to say. *I will carry your message. I will keep watch over you.* I understand now why it's said a raven's magic can never be understood. The more answers I seek, the more questions arise. It's a formula designed to keep the divine lessons coming, and I'm learning that as long as my heart remains open, at some points, I will experience the extraordinary.

To quote the single word spoken by The Raven in Edgar Allan Poe's classic poem of the same name: *Nevermore,* will there be spiritual dryness in my life.

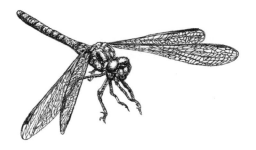

DRAGONFLY
unexpected change

7

It's two days after summer solstice, June 23, 2001, a time of warmth when a steadfast sun vanquishes darkness and stars from a northern night, and a black dragon is perched atop my neighbour's wood stove. Without a fire in the stove's belly, the papier-mâché wings and torso of the handmade dragon piñata are safely stretched across its plate-steel surface. Long after most creatures of the forest have gone to sleep, the dragon's pupil-less, gold-painted eyes are wide, fixing me with a zombie stare. Normally I don't care about dragons, but this one, I want to smash to pieces.

In Babylonian myth, the sea-monster Tiamat—a watery, dragon repre-sentation of the Great Mother, who gives birth to all Creation, but who also has the power to destroy it—is challenged to a single battle by Marduk, god of the Spring Sun and Thunder.

Piñata's are a staple of the family solstice celebration held each June across our lake—a medieval pig roast replete with period costumes, joust-ing demonstrations, a water-balloon-flinging trebuchet and a spectacular feast. I've never partaken in piñata-bashing, seeing as I'm averse to wear-ing a black bucket on my head and being spun to the point of dizziness. I'm better known for tossing a tire-sized cast-iron fry pan the furthest distance in a women-only competition. But this year I can't defend my title. Doctors have advised me not to do any heavy lifting until the wound from my breast biopsy heals over.

I hate cancer.

Fear of cancer has pervaded my psyche since I was small. I watched my grandfather's nose deteriorate from melanoma until he needed a prosthetic. After his death, geneticists took note when his brother and son succumbed to the same, rare form of the disease. Then, my aunt's two-pack-a-day cigarette addiction fuelled fatal lung cancer. The past year, at age eighty-two, my grandmother—who remarried and moved to the United States—secretly had her breast removed after hiding her tumour from us for four years. Given her advanced years and the fact she'd watched her loved ones endure treatments that didn't cure, she opted to let her cancer take its course. The tumour grew to the size of a grapefruit and restricted her breathing to the point she was finally rushed to hospital. At the precise moment that she was undergoing an emergency mastectomy in a small-town Pennsylvania hospital, unbeknownst to anyone in our family, I sat at work at my computer thousands of kilometres away in Yellowknife feeling worrisome pangs of pain in the same region of my breast and underarm. This must be breast cancer, I thought, and booked a doctor's appointment.

I discussed my fear that every mole, every tiny ache, was a sign my cancer time had come, with a very rational female doctor who explained that breast cancer *per se* does not cause pain. Then she said that beyond a healthy diet and lifestyle choices, regular screenings and a daily glass of red wine, there was little more I could do to prevent cancer. Worrying needlessly only diminishes the quality of the life I'm leading now. I felt better and went back to work.

That afternoon she called me. "I don't know why I didn't mention this when you were here, but would you like me to refer you for a mammogram?"

A mammogram? Those are for older women, I thought. She pointed out that I was turning 39 and it wouldn't hurt to start having them, just to ease my mind.

But it didn't. Far from it. The initial screening showed tiny spots of calcium called microcalcifications covering about a third of a breast. I was referred to a surgeon. On the X-ray, he showed me wee flecks resembling talcum powder that snaked in a cylindrical shape along one side, like the islands of Japan.

The Japanese archipelago is sometimes referred to as Akitsushima, or the Dragonfly Island, because it shares the same shape as the insect, highly revered amongst the Japanese—like its namesake relative, the dragon itself—as a symbol of courage.

The aged doctor sounded concerned. In all his years he'd never seen microcalcifications, a possible indicator of cancer, present in such a long, slithering formation. I lay on my back in the examining room receiving his words with quiet resignation while my support team, Francois and our friend Deb, stood frozen at the foot of the bed. Just slightly older than I, Deb had been diagnosed with breast cancer ten months earlier, but insisted, with typical gallantry, that she accompany me to this consultation. The abject terror on her blanched face travelled through her chemo-weary body to her fingers, which tightened their grip on my toes. I would need to have the entire eight-centimetre-long area removed for biopsy.

∾

Just as late June had come to herald the Medieval Pig Roast for my children (an event as anticipated as Christmas) so too had late August come to bear its own seasonal significance. That's when Francois travels to the Barrenlands to hunt caribou, following the time-honoured tradition of the Weledeh Yellowknives Dene, who, for thousands of generations left their family fish camps along the Weledeh (Yellowknife) River to canoe north, intercepting the Bathurst caribou herd's migration to its boreal wintering grounds. Last August, Francois took a floatplane to a caribou camp where he worked with a man named Jeff installing electric fences around the camp's perimeter, a joint safety feature to protect the grizzly bears they aimed to keep out, and the hunters who lodged within. Jeff had a small business in Alberta that offered wildlife control, and he had a son near Max's age, so he and Francois decided to take both boys along.

It would hardly be possible to script a potentially more dangerous scenario for an eight-year-old's first outing away from his mother—floatplanes, whose pilots can face sudden and wicked weather changes that hamper flying and landing: dense fog, high winds, sleet and snow, sometimes all in the same trip; fathers, whose attention I anticipated would be more focused on their physical labours than their caregiver roles; all the incumbent facets of a hunting camp that might avail themselves to curious little boys: guns, ammunition, motors, fishing lures, lakes. And then there were the grizzlies... I insisted a large tub of Lego accompany the children to keep them occupied.

But I also sensed that Max, who had been so finely tuned to his environment since birth, was destined to know the caribou and the treeless mysteries of the Barrens, a vast, glaciated tundra prairie that bursts into fiery reds each fall—a final shout-out from the mosses, lichens, grasses and berries before snow brings water and blankets them for winter sleep, and cold delivers a long, dark kiss goodnight. I said a silent prayer on our driveway for everyone's safe return. While Max, Jeff and his son waited in the truck for Francois, Levi noticed a bald eagle circling above them.

Max craned his neck excitedly from his seat for a look. Jeff commented that he was "pretty blasé," about eagles. "We see a lot of them where I live."

The eagle continued to adjust its expansive wingspread ever so slightly, a languid spiral downward in a funnel formation closer and closer to the truck, until it could no longer maintain its tight turning radius without furling its wings. Just a few metres above the truck, it attempted to hover with its body upright, flapping furiously like a child splashing water with both hands, or a loon propelling itself vertically from the lake in its summer mating ritual.

"Okay, this is getting kind of creepy," Jeff said. My heart pounded with excitement and gratitude. I've called Max 'Eagle Eyes' since he was a toddler because of his uncanny ability to spot eagles and other birds and animals at a great distance, always long before they'd come into my view. The Dene, as with other North American First Nations, hold the eagle in highest regard, a healing link to the Creator, and to the element of air, where the mental plane and higher mind are nourished. It's said to be a rare and special person who is able to earn, and carry, the essence of eagle medicine. I knew, without a doubt, Max would be fine.

I watched the truck roll away and gathered up the twins. My thoughts returned to the eagle and I looked up. There it was, now hovering upright directly over my head, its wings again flapping furiously.

Once inside, I was enveloped in a delicious calm, a rare sensation of being both light and fluid, like standing inside a warm hum. There is a place said to hold knowledge and wisdom that the ancient yogis called *kumbhaka*: the minute pause at the end and beginning of each inhalation and exhalation, the only place our minds are totally at peace. I felt there. I stopped to savour the moment, recognizing it as joy.

Then, as sure as my next step, a thought thundered across my mind. *Someone I love has cancer.* So much for joy. I admonished myself for not being able to wrest more time from the happy place, blaming my psyche for the negativity that breathed down my neck like the fire of a dragon, always on the ready to devour, and believing that I should, or somehow could, exercise more control over the negative feelings. Years later, I would read in the book *Emotional Freedom*, by American psychiatrist Dr. Judith Orloff, that negative emotional energy, one of those "subtle energies" that emanate from us like a force field—what the Chinese call *ch'i*, or the Hawaiians call *mana*—is basically louder and wilder than the positive, and so grabs our intuitive attention more seductively, just as war and conflict grab more headlines than peace. She gives the example of a bucking bronco versus a contented cat warming its belly in the sun. Where would your attention go, if both were in front of you?

In an effort to make the most of the lingering last days of summer, I phoned Deb to ask if she and her husband Miles would like to go camping. Miles picked up. He sounded tired, as he reluctantly explained that Deb had just returned from the hospital after having a lumpectomy. She hadn't wanted to tell her friends yet about her breast cancer.

∼

The man who's suing me isn't returning my calls, or at least his lawyer isn't returning my lawyer's calls. It's a strange predicament. I want the case to move forward, to end, but now he's stalling the process, his attentions focused on new lawsuits and appeals of his claim of wrongful dismissal. My lawyer suggests I subpoena him to force him to continue suing me, as the only means to make it end. That makes so little sense that I outright quash the idea.

Linda and her family have moved away, reluctantly. They loved the North, but her ordeal was of a magnitude that a clean start made more sense. Before she left, she told me there'd been no reports to social services about suspected child abuse since she took sick leave from the school. She believed staff members were too scared. A chill had descended upon the system. When I wrote to the Northwest Territories minister of education and the minister of health and social services, asking them to investigate the entire matter, I asked for statistics on the number of child abuse reports from the school in the past year. Citing privacy issues, they refused to release those numbers. If what Linda said was true, children were not being afforded the protection they needed, which had been our greatest fear all along. Abused children have a greater likelihood of growing up to be abusers, and frequently suffer from addictions as a means to cope with their trauma. The legacy of sexual abuse at residential schools was reverberating in this way. It is time to stop the cycle, I'd written. I remember clearly what happened the day I was composing that letter to the ministers.

"Mom, you got thunder and lightning eyes," Levi told me as I was typing.

"Sorry, what Levi? What are you talking about?" I asked, turning to look down into his cherubic face. He looked away.

"In your eyes Mom. It's clouds and thunder and lightning stuff, behind your glasses."

From East to West, the dragon as a symbol has been used by virtually every culture throughout history with changing attributes. Most mythologies agree it was born of clouds and water, a weather-lord of tempests, often associated with primordial chaos.

I looked behind me out the window, where there was nothing but blue sky.

I asked Levi to explain, but he doesn't want to talk about it anymore and runs away. This is not the first time he's spoken like this. When we were visiting my grandmother earlier that summer after her mastectomy, he said she had "war eyes," spears going into the black part of her eyes, reflections of soldiers, cannons; something he also saw in another relative we'd visited who was pinned under a mountain of family problems.

I was first given proof that this spirited four-year-old had the gift of second sight, an ability to detect elements of people's inner consciousness, in the aftermath of Francois discovering him and his twin brother

Calvin playing with matches. They burned their hands and, crying inconsolably, were treated and taken to their room. Each sitting on the lower bunk bed, their sobs dimmed to intermittent sniffles, I began my dissertation on the dangers of fire. Partway through, I stopped to ask if they had any questions.

"Mom, you gots three eyes," Levi asserts.

"Why do you say that Levi?"

"Because I see them."

"Where? Here?" I ask, pointing to my chin as a test.

"No, right there," says Levi, walking over and touching my forehead between my eyebrows.

Before my trip to the writing workshop in the Gulf Islands, where I befriended the clairvoyant Ruth and the crone Phairee, and met the insightful author Sharon Butala, I'd never heard of a third eye. Now, just weeks later, here's Levi telling me he can literally see mine. Indeed, Ruth flew to the Northwest Territories to visit me shortly after we met and Levi drew a picture of her with a purple third eye. His ability to use his physical eyes to glimpse into people's metaphysical elements fascinated me, creating an insatiable curiosity to understand more. Orloff describes the third eye as a mystical organ of inner perception, a place where images, archetypes, intuition, imagination, memory and fantasy are on constant display. In Sanskrit, this place is called *Ajna*, which means both to perceive and to command. For centuries, and to this day, scientists and philosophers continue to probe the possibility that our pineal gland, located in the direct centre of the brain, is a vestigial third eye. Descartes called the pineal the "principal seat of the soul."

Levi's water paintings during this time were a fascinating glimpse into these perceptions: free and fearless, colourful self-expressions before he became aware that most others did not see the world with such vivid intimacy. (Given Levi's reluctance to talk freely about his intuitive abilities as he grew older and more self-conscious, and not wanting to exploit his gifts in a way that could ostracize him from his peers, I gave careful consideration as to whether to include them in this book. I asked Levi's permission when he was a teenager, fully anticipating he'd say no, but in fact his response was unequivocal, and immediate, "Yes, do it." I believe people who have such healing gifts also understand they have an obligation to share them, with intent to uplift and illuminate the aching world around them and let others with intuitive gifts know they're not alone.)

In one piece of art, he painted two pools of blue with black centres and outlined them both in black. Between them, in the *Ajna* chakra, he painted an almond-shaped solid black eye. Behind all of this was a background of green and red swirling around each of the circles. He called the painting "Max's big blues eyes, with his eyebrow eye" (Max has hazel-coloured eyes). Levi often talked of seeing colours on people's faces (perhaps auric fields, sometimes in their eyes) that were always one of the seven shades of the rainbow. These colours correspond with the seven chakras, or major energy centres, located between the base of the spine and the crown of the head. Often he told me I had "lots of eye," that is, more than three. Once he counted as many as sixteen. He also spoke of auric colours around trees and plants.

A psychotherapist I consulted told me Levi might be an "Indigo child," a term used to describe particularly intuitive and psychic children said to be part of a new wave of beings (ones often diagnosed as having attention deficit disorder). These children mark a Darwinian-like evolutionary change, but instead of an outward, physical body adaption there's a shift to a more empathetic, energetic consciousness resulting from a new chakra area close to the heart. When I heard a film about Indigo children was being presented in Yellowknife, I took Levi to see it. The opening credits featured dozens of children's paintings, all showing remarkable resemblance to Levi's, with bold close-ups of multiple eyes shaded in various colours of the rainbow. Levi became visibly disturbed by the paintings. Maybe it was overwhelming to have so many other interpretations of his inner world placed so blatantly before him. He left his seat to crawl into my lap, where he wrapped my arms around him, his heartbeat racing. At first he wanted to leave, but eventually settled in and enjoyed the film.

When Levi informed me one day when he was four that he could only divulge information on people's eyes and colours "on Sundays," I confess he was starting to freak me out a little. Without having watched much television (we have no cable or satellite), without attending any preschool or having been taught by me, he suddenly knew all the days of the week, and was able to pinpoint which one we were on.

His insights into the meaning of the auric colours he would see were no less fascinating: red generally meant angry or worried; yellow and green meant I was happy; purple, which corresponds to the crown chakra, purportedly our portal to our spiritual connection with the universe, meant to him that I was "sorting things out, you know, like in school."

Indeed, I had a lot to sort out. The questions plaguing my outer world were so pervasive they began to impinge on my sleep as well. In one dream, I'm in the grocery store with a friend who's been by my side every step of the way as we pushed the school board for answers and action. The man who's suing me is there as well, and I'm certain I have put my friend in danger and try to hide her from him. Another night, I dream I have cancer and the only doctor who can help me is someone I dismissed earlier, so I spend the rest of the dream looking for him. It is just days after this dream that I have my first mammogram and am told I need a biopsy.

∼

I'm wearing the humbling green medical gown, backside exposed, awaiting surgery when a nurse informs me that the mammogram technician required to assist with the biopsy is ill. "We think she has pneumonia, so she's going home and our other technician is in Newfoundland for three weeks. I'm really sorry, your surgery will be cancelled for a while."

Saved from the knife. Still physically intact, Francois drives me home where I contemplate the ambivalence I feel toward my breasts. Not so long ago, they'd continued the deep, life-sustaining physical connection to my three babies after their birth. It's hard to think that they'd turned on me now, that they'd become potential killers.

∼

The Edmonton strip mall looks more like a place you'd go to do your laundry or pick up a chicken shwarma, not get a breast biopsy. But the minute I step foot in the Breast Centre, I feel reassured. A framed, hand-tatted Hungarian doily hangs on the wall at reception, reminiscent of my grandmother's handiwork. My Yellowknife doctor arranged a trip here a few days after my surgery was cancelled as a way of expediting my diagnosis. This is all they do here, check for cancer, and they do it with assembly-line efficiency. First I watch an information video on breast self-examination with a half-dozen other sombre-faced women, some with their husbands. Next I have an ultrasound. The technician assures me she's seen "hundreds" of similarly shaped microcalcifications. I tell her I had mastitis in that same area when I was nursing the twins and she's almost certain that's what damaged this tissue. "But let's take a sample, just to be sure." There's no escaping the biopsy, but at least here the procedure, called a mammotome, is non-surgical and will not disfigure me.

I'm instructed to lie on my stomach on a smooth, raised platform with my breast dipping into a hole, as if I've been chipped onto the ninth green and landed in the cup. My neck is twisted so my head faces the wall, and I'm ordered not to move. A doctor arrives and introduces himself, but I will only know him as the disembodied voice that will lance me repeatedly, and painlessly, with a small, sharp vacuum probe.

St. George of England, the patron of arms, upon being told by a bound and weeping king's daughter that she is being sacrificed to feed the dragon, lances the dragon several times, but does not immediately kill it. The dragon is then tied with the princess's girdle and led back to the city.

The disembodied voice exits the room and a kind nurse binds my entire, suture-less chest with a thick, girdle-like pressure bandage, so tight it restricts my breathing and redefines my upper body shape into that of an adolescent boy.

I'm told that a small bead has been placed inside of me, to mark the spot.

The beneficent dragons of China and Japan are often depicted holding a 'sacred pearl' under their chins, an egg-like emblem of the dual influences of nature, the yin (negative-feminine) and the yang (positive-masculine). It is also referred to as the 'pearl of potentiality,' a complex symbol of wisdom, of enlightenment, of self-realization of spiritual richness, which is always within sight of the life force, but which often eludes it.

"What colour is the bead," is all I can think to ask.

"Blue," the nurse says.

Chinese spiritual dragons are often blue, because this is the colour of the East, from where the rain must come—the Azure dragon being the highest in rank among all the dragons. The sighting of the Azure dragon announced the arrival of spring thunderstorms and the awakening of animals from hibernation.

I taxi to the Edmonton airport where I purchase *The Book of Bad Songs* by American humourist Dave Barry, a compilation of old pop songs with inane lyrics, most notably *MacArthur Park* with its "someone left the cake out in the rain" and Neil Diamond's *I Am*, which includes the line "and no one cared, not even the chair." I start laughing in the bookstore aisle, then carry on in the departure lounge to such a degree that I'm crying and blowing my nose while struggling to inhale, waving the book in the air by way of explanation to the fellow Yellowknifers who watch on, perplexed. Were I not so tightly bound, surely I would have died laughing, my headstone reading: Dave Barry Cracked Her Up.

~

As children, our first tangible encounter with death is said to be the moment we awaken our inner life, the dawning of our new consciousness, of awe surrounding the mystery of death, and life. This was true for me when, at age five, I bounded down the stairs for breakfast to discover my pet budgie Romeo prostrate in the gravelled newspaper lining of his cage, his lime-green body still and lifeless. The irretrievability of his companionship, of his movements, his scent and sounds, ("Romeo, Romeo, wherefore art thou?") preoccupied me well past my walk to school. German philosopher Oswald Spengler describes this shift as the time when a child "suddenly grasps the lifeless corpse for what it is, something that has become wholly matter, wholly space, and at the same moment it feels itself as an individual *being* in an alien extended world."

Romeo's passing was the first of many that alerted me to the inherent duality of our lives. Without death, there can be no new life. Having given new life to three sons, I am, with absolute certainty, becoming the dead one; but first, I must protect the new life I've created, and that's what cuts so deeply, the thought of a motherless future for my three little boys.

It's the day of the pig roast—six days before my biopsy results will be revealed—and, like my friend Deb, I have not shared my ordeal with friends, preferring normalcy over concern and compassion. I consult with Ruth, however, who has extensive contacts in the field of breast cancer through her many years as a Dragon Boat coach in Vancouver. At a time when their upper body strength is most compromised, she teaches breast cancer survivors to distill their power into one united force, twenty blades working in unison to a drummer sitting at the bow behind the protective watch of a dragon's head.

The Chinese classics teach that the dragon is thunder, resting in pools in winter and rising in the form of rain clouds each spring. Dragon boat races were organized so they seemed to represent fighting dragons in the hope that this would precipitate a real dragon fight with its accompanying heavy rains for fertile fields.

Ruth puts me in touch with an oncologist who expounds on procedures and probabilities for my situation, then orders me over the phone to "start thinking of yourself as the strong, healthy woman that you are!" Her strident voice, more commanding than consoling, is like a call to arms, a jarring realization that my ruminations have reduced the once-raging fire in my belly to an ember glow. Slowly, submissively, I had begun to think of myself as dead for the first time in my life, and in so doing, something mighty shifted deep within. I developed a profound appreciation not only for the people in my life, but also for the sundry details surrounding their upkeep and well-being. The chores and minutiae I so often spurned now seemed more like meditative labours of love. There was also a peaceful realization that I had no bucket list. My early life of relentless ambition and insatiable wanderlust meant I would not have to chase down unfulfilled dreams and pursuits. If indeed my days are numbered, I concluded I needed to spend them in greater service to others, not myself.

The Ouroboros, an ancient circular symbol depicting a dragon eating its own tail, often half in black, the other half white, represents the eternal cycle of life, death and rebirth. Self-devouring is the same as self-destruction, but the union of the dragon's tail and mouth was also thought of as self-fertilisation, sometimes expressed philosophically as a cycle of 'exist, destroy and create.'

Before I don my medieval dress, Francois unwraps the bandage from my upper body, the blood from my wound successfully staunched.

The dragon, wrapped in the girdle of the King's daughter and lanced several times by St.George the dragon-slayer, is taken to the city to be slain before the people.

I luxuriate in a few expansive breaths before helping the boys into their costumes and making our way to the neighbour's house. After seeing me eye the dragon piñata on their wood stove, Francois encourages me to take a crack at it this year.

Another neighbour, Wendy, a psychiatric nurse from the hospital whom I affectionately call my Sister of the Lake, is the first to greet me. She looks energized and robust, even though four months previous doctors discovered a rare type of tumour attacking her adrenal glands, and recently she discovered a lump on her breast. I ask her how she's feeling.

"I was writing my obituary, I thought I was through," she says, "but I'm cancer free! I went for a nuclear medicine scan in Edmonton so they could stage my tumours and they couldn't find any. They're all gone," she tells me.

"That's fantastic. How did you do that?"

Wendy explains that while she was waiting for her medical appointments, she did everything she could think of that might be beneficial in trying to rid her body of the tumours and the excessive hormones surging through her body. She did guided imagery and swam sixty lengths a day at the pool. Afterwards, while floating, she says she put her brain into "alpha"—a deep breath, meditative state said to bridge the conscious to the unconscious: a tranquil, positive place where learning comes easily and we see the world truthfully. She did this by counting backwards from six with the colours of the rainbow, and then again from ten back to one. Then she visualized every part of her body healthy and the tumours dissolving and being flushed out. Her mother and "hundreds of other women" also did therapeutic touch on her, from a distance.

Every now and again, I hear such stories of disease being cured without conventional western medical intervention. I once interviewed an Alberta professor of anthropology who authored a book about his insights into Aboriginal medicine men and women. I was writing an article about Dene healers, one of whom had been given permission to speak with me about her practices. The professor told me he has "no doubt" that some of these healers have cured cancer. Wendy's words are like bellows, stoking the ailing fire in my belly with hope and optimism. It's time to raise a sword to the dragon.

Maids, maidens, paupers, knights, lords, monks, priests, minstrels, jesters—all gather 'round. I feel their gaze as a black bucket is placed on my head and I'm twirled a few times to further disorient me in the darkness. Despite this, my feet are well grounded and the sword feels weighted and purposeful as I raise it straight up with both hands. I take a breath and circle it, slicing down hard through the air. I make direct contact with the dragon and the crowd cheers. As is tradition, I bequeath the bucket and sword to the next in line, to allow as many people as possible to face the dragon.

"Mom! Mom!" Calvin is racing towards me. "You killed the dragon!"

"I did?"

"You whacked its head off Mom!"

I turn towards the dragon and see Max carrying its severed papier-mâché head like a trophy. Calvin is looking at me with awe. *I'm going to be fine*, I'm thinking, *even if I do have cancer.*

~

The next morning an unexpected visitor arrives at my house: Linda. I can hardly believe my eyes. It's been four years since she first made those child-abuse reports and I became her champion. She drives her rental vehicle into the driveway and when she steps out, she is surrounded by hundreds, possibly thousands, of newly hatched dragonflies sunning themselves on the gravel.

Dragonfly, or Odonata adults need sunshine and warmth for their daily activity, and that is why you never see them on cold or cloudy days. Most of their life is spent as nymphs in water, shedding their skin several times, over as many as four years. Once the nymph is fully grown and the weather is right, it crawls out of the water and climbs up a plant, where it will shed its skin once more, completing the metamorphosis.

"Well, fancy meeting you here," I say, walking up to give her a hug, dragonflies scattering in all directions.

"I'm in town tying up a few loose ends and thought I'd drop by for a visit," Linda tells me. I invite her inside for tea.

I share with Linda my anxieties over the biopsy, then our talk turns to the lawsuit. My lawyer, a kind man who first helped Linda and later took up my cause *pro bono*, has moved away, leaving everything in legal limbo.

Linda tells me she arrived two days ago. She went downtown to a bank machine and there was a young girl in front of her. When she turned around, it was one of the adolescent girls who had first come to her with an abuse complaint. She's now a high school student.

"We were both in a state of shock," says Linda. "I couldn't believe the first person I run into is her! We start talking and she was telling me how sorry she was for everything, as if my moving away was her fault, that she and the other girls had been responsible. They thought I was fired.

"All they knew is that one day I was their counsellor, and then after they told me about the basketball game, I was gone. They knew from the news that there was this lawsuit, but they didn't know that the principal's contract had not been renewed, or that the man suing you had been fired. We were hugging and crying. I kept assuring her that she had, that all the girls had, done the right thing by talking about it."

Linda and I, and the handful of other moms involved with bringing the girls' experiences and Linda's treatment to light, had always known that keeping the children safe was the first priority. But beyond that, our biggest fear was that the girls, and indeed everyone else who was watching this ordeal unfurl—teaching staff, media, the public—were taking home the message that reporting allegations of sexual abuse is not worth the hassle. Best to mind your own business. Indeed, one could look at what was happening to me as a prime example; the intimidation of a fifty-five thousand dollar defamation lawsuit had rocked my world. And Linda had chosen to relocate her family to the other side of the country rather than break the law by abiding by an illegal, written directive from the school district. She'd received no support from her union and when she eventually brought the issue to the Canadian Labour Relations Board, they said she had a case they would argue, but she was too late. Her complaint had not been made within their prescribed time limits. People she'd thought were friends had chosen to look the other way. People she barely knew, like me, had come to her defence. She'd been isolated and her reputation maligned. And still...

"I'd do it all again in a heartbeat," Linda says, as we discuss the toll of our efforts. "I really would. I personally would have no other option."

I think back to that summer day four years earlier when a neighbour first told me about what was happening to Linda at the school where Max was about to start kindergarten. Had I not chosen to investigate further, had I not demanded accountability from the school board and then the territorial government, I would not be facing this lawsuit. But would the children be safe in an environment of fear? I conclude that I too had no other option.

Max strolls in, still toting the dragon's head, and relays to Linda the story of its demise.

"Looks like Max's Mom is a dragon slayer," Linda says, prompting a long, sneaking smile from Max. Linda says we have the same smile.

~

I'm standing on our deck drinking in the magnificence of the lake and its sylvan shoreline. The evergreens seem greener, the birches are luminescent white, everything appears more brilliant, as though it's been glazed and baked in a potter's oven, since I received confirmation I don't have breast cancer. I couldn't wait for a doctor's appointment, so I had the lab results faxed to her office. The receptionist and I watched as my fate buzzed and hummed its way through the machine. She handed the paper to me just as sunbeams broke through the window. I smiled and let out a whoop, then we hugged and both cried a little.

"You've got your life back," she told me.

"Yes, yes I do."

The intense heat of the day has activated the dragonflies; they scoop and dart on their carnivorous hunt for sustenance, and sex, on the water's edge. I hold out my arms and invite them to land on me. One does. I feel the scratchy cling of its legs attach to my white tee shirt along my side, under my armpit. The same place where I'd felt the pangs the day of my grandmother's mastectomy. When I can no longer hold my arms up, I brush it away so as not to crush it.

BEE
power of cooperation

8

The view from the Riverview Inn in Lewiston, Idaho, takes in a pulp and paper mill spewing clouds of toxins into a clear blue sky. As visions of dioxins and furans dance through my head, I notice a stench akin to a sour diaper pail overpowering the smell of stale cigarette smoke and beer that hangs in the air-conditioned lobby. "That's from the mill," the friendly check-in woman explains. I glance wide-eyed at Ruth and Nancy. I'm having serious doubts this white-water rafting trip will live up to its billing—a pristine nature adventure on the last remaining wild river in the American Northwest: The Salmon.

I'm slightly assuaged to learn the river we're looking at first is the Clearwater, a major tributary of the Snake, which is a tributary of the Salmon. For those who work as river guides, the Snake is synonymous with all things evil: dams, diesel fuel, pulp mill effluent, human and agricultural waste, cottages and fuel-puking jet boats. We must travel the Snake briefly on the last afternoon of our five-day, 115-kilometre trip. The rest of the time we're to be gloriously unreachable, bathed in light as we set ourselves adrift through the ancient canyons of its exalted cousin, the mighty, mountain-fed, motor-free, at times tumultuous, Salmon River. But first, we wait at this dusty motel for the others to arrive, and our reunion to begin.

It's been a year since things went bump in the night in the cabin I shared with Ruth and Nancy at a writing workshop on the West Coast. During that time, the proceedings for my lawsuit haven't abated. I've just spent an excruciating month awaiting biopsy results on my cancer fate, which concluded in my favour, but now I'm noticing troubling changes in my mother. She's become oddly distant and detached. Slurring her words, losing track of where she is, walking stiffly. I ask the river, the sacred water, to renew me so I can find strength for the challenges ahead.

One by one the others arrive: Christa, looking revitalized with a new job and an overseas romance; Miriam, the English doctoral student from Germany; and Sheree, the Oregon geologist and river naturalist who wrote of the restorative powers of "river time." The six of us are reuniting to experience the seductive rhythms of this phenomenon together.

In the ancient world of bee shamanism—representing the zenith of the feminine potency of nature—six female apprentices, known as the Melissae, serve their Bee Mistress, also known as the Mother Bee and the Queen of Synchronicity.

There are two newcomers: Nancy's twenty-one-year-old daughter, Lisa, and Beth, a fifty-one-year-old colleague of Sheree's. Raised in Tehran until age fifteen, Beth insists she's never done anything as adventurous as white-water rafting and is apprehensive to try white-water kayaking.

It's the last week of August and the temperature in Idaho's high desert still breaks forty degrees Celsius without fanfare. We receive our safety orientation on the riverbank from our guides, Kate and Scott, before our turquoise rafts slip into the water: one main barge, two smaller rafts, plus four inflatable kayaks.

Scott is twenty-three, tall, tanned and lean, with a swirl of soft brown curls and a goatee. A special-needs teacher by trade, he bears the markings of a gentle man wedded to nature—a bone necklace, a wooden anklet, and a star tattoo on his left shin. Kate, thirty, is also a teacher. A straw hat that's ripped on top, exposing her crown to the sun, covers her shoulder-length brown hair. Her only adornment is royal purple nail polish on her toes. Quiet, serious, Kate is clearly our leader, perpetually strategizing the movement of boats and people and exuding a mature confidence that permeates and relaxes her followers.

A honeybee colony is made up of a queen, fifty thousand to seventy thousand female worker bees, and up to two thousand male bees, or drones. The queen secretes a pheromone from a gland in her head. This scent secretion is taken up by the worker bees attending to her and passed on in minute quantities to all the bees in the hive, stimulating and inhibiting certain behaviours and physiologic processes, which significantly affects the life and social order of a colony.

The slow-moving parts of the river, known as slack water, reflect knobbly, denuded hills along the banks that remind me of giant sweet potatoes. Not a single cloud will surface during this trip, just the eternal optimism of a desert-blue sky and the mysteries of the moon and stars. The heat sucks my breath and before long, I seek refuge in the river, floating freely in my life jacket, my watch long dismissed, ready to let the river take me where it will on its own time.

~

We set up camp on a white sand bank surrounded by geometric peaks of seventeen-million-year-old basalt rock. The conversation turns to insects, or the seeming lack thereof, and I'm reminded of the well-dressed, middle-aged woman I saw in Lewiston that morning who was completely unaware a large praying mantis clung to her hair just above her bangs, like a giant hat pin.

Scott is preparing baked salmon when he lets out a yelp. Either a wasp or a bee has stung him on the inside of his lip.

Only female bees have stingers. They sting to protect their honey, their hive, or their queen, and only when provoked. Many cultures revere bees for being in communication with the Spirit. A bee sting was thought to be judgment for immorality, or a message from a soul in purgatory requesting prayers.

The dearth of mosquitoes means we don't need tents. For the first time, I will sleep unobstructed from the stars, my sleeping bag burrowed into the sand like a ghost crab, the moon shining like a naked light bulb against the night sky. At daybreak, the morning sun makes the tall canyon peaks look like giant wedges of golden cheese.

We start our day with a geology lesson from Sheree, who explains the dark columns of basalt rock were formed by underground molten lava that flowed up like chocolate syrup through cracks in the surface rocks. The granite of the canyon came from the same lava, except it was trapped under a solid plate of rock for thousands of years where it hardened and had time to organize quartz crystals, their hexagonal shape making them highly stable and resistant to weathering and erosion.

The six-sided, hexagonal honeycomb is the only format or pattern of cell in the cosmos where no empty space exists between them. No gap may arise, much the same as in bee society, which manifests the optimal relationships among all constituent parts of the hive.

The Dene refer to rocks as Grandfather, a show of respect and reverence for the eons of knowledge and experience they believe rocks store within and can transfer to others. Some Shamanistic teachings hold that what lies beneath the earth is the collective equivalent of the repressed unconsciousness. The shadow realm. Dreamtime. Myths and legends.

Over millennia, the Salmon River carved North America's second-deepest canyon. Its first inhabitants arrived ten thousand years ago. Until the late 1800s, the Nimi'ipuu, meaning The Real People, now more commonly referred to as Nez Perce, set up their villages at the confluence of streams and rivers, sustaining themselves on camas roots, salmon and big game, such as deer, bear and bison. There are no more salmon in the Salmon River, their spawning runs now blocked by eight dams between the ocean and the river's entrance. The Nimi'ipuu, as well, were driven out of the canyon, nearly decimated by American armies.

"Rock is never still," says Sheree. "There's always alchemy, transformation, metamorphosis."

I, like Beth, didn't think I had the courage to kayak white water, but that morning, as we float past the calming green walls of serpentine in the next canyon, I change my mind. The inflatable kayaks are more like dinghies with holes that allow water to self-drain. All goes well until my first challenge: an ominous 'hole,' where water moving over a rock flows down, then back onto itself in an eruption of white water. A desperate attempt to back paddle away from it is futile and I'm sucked down. I feel myself grow small and insignificant as I stare up at the wall of water. Frozen in the dip, time stands still. "Paddle! Paddle!" I hear Kate cry from afar. I dig in deeply and pull out of the hole to safety. Having trumped my fear, I'm feeling renewed. Beth listens to me expound on the thrill.

I wasn't visiting with Ruth as much on this trip as I had anticipated. She'd just met an Iranian man in the aftermath of a Dragon Boat regatta, an attraction she mused that may have been spurred by her sudden desire to line her eyes with black kohl. After hearing of Beth's upbringing in Iran, Ruth began mining Beth's knowledge on the country, the people and the language, even determined to learn some Farsi. Humble Beth cheerfully complied, at times seeming dismayed by Ruth's enthusiastic attention.

That night, with the most challenging class-four rapids of the trip behind us, our guides begin to relax. This is Kate's ninth season as a river guide. She tells us she has never had a client or employee injured.

"How many river guides does it take to screw in a light bulb?" she asks. "None, 'cause they screw in their sleeping bags." Scott blushes.

Drones that are ready to mate leave their hive in early afternoon, flying near their hives or gathering in drone-congregating areas where the weather conditions are favourable. The queen bee is the sole female with developed ovaries. She chooses her partners and always mates with them in the air. The drones die in the course of copulation.

The women gather that night to reminisce about our time together the summer before. Ruth starts with her experience of flying to the Northwest Territories afterwards to visit me and tells of my son Levi, then six, drawing a portrait of her in which she had three eyes, the middle one coloured purple. Ruth had dreamt the night before her flight that she was to "work out the purple bits." Christa then recounts her dream of the previous night in which a young, blonde man in his twenties asks her to scrape the pupil off his eye, which she does, realizing only afterward that he had three eyes and none appear to have irises.

The bee has a collection of eyes. Three simple ones, or ocelli, on the top of her head navigate the dimness of the hive. Outside, she employs two bulging compound eyes, perched on her head like a pair of dark wraparound sunglasses, which are composed of thousands of rounded hexagonal facets that sense light, colour, contrast and movement as a prismatic mosaic of colour and shape.

I enjoy the way these women, academics and scientists, seamlessly weave and incorporate the metaphysical with the physical in their lives. Sheree is able to reconcile her background in western science, which deems the natural world as something material to be deciphered empirically, with a firm belief in unseen, often-inexplicable dimensions.

She does a daily meditation to send positive energy into her DNA. She believes she can take universal energy in through her crown chakra and funnel it into the earth. "We are able to channel energy that cleanses this river, cleans the hazardous waste sites. It's that simple," she tells us. I'd like to believe this, but think a more tangible and immediate solution is to stifle polluters.

I go to sleep watching the moon rise and cast shadows on the canyon wall that resemble a giant Batman logo.

~

"Coyote went to visit his friend deer," so begins Kate's daily storytelling of a Nez Perce legend. Today's is their creation story. "Coyote can't find anybody—elk, crow, otter, beaver, eagle— the giant monster's eaten them all. Coyote convinces the monster to eat him too, then pulls out a knife inside its belly and cuts everybody out. Flinging parts of the monster around, Coyote creates the oceans, mountains, plains. When the animals point out he neglected to create people, Coyote adds water to the blood of his knife and the surrounding bones and creates the Nez Perce, a tribe small in numbers, but strong in spirit."

According to information from the rafting company, the Nimi'ipuu, or Nez Perce, maintained peaceful relations with traders and trappers until American expansion and the greed of gold mining caused the tribe's displacement. Between the mid-1840s and 1863, many tribes were forced to cede their ancestral land in a series of treaties, but a group of chiefs steadfastly refused: among them were Chiefs Whitebird, Looking Glass, Eagle-from-the-Light and Old Chief Joseph. They took up the fight. As Old Chief Joseph lay dying in 1871, he told his son, "This country holds your father's body. Never sell the bones of your father and your mother."

The violent confrontations escalated into the Nez Perce War. By 1877, Chief Joseph's son was forced to surrender the last weary remnants of his warriors in order to save what was left of his tribe. The two hundred sixty-eight Nez Perce who survived a brutal, thirteen hundred-kilometre winter trek to South Dakota were eventually moved to a reservation in Washington. Chief Joseph died in 1904, still clinging to the hope he'd return with his people to the land of his ancestors. The doctor reported Joseph died of a broken heart while sitting before his tepee fire.

We steer our rafts and kayaks into Horseshoe Bend, where the Nez Perce fled across the Salmon after defeating a reckless early morning attack in 1877. The crux of this oxbow is just before the rapids at China Bar, so named for an old mining cabin that belonged to seven Chinese gold miners. As legend goes, they mined better than the whites, so they were slaughtered and their dead bodies were thrown in the river. Each one grew into a large boulder. Were it not for the legend of the boulders, I would have no sense that this magnificent point in the river had absorbed so much violence. It's like the Dene belief that Grandfather Rock stores knowledge over the ages; the boulders, and their legend, keep the racist atrocities of the past alive so future generations can remember, and do better.

~

"It's Salmon hot," says Kate. "That's like Africa hot." The temperature reads forty degrees Celsius on the river, thirty-four in the shade. Kate guesses the time is 2:40. Beth confirms it's 2:42.

"How did you do that?" asks Scott.

"Look at the light on the tree," says Kate.

Bees use the sun as a reference point to convey the direction in which to find food. The bee does a dance that follows the formation of a lemniscate, or sideways figure eight, the symbol of infinity. The dance is done on the surface of the combs, which hang down vertically. The angle formed by the line from hive to the sun and the line from the hive to the food source is the same as the angle between the comb's vertical line and the straight line of the dance. If the straight line of the dance points straight up, this means that food is to be found by flying directly in the direction of the sun.

I'm sitting in the shade beneath the tree, a massive Ponderosa Pine so wide my arms reach only halfway around it. Sheree is sitting on a chair in the shallows, water painting, while Nancy and Ruth let a back eddy swoop them upstream, laughing over and over. Christa, meanwhile, is melting.

The petite redhead is physically unsuited for this climate. Her pale, practically translucent skin can't tolerate the punishing intensity of the sun. I wet her blouse and sun hat in the river, then settle under the shade of the tree with Miriam to fan her.

At temperatures much above thirty-five degrees Celsius, bees slow down. They stop flying at forty-three degrees. To cool the hive, workers spread drops of water on the interior, then fan it with their wings to evaporate it and blow the heat-absorbing water vapour out.

When the group sets off again, Christa and I enjoy a long, languorous stretch of rolling river together in the water, floating in our life jackets. Our duck's-eye view of the churning froth conjures up an image of bathing in a sea of soft, bursting diamonds. The beauty of this canyon, the carefree camaraderie of these women, the excellent food and care from our guides has infiltrated my every molecule. Rarely, if ever, have I felt so relaxed. So happy.

This profound sense of well-being follows me to bed. I lie in the sand in my sleeping bag at a perfect right angle to the peak of a mountain, its apex splitting me in two, and feel the now-familiar tug of the earth rooting me down closer to it, grounding me. My gaze travels up towards a three-quarter moon and the stillness of the stars. There's a stirring in my chest and my body begins to heat and quake ever so slightly and I realize I am about to weep. Tears of joy. Instead, at that moment I see a burst of light just above the apex of the mountain, a brilliant explosion, perhaps a meteorite. There is no vapour trail, no other movement. I sleep like a baby.

∾

It's day four. As testimony to my positivism, instead of lamenting the winding down of this trip, I awake relishing that I will enjoy two more complete days on the water. I start the day in a kayak, as does Lisa, Ruth and, surprisingly, Beth, in her first venture off a raft. The long stretch of gentle, fast-moving water is a sparkling delight to paddle. I'm enjoying myself immensely when a hairy white bumblebee, almost the size of a marshmallow, lands on my right hand. Without missing a stroke, and without panic, I dip my right hand slowly into the water while saying aloud, "Not today."

The bee recoups from its quick dunk and flies ahead, past Lisa and Ruth and past Kate's raft until I can no longer see it, but I hear Beth, yell, "Ouch!" as she swipes at her neck.

When a honeybee stings a human or some other mammal, the barbs of

the stinger implant a venom sac which injects eight or more toxic proteins,
including minute amounts of nerve poison similar to cobra venom. Bee ven-
om also delivers dopamine and norepinephrine, neurotransmitters that ac-
centuate fear and excitement. When the bee flies off, her weapon tears from
her body, leaving parts of her abdomen and nerve strands behind while the
venom sac continues to pulse and inject poison. The bee quickly dies, but
during her sting, she emits a scent that incites other bees to attack in greater
numbers.

I can't help but feel the sting was meant for me. By the time I catch up
with Beth at lunch, she's long recovered from the trauma and is so exhil-
arated by her first kayak experience she declares she will try more challenging white water this afternoon. We dub her "The Adventure Diva."

When the appropriate place comes for Beth to transfer into a kayak,
we drift all three rafts to shore and hug the riverbank. Sheree begins another rock talk as Beth hastily crosses the raft I'm in. In her excitement,
her right leg misses her kayak and slips into the water, forcing her left
leg down hard onto the raft's open metal ore lock. The u-shaped lock is
the size of a horseshoe but has the thickness of a garden hose, slimming
slightly at its top. Beth's hanging by the back of her knee on this rounded
hunk of steel, which is now completely consumed by her flesh. I'm sitting
just inches away.

"Help me! Please lift my leg off. Hurry," Beth shouts.

Scott rushes over and lifts her under her armpits. I hear a sickening
suction sound as the metal slides slowly out of her leg. I whip off my long-
sleeved sun shirt and wrap it tightly around the wound while Beth grabs
at it to apply pressure. Blood trickles down her hands and shorts.

"I'm sorry. I'm sorry. I was so anxious to get into the kayak!" she cries.

Kate asks Beth to lie on her stomach along the pad of the raft where
I'm sitting while she and Scott don surgical gloves. Ruth is now beside
us, her long slim hands outstretched over Beth's leg, her face a picture
of concentration as she speaks soft words of encouragement. Ruth is
performing Reiki, channelling healing energy through her own body to
Beth's.

Kate unwraps my shirt from Beth's leg. The puncture is a few inches
long. Subcutaneous fatty tissues hang on the outside like cheese curds.

Miriam's also in our raft. She tells us she'll perform the new energy work techniques she's just learned in training.

"It doesn't hurt, really," says Beth. "Probably just needs a butterfly bandage."

"No, it's too big for that," says Kate.

I hand Scott my water bottle so Kate can dip a syringe into it.

"This is an irrigation syringe, without a needle," Kate tells Beth. "I'm going to flush water into your leg, it might hurt." Beth winces as Kate cleanses the wound.

"That was great, you're doing great," Ruth tells Beth. Ruth looks over at Miriam to see that she's fading and asks Lisa to bring Miriam some water. I glance over and see Miriam throwing up.

Honey from the bee is a very sweet and pure form of vomit. A bee absorbs nectar, with her tongue, or proboscis, and puts it in her honey sac. She absorbs only as much nectar into her digestive system as is needed for her survival. On the way back to the hive, water is eliminated from the nectar and passed to the intestines and the nectar is enriched by various glands of the bee. When the field bee returns to the hive, she unloads the processed contents of her honey sac into empty cells of the comb or passes on the nectar to hive bees for them to process.

"Good spotting there, Ruth," says Kate. I lift Beth's leg while Scott wraps it.

"I'm going to do a head-to-toe exam on you, and then we're going to talk about evacuation," Kate says with composure.

"Oh no, I'll be fine, please don't change the trip!" begs Beth.

We have no communication with the outside world. The canyons don't support radios or cell phones. Kate's concern is Beth could lose a serious amount of blood, her wound could become infected, or she could go into shock.

Kate says she'll stay in the raft with Beth and use a small six-horsepower motor on board to try to speed their journey through slack water to the edge of Hell's Canyon, the deepest gorge in North America and the confluence of the Snake. Once on the Snake, she's hoping they'll find a jet boat that can travel the twenty-five kilometres to the Heller Bar takeout point in Washington.

"We're going to need another person besides the driver to be with Beth," says Scott.

"Oh yes, I was thinking Ruth, and at least one other," says Kate. It's no surprise Ruth's calm, capable demeanour, her selfless concern for others, would make her Kate's obvious first choice. But who will accompany her?

I do the math. Sheree and Scott are paddling rafts. Miriam is faint. Christa is easily overcome by the sun. Nancy and Lisa are a team. It looks like I'm going to the hospital emergency ward.

There are few things less fun than a hospital emergency ward. The mindless waiting, the steady stream of sick and wounded, the pale-yellow cinder-block walls, the worry. The experience could scarcely be more opposed to river time beneath the stars. I hearken back to the lessons of the year before with these women—their selfless giving, their kindness. Of course my primary concern must be the overall safety of our group, which means as we split up, each unit must function at its optimum.

The division of labour within a honeybee colony demands constant toil of its worker bees. She begins cleaning her cell as soon as she has hatched. She then feeds honey and pollen to the older larvae for a few days. By the third day, her brood-food glands have developed, which allow her to feed the young larvae. Next, she relieves the field bees of their nectar, cleans the hive, builds honeycomb and guards the entrance. In her final stage, she makes up to fifty forays a day in search of food for the colony.

"I'm not ready to go," I say quietly to Ruth, but I resolve that if I'm needed, I'll make the journey out without complaint.

Kate announces an improved plan. She'll offload the group's camp gear at the confluence. If a jet boat comes by soon, Beth and Ruth will transfer onto that and Kate will stay at camp. If no jet boat appears, they'll all take the raft and its tiny motor to the takeout point.

"Do you need me to go, Kate?" I ask.

"I think we only need one other person to assist," she says, "and that will be Ruth."

I kiss Beth and Ruth before leaving the raft.

I sit in Sheree's raft beside Christa and Miriam as we drift down Blue Canyon. I ask Miriam how she's doing.

"I'm just amazed at what happened to me. I was sending her this healing energy and all of a sudden a huge surge of energy just left me and I felt very odd. Dizzy. Faint. I tried to loosen my life jacket because I couldn't breathe. Thank goodness Lisa came over to help me."

"Well, perhaps that helped Beth," says Christa.

"Are you squeamish at all, did the sight of the wound have any effect?" I ask.

"I don't think so, because I wasn't looking. I was putting all my energy into Beth."

But when I start describing the wound, Miriam closes her eyes and asks me to stop. "We don't need to go into details."

The rest of the afternoon is spectacular, filled with long, powerful rapid runs. When we get to the confluence of the Snake and Salmon Rivers, Kate is at the campsite with the raft, the gear unloaded and organized. Ruth has gone with Beth on a jet boat to hospital.

Kate explains that within minutes of arriving there, the last scheduled jet boat trip of the day came by.

"Had we taken five minutes longer at any point, we would've missed it," she says. "We would've gotten her out, but it would have taken a very long time."

We're finally on the Snake River, in Hell's Canyon, so named because of the radiant heat from the rocks. The jet boats won't start until morning, so it's quiet and peaceful, not much different from being on the Salmon, except we can't swim because of the pollution, and when I plant my sleeping bag in the sand, I find cigarette butts and dental floss.

At ten a.m., we hear the droning buzz of two 350-horsepower engines from the first jet boat of the day, signalling our return to civilization. The boat slows, as if to give its sightseers a better view of us, then stops altogether and Ruth pops up.

Ruth steps off looking refreshed. She tells us Beth took some stitches and is fine, resting in the hotel surrounded by over a hundred dollars' worth of food Ruth foraged on an excessive shopping spree. The doctors said she was lucky. Had the ore lock punctured a few millimetres to the side of where she landed, it would have severed a major artery in her leg. The canyon may have taken more of Beth's blood than she could have withstood.

~

In 2003, a year after this trip, I'm still pondering the meaning of this event and its connection to the large white bee. As with most accidents, I wonder if Beth was spared some more serious fate. Perhaps she wasn't intended to tackle the white water. I call Ruth in Vancouver to get her thoughts.

"Maybe the release of adrenalin after the sting helped prepare her for the accident," she muses.

"Or caused it," I say.

Ruth reads me her journal from the trip. One page has a life-sized drawing of an ore lock. She's always been terrified of them, even as a little girl at their cottage.

"I finally got to ride a jet boat," she begins. "I'd been dreaming about it since going to Dessa's wedding in 1988. Thirty-four foot aluminum jet boat with two intake drains that required..."

"Wait, wait," I interrupt. "You *wanted* to take a jet boat?"

"Oh yah, ever since I saw them at a wedding in Greece. The only thing that would've made it even better is if I could have driven it."

"Really! Okay. What else?"

"The gift I was able to give Beth was love and support. I'm able to interpret and anticipate peoples' needs. I'm truly trusting in the Divine. It really has moved beyond words and become a way of living on this planet."

This is classic Ruth.

"Did you ever find anything out about the black and white bee," she asks. "Is it albino?"

"I don't think so. I found one description that's close. If it's the same type of bee, it's called a collenette and it's rare. Funny thing is, after I write all of this about the cooperation of a hive, I find out this white bee digs into sand and pupates its young there. It's solitary. Sometimes we're meant to do things on our own, I guess."

"Well, I was pretty happy to be alone," Ruth tells me.

"You *wanted* to leave the river?" I ask, incredulous.

"I can only handle being around people for so long. It was perfect being in the hotel that night while Beth slept. But the next morning I was ready to get back on the water."

It occurs to me that Ruth and Beth's explosive new friendship on that trip in many ways mirrored the profound personal growth Ruth and I experienced when we first met, a give and take of huge magnitudes.

I ask her if she wrote anything else in her journal.

"Well, the last thing I have here is, 'and the best part, no wasp sting. Zen with wasps.'"

"What! Why'd you write that?"

"I'm horribly allergic to wasps and that was the only thing I feared could go wrong on that trip, getting stung and being stuck out there."

"Are you allergic to bees, too?" I ask.

"I don't know, I've never been stung by one."

Two hundred million years ago, before humans or bees existed, large, fierce wasps known as Hymenoptera scoured Asia in search of food. Some gave up their predatory, carnivorous ways fifty million years later, their bodies evolving and their dispositions softening, to take peaceful advantage of the advent of flowering plants.

PRAYING MANTIS
the prophet

In 1967, the year I first saw a praying mantis, I knew my world would never be the same. When you're five and something that foreign drops onto your forearm, how could it be? Green, with bulging eyes darting on an articulating triangular head, four legs as delicate as leaf stems supporting a boat-shaped body, and two thicker front ones protruding from its thorax like spiked, muscly arms bent in prayer. There's much I didn't know and hadn't seen at that age, but no one could've prepared me for the excitement of being in direct contact with something at once so startling, grotesque and beautiful. If I hadn't seen it with my own eyes, I wouldn't have believed this alien and I moved in the same circle.

The praying mantis is the only insect capable of moving its head from side to side like humans. Large compound eyes that can move one hundred eighty degrees, and three simple eyes in a triangle between the antennae give it good eyesight, but the mantis must move its head to centre its vision optimally, much like people.

After just enough time to register its physical details, I shook it loose from my arm. It landed silently and without protest on a stick inside my 'secret' fort—a hand-built, ramshackle abode comprised of discarded plywood and construction lumber, but a place of pride nonetheless. I crouched down for a closer look. We were both still staring, waiting for the next move.

I ran home to get a jar.

I had no idea if this creature was friend or foe, didn't know if its jaws were capable of puncturing my flesh or if its slender body secreted unseen poisons. But instead of wanting to flee from it, or shoo it from my inner sanctum, I yearned to keep its presence, its mystique, nearby. I definitely didn't want to kill it. By capturing it in a glass jar, I thought I could bottle up its secrets and let them unfold to me through a transparent wall, safely and on my own time. I also wanted a pet. My parents hadn't yet heeded my incessant pleas for a dog, and here was something that could sit on its four 'hind' legs, and fold its front 'paws,' practically begging for my attention.

Yet once I'd removed its ability to interact with me, our time together lacked the predator-prey dimension and some of its intrigue. Capturing wild things allows us to observe them without fear of attack, but the barriers between us greatly diminish an animal's ability to behave the way we so crave—wildly—which in turn lessons our own experience in its presence. This was certainly true for my praying mantis, which did little except cling to the twig I included in its sparse new observatory.

It also wasn't interested in the dead fly I dropped inside. It became virtually comatose, giving up none of its secrets, providing little entertainment and even less companionship. I released it into the tall green grasses and flowery weeds that grew alongside the fence just outside my fort.

The praying mantis is a highly predacious and efficient hunter, capturing and eating up to sixteen crickets a day. It prefers soft-bodied insects like flies, but will only eat live prey.

I'd chosen to build my fort beside this particular fence because it contained another object of my desire—a horse. I happened upon her the first time I skipped around the crescent in our new subdivision. My family had just moved to Guelph, Ontario, for my dad's teaching job, an hour's drive away from Brantford where both Hungarian families and a tight-knit Hungarian immigrant community had cocooned us like leaves on a cabbage roll. I may have inherited my love of horses from my great grandfather, who'd been a horse breeder throughout the expanses of the Austro-Hungarian Empire. A devout Catholic, he'd come to North America by ship, hired by the church to escort twelve nuns and a Mother Superior from Budapest to New York near the turn of the century, before eventually migrating into southern Ontario.

The praying mantis (mantis religiosa) is not an indigenous species to North America. It is believed to have travelled on a ship from Europe to New York in 1899, subsequently making its way into southern Ontario and Quebec.

Except for the muted greys and occasional red brick of the new houses, most everything in my neighbourhood was brown—bulging slabs of bald, churned earth that smelled of roots and rain and the memory of leaves alongside hard-packed dirt roads and driveways. The horse was brown too, but it popped out against a backdrop of wild green meadow and towering maples. Scarcely could I believe that around the corner, and just out of sight from the noisy, treeless construction on my street, there existed a forest and a farm.

In short order I had dragged over my own construction supplies and built shelter from the elements so I could steal away, come rain or shine, to my own personal Shangri-La. Resting my head dreamily on weathered fence posts, I would rip tall, fat grasses to feed the horse through the barbed wire, never tiring of the noisy chomp or the yank and quiver of her searching muzzle. As much as I loved her—and it was true love—I was too fearful to cross through the fence. Like the bounties of nature beginning to unfold to me, everything about the horse wreaked of strength and power, beauty and mystery. Her legs more than spanned the top of my head. I had my tiny hands full contending with her all-devouring mouth.

When she remained too distant to feed, I shared my fort with garter snakes, frogs, toads, grasshoppers and butterflies—all of which I captured by hand for closer inspection. Occasionally, a rabbit would hop by. I was never alone and buzzed from the inside out with the industry and whiffs of excitement and danger that accompanied my exploration of this natural space.

I could never predict when or where the praying mantis would arrive. Its appearances were rare, which only heightened my sense of awe and respect for it. While it's relatively small and wouldn't be considered ferocious (unless you are an insect being sized up for dinner), it came as little surprise to me in later years to learn that the praying mantis, one of twenty-four hundred species worldwide in the mantis order of insects, is highly revered in several cultures, and is even the supreme god to one, the

San. Also known as Basarwa (meaning those without cattle) or Bushmen of Southern Africa's Kalahari Basin, the San worship the praying mantis for its hunting prowess, but also for its enigmatic, trickster qualities.

The name mantis, which means prophet, diviner, or magician ordained with spiritual qualities, was given to this insect by the ancient Greeks because they believed it had supernatural powers. In the Muslim world, it was thought a praying mantis always prayed pointing to Mecca, and in parts of southern Europe, the belief was that a praying mantis would point a lost child home.

I can't remember the last time a praying mantis visited my fort, but I remember with painful clarity the day I skipped around the crescent to discover my plywood sanctuary was gone. Disappeared without a trace.

With each breath, I seemed to suck in the emptiness of where it once stood until my hollowness filled me to the point of bursting, and I ran home sobbing. Within days, the horse and its fence disappeared, too. In their place, a giant backhoe razed the very earth that was home to the plants, animals and insects of my untamed world, not stopping until the last vestiges of its despoliation was complete.

Among the legions of lore surrounding the praying mantis is a superstition that the brown saliva of the insect can cause blindness in a man, and a mantis, if eaten, can kill a horse. Through my five-year-old eyes, it did feel as if the backhoe operator must've been blind to the death and upheaval being caused by the steel teeth of his machine. Surely, he couldn't know all that was at stake. As for the horse, it's entirely possible it swallowed a mantis, still and camouflaged, clinging for life on a thick blade of wild grass in the meadow; both of them providing a type of poison pill to the other, a hastening of the otherwise slow and gruelling death by starvation that is a hallmark of an animal's habitat destruction.

~

With the advent of school, an entire new world opened up to take my mind off paradise lost. I took to words quickly and became so absorbed in books I barely thought about the horse. Sometimes I'd walk home from my nearby school past the place where the animal once lived, but the landscape was so completely altered—the forest felled, the meadow now lined with houses and a matrix of front and back yards, each newly sodded and with a spindly maple sapling planted curbside—that there were no tremors of recognition inside my body, no smells of sweat or manure or honeysuckle, no spongy leaf floor to denote this was once holy ground that imbued me with spirit.

In the opposite direction from the horse's old domain, there was a hill we used to tumble down. That stopped when a cement walkway edged with a chain link fence was installed there. I felt like Dorothy on the Yellow Brick Road the first time we marched up the cement path on our way to the city's newest attraction: Guelph's first mall! The magnificent brown edifice, with celebrity Mr. Dressup and prizes on its opening day, was the closest thing to Disneyland any of us had ever seen.

Homes radiating out from my street attracted Portuguese and Italian families that planted all-encompassing backyard gardens with grape arbours. The praying mantis all but disappeared, despite its attraction to gardens, but its relative, the grasshopper, thrived in this changing environment. My friend Leah and I would collect them under a bucket, diligently re-capturing those that had tried to sneak out. When the bucket was full, we'd lift it and stand near the pulsating pile and shriek as each insect clambered to escape, ricocheting off our legs and hopping into our hair.

~

When fault lines in my parent's marriage cracked wide open, the resulting divorce meant relocating with my mother and brother into a downtown apartment. It was a lone high rise in a sea of pavement and shops, only a short drive from my house but worlds away from the pastoral countryside that had so profoundly marked my initiation into nature's wiles and connected me to the praying mantis. The insect now had no tangible presence in my day-to-day existence as a twelve-year-old, except as a distant reminder of all that was disappearing in my life.

It would be twenty-five years before I saw another, after I had children of my own. We were visiting a cousin in Kingston, Ontario. She lived in a unique subdivision where spacious homes with swimming pools were built into the natural flora and fauna: mixed forests of oak, maple and birch were largely intact instead of razed down, mingling with ferny stalks of fleabane, giant foxtail and purple thistle. My boys ran through the colourful, "weedy" grasses yelping with glee each time a displaced grasshopper was rustled into action, until Levi suddenly halted and shrieked out in panic.

"Mom! What is *this*?"

There were gasps as the children glimpsed their first praying mantis. I sighed with relief. I hadn't realized how much I missed that creature. Maybe it wasn't the insect itself I'd missed, but all it had come to represent—an ecosystem where seeds flung by the wind, released from the bowels of a bird, or perhaps nudged from a pod by the clomp of a hoof, were welcomed into the soil. A place where water could pool in ravines, bees could pollinate and a little girl could play and explore, secure in the knowledge that her mother, father and brother were a short skip away.

I'd had difficulties visiting Ontario after I moved to Western Canada. I couldn't bear witnessing the seemingly incessant urbanization during the eighties and nineties. Farmland, marshes, orchards and forests were being gobbled up at breakneck speed, and in their place rose subdivisions enclosed by brick walls and sodded berms. Inside those walls, vigilant care was taken to ensure lawns and landscaped playgrounds remained monocultures of green by plying them with cocktails of pesticides—insects, birds and bunnies be damned—that attached to the soft skin of innocent children playing barefoot. What chance would a praying mantis have in the face of all this? Yet here was one right before my eyes, defying extinction and dazzling its onlookers with all of the same mystery and challenge it had presented to me as a child.

In my children's eyes, it was Pokémon and Transformers incarnate. Something alive. Unpredictable. Breathing the same air. Levi carried it on a twig until the mantis flew off and none of us could find it again.

Praying Mantis exhibit flash behaviour to escape. Their hind wings are exposed during flight and concealed when at rest. In evading a predator, the insect jumps or flies a short distance and then suddenly assumes a stationary, camouflaged position.

∼

Because newspaper jobs had lured me to Alberta in 1984, and then the North—into climes too cold to sustain the praying mantis—my adult life had been largely bereft of them, until I returned to the heat of Africa with my family in 2004. The decision to drive and camp through South Africa, Botswana and Namibia with our pre-teen sons was homage to Francois' Southern African heritage, but it felt much like my homecoming too. I hadn't lost a speck of the zeal or commitment I'd had to further explore the continent since my first fateful trip sixteen years prior when I'd fallen in love with my expedition leader, Ian. And while those original plans with him had fallen through, this was the second time Francois and I had made a low-budget trek through some of Africa's most remote and wild places. Neither of us, it seemed, could get enough of them.

Our first trip was to Zimbabwe, early in our marriage, to spend time with his maternal grandmother and aunt in Harare. We had no children then and toured the politically ravaged country with risky, youthful abandon, booking a last-minute, five-day canoe trip down the muddy Zambezi River at the height of the rainy season with scores of crocodiles and marauding hippos and an outfitter we knew nothing about. Our sole criterion for choosing that company was that it was the only one that took Zimbabwean dollars, which we had in abundance, having just completed a seedy black-market money exchange in an empty warehouse building in downtown Harare. Once on the river trip, we fell asleep on white sand islands listening to the pound of African drums from the Zambian side and the distant roar of lions, both of which were wonderfully soothing to me. Central Africa is the cradle of all humankind—the evolutionary hub from which our earliest ancestors struck out to inhabit the earth some fifty thousand to seventy thousand years ago. Hominid fossils dating back ten million years have been unearthed from sediments of the Rift Valley. In effect, a sojourn to Africa is a homecoming for everyone.

The throbbing hum of huge bird colonies, canoes bobbing in the wake of elephants waltzing across the river, people and backpacks quick-drying under a searing sun after rains pour like panes of glass from hot, thunderous skies—this is half an hour in Africa. Africa seduces.

We're reminiscing about that trip as Francois and I sit with our three sons beside our campfire in Botswana's Moremi Game Reserve, a protected habitat for elephants, zebras, and hundreds of other species. The reserve is in the heart of the Okavango Delta, a flat and profusely green oasis on the edge of the Kalahari Desert, home to the San. It's April, a time when the Okavango River, swollen from rains at its source in the highlands of Angola, meanders its way east like blood through capillaries, slowly pulsing life into parched channels, lagoons and knee-deep flood plains, until the fan-shaped wetland covers an area half the size of Lake Erie. None of the floodwater reaches any sea or ocean, caught up instead in its own rapid evaporation and transpiration until much of the delta dries and the cycle starts again.

"What gave us the audacity to think we could just go and do that?" Francois asks me, poking a stick in the fire.

"What? Change our money with that sleazy expat?"

"No, just canoe down the Zambezi like that?"

I laugh because we're camping close enough to the marsh to hear the slosh and nasally snort of hippos munching on reeds. A black sky affords no clues as to what fierce and primeval activity lurks beyond the small glow of our fire—lions and wild dogs making their dinner rounds, scorpions paralysing their prey—while our twelve-year-old and two nine-year-old sons drift to sleep in a tent perched on the roof of our rented Land Rover, which we've sprayed with bug repellent to ward off malaria. Yet I know he'd not thought *this* audacious.

Something bounces off my forearm, startling me from my thoughts, and lands on the concrete table before me. A praying mantis! Then another... and another. How wonderful to be visited again by this insect that held my enthrall during the brief era of my childhood when my nuclear family had been loving and cohesive.

In San cosmology, Mantis's family is associated with the camp, the location that embodies concepts of harmony and cooperation. Their god Mantis is married to a rock rabbit, an earth mother whose preoccupation with daily tasks means she has somehow lost her imagination. Their two sons are stars and they have an adopted daughter, Porcupine. Porcupine is married to Kwammang-a, whose name can best be translated as 'something visible within a rainbow.' Kwammang-a and Porcupine have two sons. One is also an element of the rainbow, gentle and wise. The other is Mongoose, a courageous fighter.

"Mo-o-o-m. Da-a-a-d. I don't think you should be sitting out there right now," Levi yells down, his voice muffled through the thick tent canvas. "I think you should go to bed." I'm admiring the three insects facing me.

"Why's that Levi?" I ask, unable to take my eyes off of these specimens, larger than the ones I remember as a child.

"Because I'm really worried about the hyenas and I think you should come into the tent right now," he replies, his voice growing in urgency. I can tell by its wavering that he's crying.

We'd all read a warning in the game reserve brochure not to let small children sleep out in the open, as, in the past, hyenas had attacked their faces.

"Ahhh. He must be worried about hyenas because of that brochure," I whisper to Francois, the mantises now feeling their way around the table.

"It's alright Levi," I assure him. "You're safe up there on the roof with your brothers."

"No Mom! I'm worried about you and Dad, and I think you should go to bed RIGHT NOW!" he croaks through his sobs.

"Levi, we're fine. They won't come around; we have a fire."

"It won't work, Mom. You need to go now!"

A bright, columnar beam of white cuts through the darkness like a spotlight to a blackened stage as footsteps draw closer to us.

"Hello... did you... see it?" a breathless South African from a neighbouring campsite asks as he reaches our table, his strong, game-viewing light bobbing in his hand.

"Sorry? See what?" Francois asks.

"The hyena! It passed right by here."

Francois and I shoot silent glances at one another, and then the tent, which is shut tight against the inky blackness of the night. There's no way Levi could have seen a thing. It's as if he'd intuitively been able to sense the animal's presence, the danger. His warnings to get out of harm's way had been clear and unequivocal and coincided with the arrival of the mantises. If they had come to signal pending danger, to augment Levi's concerns, my own intuition didn't pick up on that. Nothing in my gut was flashing caution yellow. Quite the contrary. The insects beguiled and enchanted me to the extent that Levi's wailings felt distracting and intrusive, like the phone ringing during a delicious dinner. Perhaps these tiny trickster gods of the San had acted as sentries, warning the hyena to back away from these unsuspecting Canadians. Maybe, as I would come to think later, they had bigger plans for me.

We tell our neighbour we hadn't detected any movements. He shines his light on the ground and points to hyena tracks. It takes me five steps to reach them. The praying mantises disappear in the commotion.

The San have a song of the hyena, hauntingly sung with the call of this creature, which describes the final stage of San life. They are not shocked by the ending and beginning of their own story. Though it is eerie, they sing lightly of this burial, and their final end as the hyenas drag their bodies out of the earth to devour them once again, bones and all.

~

We had never planned on venturing into the Kalahari. Jesus Christ drove us there. Not that I believe he had anything to do with the heavy rains (granted, they were of biblical proportions) that flooded dirt roads and forced neighbouring game parks to close their gates to us. We just hadn't factored the Easter Holidays into our travel plans, hadn't realized that Africans would be travelling then too. So when we arrived at Botswana's national parks office in Maun, all of the camp reservations in the popular saltpans, now brimming with water and wildlife, were booked. We were hungry, tired and heat-stroked. Not only did our aging Land Rover *not* have air conditioning, it would overheat and shut down at high speeds unless we drove with the heater on, which drew the excess heat away from the engine and onto us. It's hard to imagine my family could ever be more wilted, desperate, or exhausted.

"We only have three nights of camping available in the Central Kalahari Game Reserve," the composed and not overly sympathetic parks clerk had told us.

Francois and I had one of those nonsensical quarrels that happen between couples when fatigue borders delirium, debating the prudence of detouring into the harsh Kalahari Desert without research or preparation, before we concluded we had little choice.

"We'll take them," I told the clerk.

According to the old Shell maps we'd been given by Francois' cousin in South Africa, there were several San villages within the expansive reserve, which, with some planning for the long drive, we could possibly reach. We'd briefly stopped in the San village of Khwai earlier that day after leaving Moremi Game Reserve, and the experience had left a colonial pit of guilt in my stomach. The people had clambered around our decrepit Land Rover as if it were dripping gold, and while we were now short on food and had brought only a bare minimum of clothing and supplies—not much more can fit in such a vehicle with five passengers—our material wealth likely outstripped that of the entire village. I bought a basket from a woman and some Fantas for the kids. It struck me as odd that we'd not seen a single San during our stay in the reserve, prompting me to research the area's sordid, and deeply racist, history.

To leave the north exit of Moremi, you must cross the Bridge over the River Khwai. Not unlike the Thai bridge featured in the 1957 movie of the same name, this is no ordinary bridge. There's no steel in sight, only tightly bound logs weathered to a blue-grey sheen, hatched crossways to form a narrow lane upon which you must balance your tires. On the other side sits the dusty village of Khwai.

Khwai feels like the souvenir shop at the end of a museum exhibit. After days of encountering only well-equipped tourists alongside crowds of zebra, antelope and wildebeest, here are people indigenous to the area, yet clearly partitioned from its bounty, like bees separated from a field of wildflowers. Unlike nomadic San tribes, the River San once lived in Old Khwai village, along the river within the current game reserve. They were forced to move after helping define its boundaries in 1963.

All of the multi-ethnic factions of the region, including the Basawana (whose Queen Moremi created the reserve to protect wildlife from encroaching cattle and from increased hunting) agree the San were the first in the region. The San refused to relocate to outlying communities and instead set up in their current location, as near as possible to the river that had sustained their ancestors for more than twenty thousand years. As punishment for their defiance, the Botswana government refused to provide water services, schools or clinics. In what seems an insulting concession, villagers are now permitted into the reserve to collect straw, which I see lined and strapped in bundles along a fence, to sell as thatch to three tourism lodges operating in prime riverside locations.

The San are the most picked on and persecuted people in all of Africa. The small, lithe hunters with the click language once inhabited much of southern Africa, and pre-dated the arrival of Egyptians, Phoenicians, Greeks and Romans to the North. Their pre-historic rock paintings are testament to a lifestyle in lockstep with nature, a reverence for their liminal relationship with the animals that gave them life. As a people, they embody the characteristics of their chosen Creator symbol, the praying mantis—an adept hunter that's also gentle and walks lightly in its surroundings—and many of their drawings combine human and mantis features. The San took only what they needed for food or tools and left little trace of their nomadic existence, with the exception of their detailed murals.

American writer Elizabeth Marshall, whose family spent time with the San during the fifties, called them *The Harmless People* (and wrote a book of the same name). They believed they were connected to the cosmos, and every living creature beneath it, through a network of strings that set up a vibrational communication, an altered state of consciousness, that afforded them extraordinary perceptions as hunter-gatherers. Many anthropologists studied their hypnotic trance dances, in which shamans travelled these strings to the spirit world in the sky, or flew through the stars to other villages, or shifted themselves into animals, such as a lion. But these connections were largely severed with the arrival of the Boers and migrating African tribes.

Black and white invaders of southern Africa hunted down the San with genocidal fervency during two hundred years of land grabbing. Their game displaced, the starving San (with actual bounties on their heads) turned to cattle and sheep for sustenance, earning them a reputation as thieves. In his book *A Mantis Carol*, South African author Laurens Van Der Post writes that the rationalized justifications produced by his countrymen—Afrikaners, Bantu sages, and chiefs of all kinds—for the near extermination of the San all boiled down to one: The Bushmen just refused to be "tamed." In other words, they refused to abandon their culture and assimilate.

Today, about ninety thousand San, belonging to several different tribal groups, live in South West Africa, southern Angola and Botswana's Kalahari Desert.

~

Flocks of butterflies the colour of butter, so thick and abundant they're like sprays of yellow rose petals, are being mowed down by the Land Rover's tires and tangled up in the grill as we grind our way through the tall, sun-bleached grasses of the Kalahari Desert. This is no bald sand dune; it's more a vast, open grassland covered with barbed, scrubby bushes. In some areas, pockets of acacia trees and an occasional baobab tower like mountainous mirages on a distant horizon.

I feel terrible about the butterflies. "There's no way around it, Laurie," says Francois with typical resignation. And it's true. We have to keep to the faint track, the 'road' forged in the sand for vehicles. (One of only two such tracks that we see in three days.) The butterflies, seeking shade and moisture from the grasses, are everywhere. The only way not to kill them is to not be driving here.

We'd entered from the northeast by opening an unlocked gate through a chain link fence. Known as the Kuke Veterinary Fence, it's meant to keep wildlife from spreading foot-and-mouth disease to cattle. But in times of prolonged drought, tens of thousands of wildebeest, eland and hartebeest have perished along the fence trying to migrate to areas with water. Still, for all its controversy as a death trap, the fence has preserved the Central Kalahari Game Reserve from the infiltration of intense cattle grazing. It's kept it as a place for wild things.

The boys and I climb to the roof of our vehicle, so we can drink in the panoramic views of the plains, now lush from summer rains that fill the dried lakes and riverbeds like water in a dog's bowl, attracting thirsty, black-masked oryx and shaggy wildebeest. Giraffes feed among the stiff thorns of acacia trees and herds of fleet-footed springbok dot the grasses like white daisies in a meadow. I've always preferred the expansive skies of a prairie to the claustrophobic press of a mountain landscape. The Kalahari feels like 90 percent blue sky and billowing clouds, with a mere strip of land beneath.

While driving to our first campsite, Francois notices a family of ostriches, five adults and about thirty chicks, their drab brown colour a perfect camouflage. Upon seeing us, one adult starts hurtling our way like a drunk looking for a fight, her spindly legs stumbling while one wing sags as if broken. She runs in front of the vehicle, so close I can see the panic in her bulbous, feathery-lashed eyes. Francois slows to a crawl. The ostrich plummets to the ground, as if she could not take the next step, and flails about with intense drama.

In the Promethean-like myth explaining where fire came from, the San believe that Mantis, through a con act, stole fire out from under a wing of an ostrich. Ostrich never lifts her wings to fly again, for fear she will lose what little fire she has left. But perhaps Ostrich was hoarding the fire and had too much to begin with. Perhaps she was not supposed to fly, but to run very fast and protect her eggs on the ground. If so, did Mantis step in to create balance and bring fire to all mankind?

"Look, she's pretending she's injured to distract us from her young," Francois says with apparent delight. As soon as we're safely past her brood, she lifts herself off the ground and trots back to her kin, perfectly fine. I marvel at her bravery, and her Academy Award-worthy performance.

~

Max turns twelve in the Kalahari. I'd found a chocolate cake mix in Maun, which I manage to bake in a covered aluminum pot on top of the gas hot plate. It tastes foreign and hot and delicious under the canopy of an acacia grove where we've settled for the night because Max had spotted the spiralled horns of a kudu laying on the ground and proclaimed this was where we should stop. He'd always been attracted to animal parts—feathers, fish spines, bones, antlers—and this is the first skull he'd discovered in Africa, presenting itself as the perfect gift.

There are moments in the history of a family that stand out because of the shared intimacy they hold. This night by the light of an evening fire, under a black sky awash with milky layers of stars, was certainly one of them. In discussing birthdays and the layout of our family, I casually mentioned there was such a large gap in ages between Max and his brothers because of the miscarriage.

The boys became completely still, as if to better absorb this shocking statement.

"What?" says Max eventually. "You had a miscarriage! Why didn't you tell us?"

"I thought you knew that," I reply.

"No, we never knew that," says Levi.

"You mean, we could have had a brother or a sister?" chimes in Calvin. "How could you not tell us *that*?"

"I don't know. I guess I thought you already knew, or else I just don't think about it very often," I say, pointing out that had that baby lived, there wouldn't have been more children. There wouldn't have been the twins.

I seize this moment to tell them that early in my pregnancy with Max, while on assignment in Whitehorse, Yukon, I had signs of a miscarriage. I checked into the hospital, but the medical staff there said I seemed fine and advised me take it easy for a few days. Years later, my doctor said it was likely I did miscarry, that Max had also had a twin.

The boys continue muttering dismay, shock and awe long after they've climbed into their tent, unable to let go of the mystery of not one, but two missing siblings having suddenly been woven into the web of their lives. Meanwhile, Francois and I discuss the wisdom of trying to push south to the San village of Xade the next day. We sit at our portable foldout table with two candles lighting a map we've discovered is sorely lacking in both accuracy and place names. Two praying mantises join us. They perch near to the flame on the side of my glass candleholders (which I won at a Bingo in South Africa). As Francois speaks, I see one is placing its head right into the fire.

"Don't do that," I say out loud, brushing it back gently, while the other begins to do the same.

I continue brushing them away until Francois is prompted to ask what I'm doing.

"These praying mantises. They seem determined to burn themselves. They keep sticking their heads in the fire, almost like they're washing their faces in it, waking themselves up."

In the San's all-devouring myth, Mantis feels sick from eating zebra, an animal of flight and evasion. Mantis is saying I can't swallow any more flight, any more evasion. He tells his adopted daughter Porcupine to call her father the All-Devourer, bushfire, to come and eat sheep with him, the meat of acceptance. Horrified, Porcupine knows her father will eat everything. She hides a little bit of her own food and summons her father. The sky grows black. He sits down to eat with Mantis. Soon everything vanishes into the All-Devourer's stomach, including Mantis and his wife and sons. Porcupine is protected because she, the soul, is the daughter of the All-Devourer's Source. She stands with her father and has her fierce son stand on her father's right, and her gentle son on his left. Then they cut the belly of the All-Devourer open. Out comes the vanished world, including Mantis and his family. She gives them some of the nourishment she has preserved. They have been altered and renewed. She has led them to a new element of being.

∼

We never did meet the San in Xade. The enormity of the Central Kalahari Game Reserve, combined with our poor maps, lack of cell or satellite phone, and a stark warning from another traveller that we should've put a screen over our vehicle's grill to keep the seeds and brush from entering our engine block and starting a fire, all factored into our decision to exit through the west and carry on to Namibia. Weeks later, as we're packing to fly back to Canada, I notice a headline in a South African newspaper saying the San were going to court for the right to return to the Kalahari. The village of Xade no longer existed. The Botswana government had evicted the San from Xade and other villages, forcibly removing them off the Kalahari Game Reserve. Their huts, just like my childhood fort, were destroyed.

Upon investigation I learned the entire reserve area, established in 1961 as a sanctuary for the San and their hunter-gatherer way of life, had been claimed by large companies for mining diamonds. In three waves between 1997 and 2005, virtually all of the five thousand San had been cleared from the reserve and put into resettlement camps. The government claimed it was trying to improve their lives with modern services, but the San said they were told their removal was to make way for diamond mining. Unable to hunt or re-enter their homeland—and beaten when they tried—the San lived a predictably dire life in the resettlement camps. In 2006, Botswana's high court ruled the evictions were illegal and the San could return to their ancestral lands in the reserve. But the government hasn't made life easy for them, depriving them of water boreholes while it drills new ones for wildlife, and new safari lodges with swimming pools.

Perhaps most telling, in 2011, Gem Diamonds began an underground mine at Gope, a former San gathering place for picking wild fruit on the reserve's eastern border. A condition of government approval of the company's environmental impact assessment was that Gem's boreholes be used solely for mining.

The mining companies staking claims to the Kalahari were the same ones doing business in Canada's North, where they are compelled by government to negotiate jobs and compensation with the Dene and Inuit. In preparation for a 2005 *Canadian Diamonds* magazine article about the different approaches of the two countries to Aboriginal rights, I interviewed San activist, Roy Sesana, with the help of an interpreter. His click language through a crackling speakerphone describing the simple wish of his people to "go home," to join their ancestors, made me weary. Had these harmless people not suffered enough? Would there be no end to their oppression?

For twenty thousand years they'd lived in the Kalahari. The bones and flesh of every grandmother and grandfather of every family for at least twenty millennia have been absorbed into the sands, consumed by the animals, wetted by the rains or swept by the wind. I have no doubt the San have developed a special consciousness through those attachments.

Just seconds after we'd hung up I realized I'd forgotten to ask Sesana a pressing personal question: What did he make of all the praying mantis encounters I'd had in the Kalahari? Were these mantises—these gods that were never prayed to for rain or good hunting, but which existed in kinship with every creature in the giant cathedral of plains, saltpans and ancient river beds—missing their brethren? Had they come to me at a time when Sesana was travelling to Hollywood and London, explaining his people's plight, imploring the world to help, so I could help spread the word, too? Had mantis, the creature in the all-devouring myth that had tired of evasion and flight and called in fire for renewal, sensed my reverence, my sympathies towards it?

In 2008, three years after my story was published, a huge bush fire burned about 80 percent of the Central Kalahari Game Reserve. The origin of the fire remains unknown.

∼

Twenty thousand years ago, year-round fields of ice and snow had melted and mastodons and caribou mingled with paleo-Indians in the now heavily populated area of southern Ontario where I was born. Following that, vast tracts of unbroken forest sprung from the fertile soil, becoming the hunting grounds of the Huron, Neutral and Iroquois Nations. After their arrival, the Europeans forever changed the landscape with their intensive industrial development and agriculture, forcing First Nations onto patches of reserves, not unlike the San resettlement areas.

Today in Guelph, the neighbourhood where I first became conscious of sharing my world with nature, is feeling the effects of urban decay. The once "glorious" mall is like a half-empty ice cube tray no one's bothered to refill. I hadn't been back since my early teens when my father sold our childhood home, post-divorce. Then, out of the blue while writing about praying mantis, I received a message from my first friend on our street, Leah, the girl who'd helped me collect grasshoppers. Our exchange was a fascinating reminder that while we constantly recreate ourselves within our own minds, what we are to people from our past is frozen at the moment of impact. "You were my Anne of Green Gables," she told me. "Your imaginative play and enthusiasm inspired me."

Really? It felt hard to believe there was ever a period when I wasn't tired and weighted down by the lawsuit or parenting demands. I longed to go back to that place where the praying mantis challenged me to explore, discover and imagine. And so I did.

~

My aunt and uncle drive me and wait in the car while I run around the Guelph neighbourhood of my childhood during a torrential downpour. My body is light and free, coursing with energy. My knees and back feel none of the creeping aches and pains that have marked my initiation into middle age. I'm possessed by a grounding sense of happiness that everything is *still here*.

I run past the spot where my horse and farm and forest used to be and the houses still stand. I run as if late for class onto the asphalt path that leads to my grade school, past the playground and the woods, which are now an off-leash dog park—a sign instructs people to please pick up after their pets. I run up to the front doors of my old school, breathless, soaked, a solid forty-five years after my mom had walked me there for my first day of kindergarten.

I turn my head towards the sports field of my adjacent middle school and am suddenly awash in a long-forgotten memory of riding a horse for the first time. Not *the* horse that welcomed me to the neighbourhood, but one belonging to a Grade seven classmate, who somehow managed to stable a horse in the city. (I couldn't have been more envious.)

One night, she clip-clopped down the road, cars whizzing by, to our softball game on her dappled grey mare. Bareback, no reins—that was her style. She invited me to take a ride. Intense with desire, I was hoisted up onto the warm curve of the horse's back and instructed to kick. My surroundings blurred as the horse galloped off. My hands clenched the straw-like, ivory hairs of her main, but I was powerless to slow her down or stop her. Nor did I want to. My hips and spine hinged and straightened in dreamy, rhythmic sync with the horse's strides. The little girl who was once too fearful to enter into a horse's corral was now a young woman riding high on a beast she couldn't control or fully understand, but seemed destined to accompany at a dizzying speed.

The horse intuitively returned me to my starting point unharmed, but a bit jostled and a little wiser.

If returning to my roots, as tangled as they were, could have such a visceral effect on me (perhaps awakening my inner child to both the exhilaration and the confusion of my early days on earth) how utterly discomposing it must be for the San to be displaced from their lands, forcibly resettled into impoverished camps and forbidden to hunt. Then came the added misery of alcohol, drugs, and prostitution along with diseases, such as AIDS and TB and a rise in suicides. This is what happens when you deny someone their culture, their birthright. When you imprison them in a world that's not theirs.

Praying mantis, the prophet, the trickster God of the San, is most famously noted in the West for the female's reputation as a femme fatale, devouring the male after sex. But scientists have learned this is not a natural phenomenon. This deviant behaviour happens only in captivity.

At the front doors to my old kindergarten class, there's a colourful sign denoting the brick building is now a "Village of Support," home to employment counselling, a women's crisis centre, pre-school, health and police services, adult education—catering to the largely immigrant population in surrounding high-density housing. Like the praying mantis, they are not originally from here. But they're trying to make their way in a strange new land.

An outdoor mural, a modern-day equivalent of a San rock painting, spans the other side of the building. Black, unclad silhouettes, like the empty spaces in cut-out paper dolls, are jumping and somersaulting over grasses and flowers where multi-coloured hand prints mingle with butterflies, bugs and dragonflies—all beneath the thick rays of a towering, Kalahari-like sun.

Praying mantis, the prophet, called me back in the rain to see this. To show the interconnectedness of creatures and landscapes and concepts and principles that have ruled my life and drawn me to faraway places. To encourage me to keep disseminating the message that we are one world and one people, all dependent on the same elements; all with responsibility to protect those very life forces that sustain us... earth, water, air and fire.

People sometimes ask me where my environmentalism comes from. I wasn't raised in a family where nature was spoken of with reverence, or spoken of at all. I can trace my allegiance to the natural world back to that brief, solitary era of discovery in this neighbourhood, when my glass confinement of a praying mantis deprived it of its hunting grounds, oxygen, food and water; starved it of life itself. This is the plight of the San and Indigenous peoples worldwide who forcibly lose their lifeline attachment to The Land. I wonder if I hadn't eked out that short window of time in childhood to commune with mantis and other creatures in an untamed world, if I'd known only supervised play dates at the jungle gym and one-dimensional wild creatures on a computer screen, if I would care today what happens to the San. Or recognize that everything we do to nature, we do to ourselves.

10

SEAGULL
subtleties of communication

I'm standing in the middle of the ragged highway that passes my home when a wildlife officer offers me a seagull egg sandwich. I've never been an egg-salad fan, but I'm intrigued. I stammer before accepting, weighing whether to tell him that seagulls have become spiritually symbolic of my dying mother.

It's June 2007, the month the Tlicho of the Dene Nation call *Eye Zaa*, or "egg month" because the birds are laying their eggs. It's also our annual highway cleanup time. Our job today is to warn vehicles to drive with caution so they don't injure volunteers wrestling garbage from the ditches. The road winds northeast from Yellowknife seventy-five kilometres then ends abruptly with a giant stop sign. If caught unawares, drivers could drop off the highway into the slack water of a river that heralds the return of nature in all directions (this in fact happened to Peruvian-born trapeze artist Janzy Jimenez, who in July 2003 thought he was exiting Yellowknife, but instead drove his Bailey Brothers Circus truck containing a six-foot python over the brink, later saying he was surprised to see water open up before him where he thought there would be road. The python escaped and was never found).

I bite into the sandwich. It's soft as clouds. Chewing feels superfluous. The egg's mostly white, the bread a puffy brown, and nothing falls out.

"This is incredible!" I say.

The officer shows little reaction when I tell him my mom has a brain disease and lives in Ontario, and I think seagulls are trying to teach me how to make sense of losing her bit by bit, year after year. We are leaning against his white work truck, its pulsating red light casting an eerie glow on our faces.

The common seagull's long, yellow beak has a red dot on its lower mandible. Newborn chicks peck at the red dot, prompting the mother to regurgitate her food. Dutch naturalist and Nobel Laureate Niko Tinbergen noted that the colour red draws a pecking response from chicks, whether it's attached to a mother bird or not. Red stripes on a stick caused chicks to go into a frenzy. Through millions of years of evolution, red simply came to mean mother.

He tells me there are maybe two more weeks left for eating seagull eggs. As a young Dene growing up in Fort Resolution, Northwest Territories, he'd gather both duck eggs and seagull eggs for his mother each year around this time. They'd gorge on them until one day she'd look at him and say, "No more eggs." He'd then start to fish.

~

Exactly one year prior, I'd returned from Ontario to the shores of the lake where I live a changed woman after watching my mother's body turn to cement before my eyes. We first noticed she was changing around her sixtieth birthday, mistaking her sudden apathy and lethargy as depression. By age sixty-two, she'd given up every physical activity she'd enjoyed—skiing, golfing, biking, walks. My brother and I had a heart-to-heart with her, pointing out she had a lot more years to embrace life. "No," she corrected us, without remorse, "just five more." She'd not been given that prediction by a doctor, in fact had not even sought out medical advice, but it turns out she had astute powers of prognostication.

I booked her into a series of appointments then, but three years of peering into her brain and her spine hadn't afforded Ontario medical specialists the information they needed to diagnose why she could no longer make her legs, arms or throat work. It took ten minutes of concentration with my lifting and coaxing her feet for her to climb four steps.

My mother was sixty-five and still without a diagnosis in May 2006 when a Dene medicine woman from Yellowknife told me she was going to Ottawa to give health clinics for federal civil servants. I booked an appointment for my mom. It was a long shot, but just maybe she could exorcise her medical demons. The six-hour drive from my mom's house to Ottawa was a crash-course in the hurdles facing the handicapped. Each pit stop was an arduous ordeal to extract her from the car and assist her in a walker through doorways, grocery aisles and stairs to the nearest bathroom, where we'd struggle anew to complete the task. Once, her walker couldn't squeeze through the narrow aisles of a small grocery outlet. "Oh, if only we had a cane or something Mom we could do it!" My mother slowly lifted her fingers off the walker to point to an old-fashioned milk can loaded with new canes grazing my thigh. We laughed as I pulled one from the bunch and handed it to her, so she could hobble her way to the toilet.

On the morning of my forty-fourth birthday, we walked into the basement clinic of Ottawa's Health Canada building, fashioned after a traditional Aboriginal healing circle lodge. Everyone had sweet-smelling smoke wafted over their bodies by someone waving an eagle feather over a small pot of dried herbs and grasses. Smudging. Removing negative entities and clearing the way for good ones.

My mother lay on a table. The medicine woman began manipulating her hips and legs while her helper massaged them, telling my mother she was beautiful and glowing and getting better. They put smooth rocks on her in strategic places and kept the sweet smell of sage from a smudge pot burning. My mom's cheeks reddened with the blush of someone exercising. After years of hastened, cold, prods in sterile hospital rooms, she looked peaceful and accepting of these practices, without scepticism or fear.

At the end, the medicine woman said she'd call in the spirits. She took out her Dene drum, made of bearskin, and began singing a prayer song. I closed my stinging, tired eyes. When she stopped, my mom looked rested but had shed none of her physical ailments. Later, she asked me in her gurgly whisper, if I'd seen any spirits.

"No, I had my eyes closed."

"I did," she said. "An old man with a long white beard and white robes. He was sitting on a heating vent beside me, looking down."

I was astounded. "Maybe he's a spirit guide, coming to help you,"

I mused.

She screwed up her mouth in disgust. "Well, he's not doing a very good job!"

~

I'm thinking about that trip to Ottawa one month later as I stare out over our lake on a sultry, sun-baked June evening. It'd been difficult leaving my mother and stepfather, who were about to move from their country home to access better services in the city. Were it not for the needs of my own children, I would've stayed. I take comfort knowing my brother will arrive soon to help with the move.

These thoughts are interrupted by the sound of gunshot at the nearby park across the lake. I hope our dogs haven't fallen victim to some yahoo with a shotgun. If they have, it won't be the first time. Several years earlier, our black Husky-cross from the pound went missing during winter. We'd assumed he'd run away, or possibly been taken by wolves, but that spring we discovered his body riddled with gunshot near the park, after the snow melted.

When Francois comes home, he suggests we take advantage of the lake's perfect stillness by going for a cruise on our "motor dock," a home-spun wooden platform atop six plastic industrial barrels propelled by a small motor. We sit in Adirondack chairs, and he steers using a long piece of black PVC pipe attached to the motor's tiller.

The word *glorious* comes to mind as we inch our way through perfect reflections in the lake, its marshy shoreline an uninterrupted melange of pine and birch, and the striated greys of Pre-cambrian rock splattered with orange and green lichens. A perfect dry heat pushes my sinking body even more comfortably into the contours of the chair. I sip my drink. The only people we see are a young couple, sitting arm-in-arm at the park.

In this complete privacy, in this glory, we discuss euthanasia; at which point we'd consider life no longer worth living and how we'd expect the other to hasten the process if we got into an immovable, pain-filled state similar to my mother's. There's still a possibility her illness is genetic, a mutation of the dementia that had beset my grandmother and great-grandmother. Still, I feel lighter, hopeful, having talked aloud my fears to both the one who has pledged to stay with me forever, and the gentle, learned ears of nature.

Returning home, we pass the small island respected by our lake community as a bird sanctuary. I notice a seagull on her nest. Her mate takes chase, hovering and squawking to distract us. It's common for Arctic terns to dive-bomb passers-by, but this is my first experience with a seagull. He flies so close I cover my head and crouch down. The encounter infuses me with adrenalin. I feel beautifully awake. Revitalized.

"That was strange," I say. We carry on in silence as we near the park. I notice another gull bobbing peacefully in the water just as Francois veers the motorized dock sharply in its direction. "Where are you going?"

"There's a red spot on that seagull," he says. "I want to check it out."

I notice it then too, a red spot near its wing. The gull floats calmly, making no attempt to move away as we approach.

"Blood," he says, confirming his suspicion. "It's been shot."

My first thought is it's unfortunate we don't have a gun to kill the bird, although it shows no apparent distress. But what's my rush to take its remaining time on earth? The gunshot had penetrated its wing at the point where it joins the body, so it couldn't fly, but it's still capable in its other element: water.

Seagulls are very buoyant—equally comfortable swimming as they are flying—but they are primarily shore birds; a place of neither land nor sea, a place between, a place often associated with fairy contact.

Clearly, the bird's now more vulnerable to predation, more susceptible to infection and disease, less able to scavenge for food... old before its time. But perhaps, if it's female, it can still sit atop a nest and bring warmth and teachings to its offspring, protected by a faithful mate. Or she can float conspicuously at a distance, drawing attention away from the nest like a decoy, maybe giving her life over in the process, but sparing her offspring at least one key strike from a predator. I'm reminded of the mother ostrich I'd seen in the Kalahari Desert that feigned a broken leg to make herself look like easy-pickings as she limped in the opposite direction of her young.

Easy-pickings. Maybe that's what I can't stomach. Vulnerability. I'm also reminded of something that's haunted me since before the children were born. Francois and I were driving to work. It was April, when the first warm breaths of spring thaw the shallow ponds along the highway by day, only to have winter ice reclaim them after sunset. With no other open water, the inaugural wave of migrating ducks settle temporarily in these ditches. We discovered one such migrant frozen solid, its bill dipped partially into the ice as if searching for food, striking a perfect pose, except some carnivore had ravaged its neck. Later, Francois said the bird would've been sick and died first, the water freezing around it only after its body heat had escaped. But for the longest time, I envisioned that bird being eaten alive.

"Here, you steer," Francois says as we approach the injured seagull. "What are you going to do?" I ask. "I'm going to whack it on the head," he replies, pulling the PVC pipe off the tiller.

It hadn't occurred to me to capture the bird and nurse it back to health. Where would we begin? Although, my neighbour Doris once discovered two newly hatched kestrels fallen from their nest. She raised them, even cutting up dead, frozen mice for food, until they migrated south in the fall. They returned briefly the next summer, delighting us by landing on our heads once again before setting off. So, with dedication, there can be rehabilitation, and even release.

My husband is a hunter. Not by trade or nature, but as someone who embraces the wholesome benefits of the hunter lifestyle. We in return enjoy wild meat free of mad-cow and listeria. He's developed the stomach to kill; I haven't. My plan is to look away.

Try as I might, I can't steer the rigid rectangle towards this bird, which watches my erratic movements, but makes no attempt to leave. Eventually, Francois takes over both jobs of steering and whacking. I move to the other side and cover my ears. The slightest, most gentle spray of pink water droplets falls upon my arm and a paralysing melancholy settles over me. How could this outing start out so glorious, turn even to euphoria, only to take such a cruel, bloody twist? Where can I go to escape thoughts of death?

Francois ties the dead bird to the back of our moving dock and heads towards the park, wanting to find the people who'd shot it. I remember we still haven't seen our dogs.

The low buzz of the tiny motor morphs suddenly into silence. Out of gas.

I look at Francois, then to the back of the dock where a bloodied bird tied to a yellow rope now floats, as if saying, you *must* look at me.

Francois murmurs obscenities. Then we row and pole our way to the shore. He jumps onto land. I sit, awaiting more bad news.

A man at the park says a young couple had left earlier with a gun. He'd also seen a young boy on a bike with two big dogs. That would be our son, Max. Relief. I convince Francois we need not bring the dead seagull home. We pick up garbage left behind by the yahoos then place the dead seagull respectfully in some brush where humans will not likely encounter it.

I go back two days later to find its carcass stripped bare, save for the feathers. At least its death had not been wasted. It nourished its community.

～

The phone rings on a Friday, six weeks after the motordock fiasco. It's my stepfather. He says my mother has been taken by ambulance to hospital and doctors aren't sure if she'll make it through the weekend. While her as-yet-undiagnosed disease continues to rob her of her voice and motor skills, the fact she's deteriorated to a near-death state is a shock to everyone. By the time my brother and I can book flights and get to her hospital room, two days later, she's rallied. "I guess I just really wanted to see you both," she whispers with her gentle smile.

It's clear she can no longer be cared for at home, with legs and a waist that don't bend and arms that can barely bring morsels of food to her mouth. The four-year wait for a nursing home turns into two days once Ontario's health-care system gets wind she is parked in a hospital bed with the meter running. "This is great news," the woman who found the placement tells my brother, stepfather and me. On some level, I agree, but know my mother will not, and that my stepfather—dreading this moment for years—will gratefully accept my offer to be the one to tell her.

She cries in the most mournful, primal way. The disease is attacking her throat and her ability to talk and swallow, so I'm startled by the resonance and power of her crying.

The seagull's mew call is a long-drawn note that has a wailing, plaintive character reminiscent of the human voice. It indicates breeding activity with the emphasis on the friendly attitude towards mate, territory, nest and young. The young gull has an innate tendency to respond to it, especially when it needs brooding.

I climb into my mother's hospital bed and hold her close, kissing her cheeks, stroking her hair, murmuring a string of consoling, loving statements. She'll get good care. We'll make her room beautiful. Her husband will be just blocks away. I'm unprepared for her terror and move on instinct, mothering instincts, to soothe and bring solace. Eventually she calms; however, knowing my kind, selfless mother, I wonder if she may have willed herself to appear so, not wanting to unduly burden *me*.

My brother, stepfather and I go to the nursing home that afternoon. It's privately owned by two Hungarian brothers who looked like my handsome Hungarian uncles. Framed samplers of embroidered flowers hang on the cinder block walls, reminders of my grandmother. The place even stinks faintly of cabbage rolls, which are on the menu. Stinking hot outside. Stinking hot inside. Ubiquitous fans blow humid air awash in the smells of urine, disinfectant and cafeteria. The colour scheme is a mash of infantile baby blues and pinks. My brother later confesses he was on the verge of telling me we will "not put her in this shithole," but something held him back. The place isn't wowing me either, but I'm looking beyond the décor to the caregivers, and my gut's telling me this is a caring lot. In short order, we all come to see them that way.

The next morning, as we're about to move in her furniture, I shut the door to her room, open the window and her closet and look seriously at my brother. "Don't ask too much about this, but I just have to do it," I say, reaching into my bag and pulling out a long braid of dried sweetgrass. I close my eyes and ground myself before lighting the ragged end, sweeping its sweet-smelling smoke along the lines where the ceiling and walls meet, along the floor, under the bed, in the closet. "What are you doing?" my brother asks. "A lot of people have died in here, and I just want Mom to have a fresh start, clear the air, so to speak." I know this is unorthodox on just about every level, which is why I opt to do it without warning or permission. I would've gotten away with it, except I linger too long in the bathroom, which is close to the hallway, and then the head nurse and staff start running about yelling "do you smell smoke?" and I sheepishly open the door to tell them it's just me, "burning incense."

The head nurse is understandably upset with me. They'd had an actual fire and evacuation the previous week. "Good for you," another staff member tells me when she sees the sweetgrass. "I wish we did more of that. It feels very nice in here now." And it does.

We move in Mom's things and she arrives that afternoon in a wheelchair. The nurses and the three other middle-aged women in her hospital room are sad to see her go. My mom makes friends quickly. Her new neighbours are now almost all hunched in wheelchairs, drooling, while most able-bodied ones suffer some form of dementia. My mom is in a netherworld, clearly about twenty years younger than most, her memory intact, her body betraying her. As I wheel her into her private room, I see her brighten. It does look nice, and while small, it has a window with a pastoral view of a farmer's field with the sweeping Blue Mountain escarpment as a backdrop. It's as good a new start as we could hope for. My brother and I leave her with our stepfather and stumble out into the soupy heat.

We walk downtown into the thick of the annual Elvis Festival. Ninety-seven Elvises are crammed onto a main street stage trying to break a world record for the most tribute artists simultaneously singing "All Shook Up." To unofficially augment the record, we're part of the sea of people holding up black and white cardboard Elvis masks to our faces, singing along... *when I'm near that girl, that I love best, my heart beats so and it scares me to death.*

I look at my brother through the holes I'd just popped out of Elvis's head. Seeing the world through my new eyes. Eyes that are starting to envision life without Mom, the hub to my wheel.

～

We hadn't expected our mother to live that summer. That she was still alive one year later, never expressing any yearning to die, in fact trying harder at everything—assisted walking, Bingo, exercise classes, jigsaw puzzles—was testimony to her strength of character, her love of family and the care and attention she received. With her pain better managed by morphine patches and cocktails of pills, she was able to turn her attention to the needs of doting staff and residents and became the darling of the place. My brother and I each flew six times to see her during the eighteen months she spent there.

Herring gulls from the Northwest Territories and Alberta have their young in northern climes, then some migrate long distances to winter in the Great Lakes area.

My quick-witted stepfather, who visited faithfully three times daily, was her cheery, affable sidekick, joking with staff and sparing my mom his grief and confusion. "Just shoot me, if I ever have to go to a place like that," he'd say to me privately. He called it warehousing people waiting to die. True, they weren't coming out alive, and maybe that's why I came to feel so privileged to be in their midst. With each visit, my worldview changed. People in wheelchairs, both inside and outside the home, became just people. The women who joked and smiled while they bathed, fed and changed the soiled diapers of residents were surely angels walking on earth. Maybe my mother's heart-wrenching demise was a continuum of the lessons I was meant to learn from her: compassion, selflessness, kindness, dignity. I no longer felt qualified to pass judgment on when someone's life isn't worth living.

A friend's mother who worked in palliative care told me if people are shown one simple kindness in a day, that's often enough to give them the will to live. My mother was awash in such kindly acts. The love motivated her to push through her agony, which seemed to augment ours.

A woman my mother used to golf with visited her daily. She'd ask my mom questions about her life, then write her whispered answers onto paper, which she later typed and printed up for me to read. Most of it I'd heard before, how she was born in Magrath, Alberta, the third of seven children to Hungarian immigrant parents who ran the local country diner and dry goods store. They moved to Brantford, Ontario, when she was two. Then I read something that stopped me cold. "When I was four, the one thing that I will never forget is going to the playground with (my sister) Priscilla. She was six and this great big man sexually assaulted me and then gave us a quarter to get an ice-cream cone at the corner store." When I pressed her for details (he'd had her sit on his lap and probed her with his fingers), I learned she'd lived with that secret until her late twenties, when she finally told her mother.

During my legal entanglements resulting from my efforts to bolster the rights of women and children to be protected from such abuse, my normally quiet and reserved mother had written an eloquent letter to the editor of the *Toronto Star*, in response to its coverage of the judicial inquiry. I was surprised by the letter's strident, powerful tone. This was unlike any conversation we'd ever had. It seemed oddly out of character, and I felt both surprised, and proud. Only after I'd read her autobiography, told to a friend in her final months of life, did I come to understand my mother's mostly understated, yet unequivocal support for me had come from a place of profound understanding of the issue.

Just before she lost her voice entirely, I called for one of our one-sided conversations. Later that day I passed a dead raven on the highway. Then two seagulls standing on the shoulder flew directly in front of my van, so slowly and for so long that I had to break hard, twice, in order not to strike them. One wobbled like a drunken sailor, its wings missing beats. In my journal that day I wrote: Mom is trying to tell me something.

∼

About a week after my first seagull egg sandwich, I run into the wildlife officer who says he's going egg hunting that night. He agrees to let my sons and me tag along. We motor in a small stainless steel boat to a flat, treeless island where hundreds of seagulls nest among the craggy rocks and lichen. They hover above us like fluttering white streamers, their rhythmic alarm call—*hahah-hahahah*—thick in the wind. The eggs are everywhere, earthy taupe shells layered with rich brown speckles.

The eggs that are a little tacky to touch are the newly laid—probably the best to eat. All eggs are dropped gently into an aluminum pot of water. If they're weighty enough to sink, it means a chick has begun developing and they're put back into the nest. If they drop, then float to the surface, it's early days and we keep them. No nest is fully depleted. The children run about with purpose while I'm invariably drawn to death: the carcass of a headless gull, its body caught in a web of thick fishing line snarled between three rocks. I work the line off the rocks to discover the bird itself is not attached, but rather ensnared in its own line. I try to untangle that mess, hoping to pocket all of the clear nylon, so I can spare another creature a similar fate, but it's too tightly woven a trap.

I ask to borrow a knife. Instead, our host cuts the line himself, rips a whole wing off for me (I said I wanted a feather) and hoys the bird into the water, its body still wrapped in its transparent killer, now lurking once more in the silent depths of the lake, waiting to take hold.

I'm suddenly reminded of a conversation I'd had with a gentle man in a wheelchair at my mother's nursing home.

"Will you please sever the line?" he asked me one night, his pale-blue eyes clear and plaintive, his skin a shiny alabaster under the fluorescent lights.

"Pardon me, sir?" I asked.

"Sever the line. Just cut it."

"What line is that, sir?"

"The line that binds us all together. I want mine cut. I'm ready to go now."

"Maybe it's not your time. That's why the line is still there."

"No. You can cut it for me."

"You really think I could?

"Yes. I've talked to two other people and they say it's possible."

And then the head nurse came and wheeled him away. I never saw him again.

When the egg pot is full, we make our way back to the boat. I try to carry out our booty, but as I step up into the boat, I slip on the slimy, wet rock and my leg slides under the bow, colliding hard with its steel bottom. I fling the pot of eggs backwards like a windmill, smashing it onto the rock.

Everyone falls silent, giving pause to my shock and humiliation. Our host helps me to my feet and once he assures I'm okay, we survey the egg damage. "Only one fell out. Pretty good," he says cheerfully, adding that a few others had cracked, but are still edible.

We're about halfway home when I comment on how incongruous a large white house looks on the otherwise undeveloped boreal shoreline of Great Slave Lake. A few seconds later, the boat's veering towards that house at a slowed pace, its motor labouring, our captain grumbling about the need for tools. Just a few paddle strokes away from shore the motor dies. The homeowners welcome our shipwrecked crew and eventually drive us all into town. I'm given half a dozen eggs to take home.

The next morning, I crack the seagull eggs into a bowl with a mix of dread and anticipation—'are you a bird, or an egg?'—while my sons look on. I'm laughing, a sort of giddy jubilation that this unusual event can be part of my life; that Indigenous peoples, despite every effort by dominant societies to rob them of their culture and identity, still retain their traditional knowledge and ties to nature, and that I'm privy to some of this knowledge. By raising our children in the wilderness, they'd come to see such events as, if not 'normal' in a mainstream sense, then at least natural, and hadn't acted squeamish. In an era when many people only have virtual experiences with nature, we're helping preserve the biodiversity of children.

That said, the scrambled seagull eggs that went down easily enough at breakfast make an explosive exit for Calvin later that afternoon, prompting Max to surmise it's the "revenge of the shit-hawk."

∼

Seagulls (which biologists point out are more appropriately termed gulls) are still on my mind a few weeks later driving home with the kids. I spot one flying, but something isn't right. It's airborne and flapping with vigour, yet not moving forward. How can this be? Then I notice a plain white plastic bag is attached to its leg, ballooning behind it like a parachute popping out of a drag-race car.

"Oh no! Look at that seagull," I tell the boys. They crane their necks for a better look. The bird lands on the side of the road and begins pecking at its leg chain. I pull the car over.

"What are you doing, Mom?" Max asks.

"I'm going to take the bag off," I tell him resolutely, then realize instantly the impossibility of that.

"It'll just keep flying away from you," he points out with typical pragmatism.

True enough. Like so many things just out of reach, there's nothing I can do to help. We watch it try unsuccessfully two more times for airborne freedom. Then I drove away slowly.

I look in my rearview mirror, unsure what I'm hoping to see behind me—one last glimpse of the bird? But all I see is Levi, his head still turned, watching the struggle.

∼

My shoulder aches with pain on par with labour, only it never ends. Mysteriously, I have dislocated it.

It's July 2008. In one week we will bury my mother's ashes in the cemetery in Brantford, Ontario, where her parents lie. I wish this had been dealt with in April when she died, but my stepfather wanted to wait, and my mom had not wanted any ceremony. It will be short. Just my brother delivering a eulogy, and I will play guitar and sing a song I wrote for her. If my shoulder doesn't hurt too much.

My mother's shoulder hurt her. In February, during the last moments I saw her alive, I asked why she was refusing her baths at the home. She pulled me closer to her in the wheelchair and whispered, "Hurts." The baths, water, hurt her, especially her shoulder, likely because of a rotator cuff injury she sustained falling off her bike during the early days of her illness, which now had a name: Progressive Supranuclear Gaze Palsy. I arranged physiotherapy and massage back then, but nothing helped. Not even mega doses of morphine. The nurse promised me she would ask the caregivers to be extra gentle bathing her and put a silk sling on her arm to reduce the pull on her shoulder. The tears were welling in the nurse's eyes. She'd come to love her, too. Then I kissed my mother and willed my trembling body to turn my back on her and walk out that door.

~

"Are you afraid to die Mom?" I asked her one afternoon in the nursing home.

"No, I want to see my father. And Priscilla."

"Do you want to live?"

She nodded yes, a glimmer of hope in her eyes, as if I were about to offer a cure.

"Not just when I'm here and you're enjoying our visit, but next week when I'm gone. Do you ever think you don't want to live?"

She nodded yes and turned her gaze down.

I felt compelled to have such conversations in case we had to decide for her about inserting feeding tubes. On this visit, she'd refused them, telling nurses she'd try harder to swallow her food. I worried she was trying to live for us, when what she really wanted was release from her pain. And then, with a cavernously deep sense of guilt, I worried maybe it was I who wanted release from mine.

I read her passages from a book of people's near-death experiences, which managed to make dying sound... well, heavenly. I took comfort in that, and she seemed to, as well.

In the final three weeks before her death all I could do was write a song on my guitar about angels whispering love. I intended to sing it to her in person, so she wouldn't be afraid when the time came. When I received a call saying she'd told the nurses she was dying, and they did, in fact, not expect her to live more than a day, I panicked.

I hadn't sung her the song. Francois was travelling, there didn't seem to be any way I could leave.

The next morning, just as my brother was arriving in her room, I had Calvin hold the phone to my mouth while I sang and played guitar.

My father so tenderly kneels on the blanket he's laid.
A smile on his face his arms wide to embrace all my fears
The window is cracked a child's voice rides the back of a breeze
Angels whisper love...

My brother said she raised her eyebrows to indicate she'd heard it. Then, through a deluge of miracles and generosity, I found myself on a plane, my brother vowing to pick me up in Toronto at midnight.

He was sleep-deprived and we used precious time to sort out his car rental and stop for water. I parked the temptation to react with agitation at the delays, opting instead to accept that every moment along this journey was perfectly timed and miraculous. Every travel encounter that day had been wrapped in kindness. My brother assured me that if she did die, his cell phone would ring, and it didn't. We pulled into the nursing home parking lot just before three a.m. and made our way to the door.

It was locked.

I buzzed the doorbell and knocked on the glass. Then I saw my stepfather exit my mother's room with a male nurse wearing a stethoscope. They stood a few moments talking in the hall... We knew she was gone.

My stepfather, exhausted, shuffled down to tell us we were too late. But I felt right on time.

When I walked into her room, the television was blaring obnoxious sales pitches from a furniture salesman. I turned him off. The stillness then was beautiful. Clearly, my mother could not have eked another moment out of her withered body and I felt relief her suffering had ended. I spent another two hours in that room, sharing time and space with my brother and two stepsisters; listening to the coroner's kind discourse on the beauty and commonness of dying at this quiet peak of night-time, when the spirit is rested and uninterrupted; trying unsuccessfully through my tears to sing my song to her spirit, which according to the near-death book was likely still hovering above us. And, with the utmost respect and gentleness, I assisted two loving staff members to change her into a fresh white gown.

Two days after my mom's death, her youngest sister, Criss, and an old boyfriend whom I hadn't seen in many years but who'd made contact by email a few months earlier, had the same dream about her. She came to them with her jet-black hair cut stylishly short, her athletic body trim and nimble, wearing white pants and a white V-neck shirt. Both said the V-neck was significant, as if my mom was trying to show off her neck and throat. Functional once again. This vision of my mother came sporadically to Criss for the next couple days during waking hours and it lifted me up just to hear about it.

~

When I return home to the lake after the memorial, I meet Maritime author Bernice Morgan at a writer's festival in Yellowknife and devour her novel *Cloud of Bones* about Shawnawdithit, the last Beothuk Indian woman. Steeped in native spirituality, one passage leaps out at me:

> Sometimes birds would follow us, flying low across our canoes. One morning Osepa the white gull flew out of the mist and perched on my shoulder—Osepa was the spirit guardian of my poor dead sister Sanagi. I knew then that she had crossed the Ghost Path and was safe with our ancestors.

For the first time in two decades at our lake, a seagull family has taken nest on the motor dock, which now floats stationery in our bay. A mother, father and just one offspring. One afternoon, I feel drawn to the deck to watch them. The young one stares back at me from the water then begins circling overhead, coming closer with each pass. I sense it wants to land on me, so I hold my arms out to each side. A heady mix of exhilaration and sorrow grips my chest. "It's okay. You can come to me," I whisper. The bird flies so close, I feel the wind from its wings. Just when I think it's going to choose my arm for a perch, it lands instead on the low roof beside me. We look at one another awhile, then it flies away. By the next day, all of them are gone.

I think back to the seagull with the white plastic bag anchoring its flight. How I'd wanted desperately to touch it, to be part of its freedom, to have it be part of mine. How I'd taken that last glimpse into the rearview mirror as I left it behind, holding such longing, but so little hope. And then had Levi cried out something that had made my heart quicken.

"She got it off, Mom! She got the bag off. I see her flying away."

"Oh, that's so great," I'd said. "Finally, a happy ending."

11

SWAN
a state of grace

While scratching my finger one day, I notice tiny red spots welling up under my wedding ring. How curious. I laugh to myself, wondering if this could be the seven-year itch. We'd just surpassed that marriage milestone, and the spots make me suddenly aware that, until now, I'd not thought about other men. I'd had no flutters of attraction, no flirtatious attempts at witty banter, not a single, pheromonal whiff of forbidden sexual intrigue at any level. The spots go away, but my new awareness doesn't.

There had been little time, or desire, to engage in sexy repartee during the early, sleepless years of child rearing when I was regularly tethered to one, and sometimes two, nursing babies. More than a lover, I needed a Seeing Eye dog, preferably a St. Bernard that could navigate the darkness of night with small barrels of liquid and sustenance. Francois, the most trusted and faithful of companions, was all this and more, preparing healthy finger-food meals and placing them on my bedside table each night, so when I awoke to nurse, I could refuel myself. For Christmas, he gave my aching, tired body a promise of three hundred sixty-five massages, one a day, a promise he kept, and there was no finer touch.

My world was largely confined to a couch with a view of the lake, a jug of water with a straw, and books, reading being one of the few activities compatible with breastfeeding's forced sedentariness. I dined on fiction with an appetite matched only by my yearning to break free of the confines of my house and the mindless tedium of keeping it in order. When my mother's youngest sister Criss (who's so close to my age I've always thought of her as my sister, not my aunt) gave me a copy of Marion Zimmer Bradley's *Mists of Avalon*—a feminist take on the legend of King Arthur's court, told through the perspective of the women who circled the Knights of the Round Table—I was ripe for fantasy.

Betrayal, lust, pagan spells, heathendom—these Druid women had a lot on the go! Tied to their spinning wheels for inordinate lengths of time, they harnessed the monotony to induce trancelike, prophetic visions termed "the Sight," by protagonist Morgaine. The Priestess was depicted on the book's cover with dark, cascading curls (like mine), sword in hand, atop a white horse standing in the foggy mists. Accompanying her at the horse's shrouded hooves is a swan, its wings half unfurled in a graceful swoop behind its arcing neck, as if floating on a cloud. The picture suggests a place of neither land nor water. The straddling of two worlds at the margin of dimensions.

I felt adrift in just such a place when, glancing up from my book, I saw a thick fog had engulfed the landscape, silently turning it the colour of cream of mushroom soup. I'd been so engrossed reading about Arthur's, Lancelot's and Gwenhwyfar's homoerotic ménage a trois, I hadn't noticed my own world misting over, or that the twins had fallen asleep at my breasts. I put them to bed and stepped outside to grab the laundry off the line. It was May, or *Tôdoo Zaà*, "month of melted ice along the shore," to the Dene. I could hear the thinning sheath of ice tinkling like wind chimes, its fused, frozen stalactites bobbing in the middle. Along the shoreline, I noticed the mist begin to swirl like a twister rising from the water where, to my astonishment, a solitary swan floated.

The Greek God Zeuss took the shape of a swan to make love to Leda, a mortal—reflecting the ability of a swan to link different worlds and dimensions.

It was common this time of year to see tundra swans, also known as whistling swans, staging at a larger, nearby lake. I once counted fifty-six resting there before they resumed their migration to breeding areas along the Arctic coast. But I'd never seen one on our lake. And why was it alone? In a move which I regret to this day, I didn't go to this lovely creature, didn't sit with it, but instead ran back to the house to retrieve my camera, as if capturing it in a flat photograph would somehow yield greater pleasure or understanding of the encounter. It was nowhere to be found when I returned, and I was left wanting.

The all-consuming busyness of those years had waned by the time I got my "seven-year" itch beneath my ring, and it continued to subdue as I skated towards middle age. Once children are in school and there are no more babies, but rather interesting little people you can comfortably entrust to others' care, space begins to open up again for coupledom. Like swans, long regarded as the gold-star standard for lifelong monogamy and good parenting, Francois and I had made a great breeding pair—attentive, protective parents with a healthy brood, nicely feathered nest and steady supply of wholesome wild foods (the ultimate organics). But all of a sudden, this newly created breathing space in our marriage felt like a vacuum—an un-oxygenated hole into which something must flow. But what?

Female swans, along with other bird species and mammals once thought to be sexually monogamous, have been proven through DNA testing to have affairs, or "extra-pair copulations, EPCs" usually in secret, at high rates.

We'd dated just ten days before our engagement, eight months later we married, nine months later we'd bought a house and within three months, I was pregnant with Max. And then a miscarriage, and then twins. "We're on the fast-life track," Francois had said to me, and it was true. There'd been no period in our relationship that wasn't marked by major change. Until now.

∽

On the day before my fortieth birthday in May, I'm strolling through Old Montreal with Francois, having joined him for a couple days at the end of his work trip. The children are staying with friends back home. My plan is to later meet Criss in Toronto and drive down to Pennsylvania with her to tend to my grandmother, her mother. As little girls, Criss and I spent our summers together in imaginative play, as teenagers we shared secrets and insecurities, and now, as mothers, we're discovering the complexities of family. We're excellent travel partners and have perfected the art of savouring the journey, as well as the destination. She rescued me from a lonely post-university year in Europe, and we'd had several adventurous road trips into the United States and Western Canada. I'm pumped.

This is the first time Francois and I have been away from the boys together. We feel a giddy and unfamiliar lightness, a sloughing off of the thick and calloused parental skin that forms under the chafe of the daily grind. I float in a sea of ease, luxuriating in the adult choices washing over me like warm water on a naked body.

"I think I know what I'd like for my birthday," I tell Francois as we stroll the weathered cobblestones of St. Antoine Street West.

"What?"

"A guitar."

"Then you should get one," he replies without hesitation.

Just then a large music store stretching nearly a city block appears before us, like a temple calling in the choir. *Steve's Music.*

We look at each other with raised eyebrows, and walk in.

I didn't actually play guitar at the time. I'd taught myself a few chords one summer in university after my dad gave me his old Framus, but hadn't picked up a guitar since. I've fond memories of my father, a top-notch yodeller, singing old country tunes in our living room when I was a very young girl and asking me to join him. For all the fraught moments of my childhood, music was a world unto its own, where family tensions weren't welcome. A place of respite and renewal.

I excelled at Royal Conservatory piano lessons under the stern tutelage of our bee-hived neighbour, Mrs. Richards, although my preference was to play air guitar and lip-sync to Partridge Family albums in our basement. As a teen, I became an audiophile, owning the best in stereo equipment to play my vinyl, cassettes and CDs (with a brief interlude of 8-track). I was a voracious consumer of live music in Toronto during the seventies and eighties, mostly UK bands—The Police, U2, Simple Minds, The Clash, Supertramp, Depeche Mode, Peter Gabriel, English Beat, David Bowie—and nearly wore out my Talking Heads and k.d. lang albums, even getting a chance to interview the torch-and-twang singer before her breakout performance at the 1988 Calgary Olympics. I could sing along to all of it. But I wasn't a singer. I loved music, but had never had musicians as friends.

That changed in Yellowknife after we hired Marie as our nanny—an amazing young Québecoise and the sole applicant for the job—so I could work full-time as a policy analyst with the government. The arrangement lasted only eight months before she moved to town to live with her future husband, but both of them had played a lot of guitar and mandolin and loved to sing. They were highly social and our house filled with instruments and musicians and late-night jams around the fire.

"I'd like to buy a good used guitar," I tell Lee, the young salesman with stringy black hair at *Steve's Music*. "I don't know how to play, so maybe you could just play some and I'll listen."

In short order, Lee convinces me I can buy a reasonable new guitar for roughly the same price as a used one. He suggests something by Québec guitar-maker Art and Luthier. I settle on a blonde acoustic for $236.

"I think you got a good one," Lee says, as he winds on new strings and tunes it up for me.

"What, aren't they all good?" I ask naively, unaware that guitars, like pottery, are handcrafted with varying degrees of excellence and results.

"Well, yah, I guess," he stumbles, "but this one is particularly good."

And it is. I walk out of *Steve's Music* that warm spring day, holding onto my guitar case with a sense that I now look like a musician, maybe even a singer. It stamps me as someone else.

~

The Rock and Roll Hall of Fame in Cleveland is closed when Criss and I arrive. We stand on the sidewalk outside the towering glass pyramid, Lake Erie lapping its shores in the background, as we ponder our next move.

Tundra swans cross Pennsylvania during spring migration, stopping on Lake Erie.

We'd left Toronto that morning, destination unknown, in a car borrowed from Criss' ex-husband. "Why don't you go to the Rock and Roll Hall of Fame?" he suggested.

"Where's that?" I asked.

"Cleveland."

"Cleveland?" both Criss and I chimed.

"It's only about an eight-hour drive."

We'd headed south towards upstate New York with a vague notion of

Ohio in the back of our minds, but no real commitment to it. Torrential rains forced us off the interstate and into a small town where we sought refuge in a diner heavily laden with artefacts from the forties and fifties. Chrome was a main feature, with swivel seats at an old-fashioned soda bar. Black and white prints from the filming of the *Wizard of Oz*, including one of a startled Judy Garland beside the quivering lion, adorned the walls. We ordered American apple pie and coffee and weren't disappointed. While glimpsing the back of the laminated menu, I noticed a small square map with a bold black arrow pointing simply to the word Cleveland.

"If we stay on this side street does it really go all the way to Cleveland?" I asked the waitress.

"Yep, stay on it for about four hours or so and you're there."

And so it was decided, we'd visit the Rock and Roll Hall of Fame. I was toting my brand new guitar, purchased the day before in Montreal. It seemed a fitting sojourn for a baptismal.

There's disappointment at the locked doors when we arrive. The tour will have to wait until the next morning. We ask a passer-by what there is to see and do at night in Cleveland. He tells us about the Warehouse District, a string of bars with the possibility of some live music. We check into a hotel with a friendly doorman who asks where we're from. We tell him and add we're here to celebrate my birthday. He guesses my age to be twenty-seven, not forty, setting the stage for my first foray as a newly minted middle-aged woman into the youthful, sexually-charged singles scene of a Friday night, in a strange city, far, far from home.

∼

The place is crowded, but not so packed we can't float over to the standing bar, where I happen to land beside an extremely tall, attractive young man so reedy thin he resembles a bean pod, one continuous width from head to toe, save for the longest and thinnest of necks.

The elaborate courting ritual of the swan often begins with a circling in the water, sometimes synchronous, sometimes not. Without touching. Either the male, or the female, may approach with its neck stretched out low over the water.

My penchant for micro-brewed ale prompts me to inquire about the taste of his. "It's good," he says. Then, in a gesture that surprises me, he tips the green bottle my way. "Do you want a sip?"

The swans begin dipping their heads repeatedly into the water as if taking sips, dunking below, blowing bubbles, as they slowly and gently circle each other. This flirtation stimulates their hormones and builds their response to each other.

It tastes fresh and bubbly. I order the same. A lengthy conversation ensues, revealing a funny and intelligent twenty-seven-year-old American with a surprising grasp of Canadian culture and geography. As the bar fills with noise and the crush of more patrons, we inch towards one another, bobbing our craned necks back and forth as we take turns placing an ear closer to the other's mouth. I'm unsure what he's feeling, but I'm swirling in an eddy of latent desires. If you're caught in an eddy and fight to get out, you may struggle to the point of exhaustion and drown. The best strategy is to patiently wait inside the vortex until it makes the next move, eventually hurling you out of its stronghold and into the river's flow.

The swans circle and dip for a very long time, moving closer to one another, occasionally their necks touch, or even gently intertwine. Sometimes, gracefully, they touch bill to bill until a perfect heart shape is formed.

∼

The morning sun blazes through the Hall of Fame's glass ceiling like a laser beam into my skull, fanning the flames of the most incendiary headache of my life. I rummage through my purse for sunglasses as the escalator silently conveys me and Criss up into Rock Heaven for a glimpse of John Lennon's bloodstained glasses (the sight of which make her weep) and Janis Joplin's 1965 psychedelic Porsche. The fact I'm hung over, wearing dark glasses in the milieu of some of the world's most excessive drug and alcohol abusers hasn't escaped me. But my child-free evening of indulgence differs from the indulgences of many rock stars' in one important way.

I'd remained faithful to my husband.

Still, something in my psyche has shifted. Long before the term Cougar joined the English vernacular, I knew I had no interest in becoming one. I recognized mine as a charmed life, not one to be risked for a purloined night of abandon. It isn't the prospect of having sex—in Cleveland no less—with a funny, intelligent beanpole (who I sensed didn't have a clue I was forty, and had he suspected, would likely have bolted) preoccupying my thoughts days later as I prepare to fly home to Yellowknife. Something else about the encounter has taken root.

"Is there a store nearby where I could buy stationery?" I ask with some urgency of the airline woman tagging my bags.

"Yes, just over there." she points. "But you better hurry, you're already late."

I'm suddenly overcome with the need to write down words that are knocking in my head. They come with a heaviness, as if their very arrival inside of me weighted me down, and I'm certain they're trying to explain the strange ways in which I'm now "different."

Not a notebook or diary is to be found, so I buy a package of office envelopes and, after I'm seated on the plane, begin scribbling down prose that has no punctuation or proper sentence structure. When I cover the front and back of one envelope, I put it down, stare out the window for a moment, then pick up a second envelope and began anew. What I'm creating looks like poems, but they aren't—they're songs. They have no accompanying melody, and I've never written a song, but I *know* that's what they are. Songs about what it is I hunger for in my life. Songs about *falling* in love.

I love, and am loved by my husband, children, extended family, many dear friends and even colleagues. Love abounds in my life. No shortage whatsoever. But I realize being in a committed marriage means, for the rest of your life, you'll never be able to experience the thrilling, dopamine-soaked emotional high of *new* love—that tumbling cascade of positive energy that lights through every pore of your being: the staggering euphoria, the quivering, exquisite curiosity and anticipation.

As a serial monogamist before marriage, I'm no stranger to new love, or the crash-and-burn devastation of a break-up that, intrinsically, has to precipitate it. Or so I thought.

~

If I was a movie director shooting this next scene in my real-life drama, I'd ponder whether the extreme winds are too trite, too cliché a mechanism to introduce the manner in which Marco blows into my life, but this is how it happens. A friend asks if he can come skating on our lake. It's November, and the water has frozen into a flawless, five-kilometre-long tableau of smooth, slate-grey ice. I'm home writing and he promises not to disturb. A quiet knock on the door announces his arrival.

"I hope you don't mind, I brought a friend," he says. "This is Marco."

I flip-flop a few times over whether to join them—it's wickedly cold and blustery—but eventually lace up my used CCM men's hockey skates and brave the elements. It's rare to have ice conditions this perfect.

Both much stronger skaters than I, their long, hockey strides out-muscle the powerful headwind, and soon they're small dots on my horizon. I lean in and will my legs to catch up with such effort that I began to sweat, despite the cold. Marco, noting my struggles, circles back to encourage me, and we manage about half the length of the lake together before deciding to turn back.

When I swivel to face my house, the winds pick me up with such force I shoot forward, as if from a slingshot. Without any skating movements, my blades propel me at speeds I'd never before experienced. I don't know how to stop. All those figure skating lessons as a kid, and I never learned. My options are a force-fall onto my behind, or to go for it. Marco is clearly relishing every moment, whooping and yipping, pushing off his edges to go faster. I lift my arms out to the side like wings and ride the wind home. It's the closest I've ever come to flying.

We're all still flushed from the exhilaration of the experience, swapping stories inside, when Marco notices my guitar.

"May I?" he inquires as he picks it up.

"By all means," I reply.

My instrument has never been played like that before. His fingers move skillfully up and down every inch of its neck, bending, pulling, muting the strings. Rock riffs, Spanish flamenco, he even makes up a folksy ditty about our skate that has me in tears laughing. When they leave, I strum the guitar and notice its warmer, more relaxed sound. It seems happier, as if Marco has released its potential after weeks of pent-up under-performance.

In his book *This is Your Brain on Music, the Science of a Human Obsession*, Daniel J. Levitin describes three phases to the sound you make on a guitar, or any instrument. The initial contact is called the "attack," a mixture of confused, noisy frequencies; followed by going "steady," when the sounds start to resonate off the instrument and make sense; and finally, there's "flux," where the tones change all on their own. The bigger and more unstable the vibrations, the longer the sound, or flux, lingers. After Marco leaves, my house has a quality buzz to it that I swear I can hear. Indeed, I sit in that state of flux, let it wrap itself around me. And I want more.

~

Six months before I bought my guitar, I took Reiki training. It was just after I learned I didn't have breast cancer, and I think, like many people awakened to their own mortality, I was seeking spiritual enrichment. I spent a weekend in an intense ceremony with a group of women and one man. They seemed oblivious to the scores of Reiki sceptics, those who, backed by studies, claim you cannot influence a person's physical, mental, emotional or spiritual state by invoking positive energy from the universe to flow through your hands and into another person. Before I'd met my medical doctor and my Reiki master, or my neighbours, Jeanette and France; before Ruth told me she could blow out streetlights; before my ailing mother saw an aged, bearded spirit in white robes sitting beside her, I certainly would've scoffed at the prospect too, but there I was, open to the idea.

Perhaps I was especially open because just prior, a psychic had come to Yellowknife to read people's auras. Not in the traditional, clairvoyant way my son Levi sees actual auric colours swirling around a person, Vikki (she did not give her last name) had a biofeedback machine with a name like a mini-van, the Aurastar 2000, hooked up to her computer. I told her nothing about myself and followed her instruction to place my left hand on a plate of sensors and think about something pleasant for a minute or two. As thoughts of a recent canoe trip with Francois danced in my head, Vikki watched her screen, her eyes widening in apparent delight. When I started to think that my minute should be up, I felt a little brain panic and slipped momentarily into thoughts of waiting for my biopsy results and Vikki's face grew grim.

She printed out my reading, splashes of colours atop Leonardo da Vinci's iconic Vitruvian Man. Greens and yellows rimmed the outer circle, purple and violet around my head, two crescents of white cupped the top of my breasts. The colour readings are to provide information on the present energy status of the seven major chakras and forty-four organs and glands of the body. By and large, my body dynamic showed a lot of high energies—white, blue, violet—indicating I'm a spiritual and creative person with an active mind. The bright greens indicated general balance and harmony, with a couple of glaring exceptions.

"Get thee to a chiropractor!" Vikki commanded, noting the grey colour emanating from parts of my spine. Since my pregnancy with the twins, when my waistline doubled to sixty-two inches, I've had lower back problems.

"And your throat is blocked. You're not expressing yourself. Wear blue scarves and pendants," she instructed. I looked and sure enough, touching the two wings of white on my breastplate, my throat was the colour of dishwater, ringed on either side by pale brown.

Baby swans, known as cygnets have two colour morphs. For the first few months of their lives, most are grey-brown, but some may be white.

I can't tell you what happened during the final stage of my Reiki training a few months later, because I had my eyes closed. I don't know what the two female Reiki masters (one a Dene woman, the other Mexican) did to me in that private room during my "attunement." I don't recall them touching me, although I felt a slight pressure on my left shoulder. I sat in a chair, eyes closed, and began to feel increasingly nauseous. I can count on one hand the number of times I've let anything travel the wrong way up my throat, so nausea is extremely uncomfortable for me, but I was so determined to stay in the darkness of my mind, I kept my eyes shut until I was on the brink of throwing up. Just as I was about to open up and seek a wastebasket, a small gong went off. The long, ringing vibration stemmed the rising tide of my stomach and my body relaxed, the sweat on my brow cooled, my breath returned to normal.

"We're done now, Laurie, you can return to the others," said the gentle voice of the Mexican woman. I opened my eyes.

The Reiki masters later told me I had two spirit guides pressing against my left shoulder the whole time (in my astonishment, I neglected to ask what, or who?). Also, my throat chakra was completely blocked, so they had to work extra hard to open it so energy could flow freely. They *cleared* my throat.

When I relayed my feelings of nausea, they said they were aware of my discomfort. This was a normal reaction to their stirring of energies that'd been trapped or stagnant in parts of my body over long times. Sort of like stirring up the orange juice pitcher, so the stuff on the bottom mixes in and can pour out. This made sense to me.

Sore throats plagued my adolescent years as surely as pimples and chronic self-doubt. Seems I was always nursing one and was forced to whisper my thoughts and wishes. Not that I would've shouted my demands from the rooftop had my throat been healthy. I wasn't raised in a liberal household where free expression was encouraged. Rather, my younger brother and I were largely mute during the tumultuous final years of our parents' disintegrating marriage—silent observers in a patriarchal world where children were seen and not heard. I spent hours in the basement drowning out the yelling by practicing scales on the piano. I had a pad of foolscap inside the piano bench, which I used to write out wildly imaginative stories about aliens and mutated animals. My diary, under lock and key, was the gateway between my inner and outer world, a repository for desperate thoughts, a place where I could ease the burden of secrets accumulating inside our middle-class home. Though my pen flowed with words, I was unable to move them through my throat.

The Mute Swan is one of the heaviest flying birds. The males are known as cobs, the females are pens.

I believe my long neck suffered so many sore throats because I was unable to express the truth about my family's situation or how it was affecting me—divorce was still largely taboo and stigmatizing in the seventies. Between the ages of seven and twelve is a time of self-expression when the fifth, or throat chakra, flowers: the realm of vibrations, sound, communication and creativity. For me, a time when I was assaulted with negative sound, while simultaneously stifled from expressing sounds that would've released the highly charged emotional energy welling inside. A metaphysical bottle "neck."

Chakras are part of our mind-body interface. Technically, they're "spinning spheres of bioenergetic activity emanating from the major nerve ganglia branching forward from the spinal column," according to

Eastern Body, Western Mind. I'd discovered this book by Anodea Judith shortly after my time with Ruth on Cortes Island. Chakras can be blocked by childhood traumas, which force us to develop coping strategies that can become chronic patterns, anchored in the body and psyche as defense structures. According to Judith, eventually these defenses create holding patterns in our musculature that restrict the free flow of energy (even when real threats cease to exist), a chronic tension known as body armour. This psychological armour affects our posture, breathing, metabolism, and emotional states, as well as our perceptions, interpretations, belief systems—even the shape of our body.

The first time I picked up this book, I opened to a page illustrating six different body types, or armours, based on character structures. I recognized myself immediately. Thin with long torso, narrow hips and broad shoulders: the Challenger-Defender. A lot of strong-willed energy from the gut—the third chakra—moving upwards in the body, especially to the neck and shoulders. We defend the underdog, the meek, with whom we unconsciously relate, and challenge the strong. Indeed, that had been my litigiously tinged adult life.

I was never sexually abused as a child, yet understand from reading this book why I relate so much to those who have been. The confusion and the helplessness they must feel, the shame, the burden of having to keep their abuse secret, sometimes under threat of harm or even death. How that debilitating childhood silence, left unchecked, can lead to teen and adult self-medicating addictions, even suicide. Speaking out against abuse of any kind has the power to prevent it, to spare children, the underdogs, trauma that can gnaw at them like a hungry ghost, draining their life force.

≈

That winter following my Reiki experience, my chronic sore throats disappear. My quiet, often froggy voice becomes louder and clearer. I overcome my fear of microphones and conduct my first on-air interview at the CBC, with David Suzuki. And I start to sing.

Though they are called Mute Swans, they are not mute. They are capable of hissing, and occasionally snorting or bleating. Their calls are quiet and do not carry very far, but their flapping wings make a throbbing, singing sound when in flight.

My guitar becomes like an extra appendage. It's sensitive to my feel-ings, absorbing them like a lover or best friend, rinsing them of their sting. There's comfort in holding the wood, in the sound of my own voice resonating with its strings, and comfort is at a premium. The preliminary court proceedings have started in the fifty-five thousand dollar defama-tion suit against me, and simultaneously, my mother is mysteriously los-ing her balance, along with key parts of her personality.

In the quiet of my living room late one night, instrument in hand, I'm moved to retrieve the lyrics I'd written on the envelope in the plane. With no real idea of how to compose a song, I begin, randomly, choosing guitar chords and rhythms, applying the words in fits and starts, until, hours later, they fit together like some primitive rock opera. Loaded with cho-ruses of ahhhhhs, it tells the story of those intimate first moments when you meet someone you sense you could fall in love with, and invite them to influence you. I love that Francois listens quietly from our bed, then proclaims it "really good."

Later, I put my second set of lyrics to a simple 12-bar blues progres-sion I learn from a book. It's a rollicking, bawdy tune about that trip to Cleveland. Another song of desire.

The third song I write, also late at night, alternates between soft and explosive tones, a yin-yang mirroring of my ongoing search to find the softer side of myself. The Challenger-Defender who refuses to bow to the patriarchy is wearing down. At the conclusion of that song-writing effort I phone Marco and sing it to him. I know if he's home, he'll be awake.

Black Swans often travel at night.

Marco and I are getting together a lot to play guitar. I feel comfort-able making mistakes around him. He's patient and encouraging, but his easy-going musicality doesn't transfer well into the real world, where employers expect him to show up on time and landlords need to be paid. He's unreliable, but people seem drawn to his offbeat humour, the way it could give them the one thing they truly ache for in life: to laugh at themselves.

His electric guitar accompaniments elevate my original songs to a level that gives me the courage to say "yes" when a friend invites us to perform at the annual fall International Music Day concert. In agreeing to do so, I purposefully invite terror into my life. I'm not a performer, or a public speaker. The last time I'd used my voice in front of a crowd of people with eyes trained on me was during my testimony at the judicial inquiry. We have less than a month to prepare.

Marco more or less flies the coup. As the concert draws near, it becomes harder and harder to locate him, let alone practice. I'm in a sweaty panic, walking around the house singing with my guitar strapped to my shoulder the night before the show, when he shows up at ten o'clock.

"Where have you been? Why didn't you answer my calls?" I demand.

With infuriating irony, I discover he hasn't arrived to practice. He was en route to a friend's place further down the road when his car broke down, right outside my house.

The black swan molts its wings after mating season, and for a period in the fall, becomes flightless.

I'm so singularly focused on not choking at the concert that I decide my indignation will have to wait. I grab Max's beginner electric guitar and amp and order Marco to the guest cabin, where we play my two songs over and over until my fingers practically bleed. With each round, our sound fuses more tightly together. Muscle memory takes charge of our hands. There's no end to my desire to stay in that room, but eventually I leave him there and return to my bed, and Francois, unable to defuse the exhilaration that keeps sleep at bay.

~

Had we not been so prepared, the performance would not have gone as well as it does. I was still nervous enough that I seemed to separate from myself while singing, but people applauded with an enthusiasm a few decibels above courtesy when it ended, and Marco is coming back to sleep in our cabin. A litany of personal problems has left him temporarily homeless, hence the troubles I had getting in touch with him.

Black Swans were once thought to be sedentary, but the species is now known to be highly nomadic. There is no set migratory pattern, but rather opportunistic responses to either rainfall or drought.

For five nights we carry on in that cabin as if we have no other cares in the world, recording and playing back new songs, trying out lyrics and riffs, laughing. All the worries and responsibilities of my high-octane life slide off my back and dissipate in a giant puddle of music. It's like being in an intensive rock camp. Sometimes Francois checks in to see if we need anything.

There's such intrigue and levity in our time together. One morning I am surprised to see the cabin door wide open, Marco fast asleep and a plastic Elvis Presley doll face down at the entrance. The doll, one of many Elvis memorabilia items given to us after Francois jokingly declared our property Graceland North, has been sitting high on a shelf in the corner. It could've fallen down, but why is it so far from its perch, as if it had crawled towards the door? And why is the door open?

"I guess Elvis is trying to leave the building," surmises Marco.

Another night while jamming out a rocking blues song, my eyes closed to better feel the good vibrations, Marco's electric guitar makes a horrible screeching sound. When we stop, literally breathless from the duration and intensity of our playing, I ask him if he'd stumbled, lost his place. No, he says. The small effects box sitting near his feet, connected by a long cord to his guitar and amp, switched itself several settings higher and slid five feet across the floor.

"Are you sure you didn't kick it?" I ask.

"Absolutely sure." He says he saw the whole thing happen.

I begin to crave our collaboration time, like an addict. My energy levels are way up. Food doesn't interest me much, and when my clothes start to hang off me, I realize I've dropped down to a weight I haven't seen since high school. Despite all the turmoil in my life, I'm optimistic and enthusiastic.

I'm falling in love.

I haven't fallen out of love with my husband, but this schoolgirl-like crush is moving perilously close to obsession. Unable to tell anyone what I'm feeling, I'm trapped in a type of love purgatory from which I can see no escape. As Buddhists and Freud have long pointed out, desire is the cause of all suffering.

When my emotions fill me to the point of bursting, like a balloon unable to absorb one more breath, I release some of the pressure by writing a song about them. But then I play it repeatedly with Marco and all those feelings amplify, his vintage Fender Telecaster riding on top of my rhythm, responding with fat, bluesy licks and occasional country whines.

With extreme apprehension, after we finish playing the song, I hint I'm experiencing some powerful feelings... towards him.

"Awwww. It's not me, Laurie. It's you!" he replies, smiling broadly, genuinely touched. "You're discovering your spirit through your music, your guitar. I just happen to be with you when you're playing, so you *think* those feelings are for me, but really, they're for yourself. You're loving yourself."

Wow, what a great answer. If this had been Hollywood, the clichéd movie response would have been long, hungry stares into each other's eyes, he would try to kiss me, our lips would brush, then I'd pull away: "I... I can't... I have to go!" I'd grab my coat and flee, leaving him in a frozen moment of anguish and desire. Cut to a close-up on his face.

Instead, he's respected everyone involved: my family, me, himself. He's given no clue as to what his feelings are towards me, and he's opened the door for deeper discussion on the endlessly mysterious subject of spirit, so we carry on in that vein. I tell him playing piano hasn't had the same effect on me. I was force-fed a classical music repertoire that didn't inspire the way the blues do, and the upright piano in my house now is largely neglected.

"Although there's this one song I learned on piano, 'The Swan,' have you heard it?" I ask him. Written in 1886 as the thirteenth movement of Camille Saint-Saëns concerto *The Carnival of the Animals*, for me, this piece evokes vulnerability, strength, sorrow and compassion. My sheet music for "The Swan" went missing several years earlier. When I bought my guitar, the song popped back into mind, and I tracked down the score for it when I was in Pennsylvania with Criss.

"I'll play it for you tomorrow," I promise him.

The next morning, I tune into classical music on the radio while driving to work. I'm already anticipating the massage I booked for later that day—part of my ongoing attempt to ease my lower back pain—when the meditative sounds of a master pianist fill me again with desire. Wouldn't it be nice, I think, to have piano music this relaxing play during my massage? When I'm lying on the massage table, the therapist asks what type of music I'd like to hear.

"Something soothing," I say.

"The Swan," performed by two pianos, is the first song to fill the room.

~

It's Francois' idea to ask Marco to stay a few nights at the house to watch the boys while we both travel for work. I'm doing a CBC television documentary for *The National* about the spiritual importance of the drum, the heartbeat, to the Dene. I need to follow a drummer on his first foray outside his small community to Toronto, where he'll accept an Aboriginal Music Award. Marco is our last hope if I want to go, and I *really* want to go.

Through some perfectly innocent labyrinthine arrangement, the boys are farmed out, Francois is already gone, and I've picked up Marco and brought him to the house the night before I leave. We're alone. Far from dispelling my feelings of desire, Marco's impeccable "it's you loving yourself" comment has fueled them. I'm well aware of my foolishness... but here's a man in touch with his emotions, and mine, and he plays guitar! I still have no idea what he thinks of me—we'd never touched, not even accidentally.

The secret world of desire is chipping away at my sanity one fantasy at a time, while the foundations of my sacred world of family and matrimony just keep getting wider and stronger—like a giant safety net that catches me if I fall, or raises me when I need picking up. Francois encourages my music at every turn. We bought the children drums, a bass and saxophone, and have morphed into a northern version of the Partridge Family of my childhood. Joy incarnate—apart from my deception. I can't go on like this.

So, hours before my flight, Marco and I are sitting on either end of the leather couch in my living room, tidy Scotches in hand, when I tell him there's something I need to say.

"Yes," he says.

"It's just that... "

"What? Go on."

"It's that, well... "

"Yes, what?"

"I, oh, this is really hard. I... "

"Whatever it is Laurie, just say it."

Then, a bit like that Reiki moment when all my bottled up emotional sediment churned and spilled out, bringing me to the brink of hurling, I have a mini blackout as I speak my truth.

"I love you."

As everyone knows, these are never words spoken lightly the first time to a potential lover. These are game-changing words that either light the way to a brighter future, or land you with a 'thud' in a reeking pile of rejection. I'm seeking neither. Truthfully, I just want release from the burden of having to cloak this shiny little part of me in darkness. I decide that telling both Marco and Francois what I'm feeling is my only hope of salvation.

Marco wastes no time pondering the implications of my confession.

"I know," he says. "So what are you going to do about it?"

Another perfect response!

"I have a plan," I say. "And I'm working on it."

"That's good."

Then, without further exploration of the subject, we turn our attention in music-geek style to my new Nora Jones CD, her sweet and salty voice singing "don't know why I didn't call."

Before he goes to sleep on the couch downstairs, I give him a stilted hug, awkward and spacious, the kind you'd give a boss. He smells like ocean.

~

My trip to Toronto is saturated with live music. In the back room of the legendary El Mocambo (a blackened bar that famously hosted a surprise Rolling Stones concert in the seventies and where I once sat in awe of U2), I hold a deep conversation with a northern rocker. I'd interviewed her after she won an Aboriginal Music Award earlier in the day, and she'd invited me down to this *Women Who Rock* showcase. She's catching her breath after a gritty, sensual performance when I comment on the obvious chemistry she has with her lead guitar player. She tells me this is a shared house band pulled together for tonight. She's just met him.

Sensing I may never have an opportunity like this again—a private conversation with a female musician who seems fused at her seams by the sexual underpinnings of rock—I confide my situation. Before dispensing any advice, she grabs my left hand and slides her thumb across my fingertips, a kind of guitar-player authenticity scan. My shiny, hardened callouses satisfy her that I do spend a lot of time pressing steel strings into place, and she opens up.

"I fall in love a little bit with every guy I play guitar with," she tells me. "You can't help it. It just happens."

I read in the paper once that modern science has proven when two guitarists get into a groove, their brain waves do too, literally synchronizing. Listening to music cues the brain for rewards and arousal, so *making* music is especially potent emotional communication. Even Darwin concluded men and women first acquired musical notes and rhythm to better their chances of getting lucky. "Thus musical tones became firmly associated with some of the strongest passions an animal is capable of feeling... " he wrote. I can attest. The question remains, what am I going to do about it?

~

The time has come to tell Francois. The next night I will be on stage by myself at an intimate club, performing all of my original songs—including one he'd never heard, about my conflicted feelings of desire—as part of a singer-songwriter festival. Right after the performance we'll leave for a nine-week trek through southern Africa with the children, a mammoth undertaking of preparations, but I worry about little else except this show.

It'll be quiet. People will listen to the words. My spirit will be naked, exposed. There'll be nowhere to hide.

"Francois, about my show," I begin, sitting on the side of the bed while he lay reading the *Globe and Mail*.

"Yes?"

"I'm going to sing a song you haven't heard."

"Okay."

"It's about something that's been on my mind and I just feel like I have to be totally honest with you about."

"Sure, what is it?"

And then, with surprising ease, the words spill out. I tell him in detail and at length about my attraction to Marco and its apparent connection to my guitar. In the weeks building up to this moment I'd tried not to anticipate his reaction. The thought of our relationship ending was something I couldn't bear. Now, in the silence that punctuates the end of my confession, I teeter on a precipice.

He looks at me, and with complete honesty says: "That's fantastic!"

Among the spectrum of possible responses, I hadn't considered this one.

"Fantastic?" I inquire, stunned. "Why do you say that?"

"Well, it's totally natural to be attracted to other people from time to time. It's healthy, it means you're alive," he says.

"You're not mad or jealous?"

"Of course not. How can I be? I can't control how you feel, or what you do."

I could've kissed him, and do.

"There's more," I go on. "When you were away and he was staying here to look after the kids, I told him... that I loved him."

"And... " says Francois, "what did he say?"

"He said... 'I know.'"

Francois starts to shake, then laughter wells up from his belly to his chest. By the time it escapes his mouth, I'm powerless against its contagion. All those months of brooding, waiting for the birth of a solution—anything—that would release me from the choking stranglehold this one secret had on my life, and this is how it ends? His and hers convulsive fits of laughter, me surfacing with great gulps of relief and gratitude after nearly drowning in a marital soup of confusion. Finally, I can breathe.

The female swan struggles under the weight of her chosen mate. For a brief moment they are one, but this requires that she submerge into the watery depths beneath him, his heaviness pressing even her long neck underwater, restricting her movements, her air. She does this willingly, knowing it will lead to new life. He understands the pressures this has come to bear upon her, and dips his head underwater, scooping his neck under hers and lifting it with tenderness above the surface. As she re-emerges to breathe, she calls out loudly and strongly.

A couple dozen people hear me sing the next night. It seems fitting that Marco can't make the show. In between songs, I talk a lot about Francois, how grateful I am for my family's support in discovering this side of myself, this softer side. And I sing the song about desire. I understand now Marco was right. The very act of creating, of songwriting, is food and water for my soul, the self-actualization of the person I truly desire: me. What I'd been craving my entire life was a place to express myself without fear of being put down, abandoned, dragged to court or skewered by the media.

After the performance, a middle-aged man walks over to me. He's from out of town, and he'd happened upon the show with some colleagues. I noticed them at their table. Quiet and respectful.

He thanks me, saying they'd enjoyed my music very much. "It's obvious you really love your husband," he says. "He must be very self-assured to have his wife up on stage and sing a song like that. It was nice."

Apart from validating that people really do listen to the words, this total stranger's ability to grasp my situation and express his gratitude for my openness is profoundly encouraging. I feel I've reached a state of grace, like the fabled ugly duckling that wanders in exile, clumsy and tormented, until he discovers he belongs with swans.

Swans have beguiled me since age five, when I rode inside the wings of one at an amusement park on Toronto's Centre Island—an electric-powered swan boat many times greater than my tiny frame, that inched without a shred of menace through a quiet lagoon. Perhaps I'd had a taste then of what it would be like to be Saraswati, the Hindu goddess of knowledge, music and creative arts, who rides the Royal Swan. The white bird, symbolic of purity and discrimination, can discern right from wrong. With swan as her carrier, the four-armed Saraswati represents the purity of the arts and their power to purify human thought. With her front hands, she plays the music of love and life on a veena, an ancient lute-like precursor to the guitar. Her message is that knowledge must be acquired and applied without ego, in perfect harmony with the world, for the welfare of all.

The swan boat of my childhood wasn't attached to an underwater line, dragging me mindlessly in circles. I could steer my swan in any direction I wanted, guided only by my gentle mother seated next to me.

I remember my disappointment a year later when my mother's job prevented her from accompanying my Grade one field trip to Kortright Waterfowl Park near Guelph, where I naively rushed up to a towering male swan with an outstretched arm and breadcrumbs in hand. He stretched his neck long and taut, as if to maximize the momentum and force of his strike—before jabbing his beak into my open palm. My measly offerings scattered to the ground, but instead of pursuing them, the swan stabbed me repeatedly in the stomach, then the legs; he pecked my head and back as I turned to flee, pulling at my hair with his angry black beak, wanting something from me that I clearly could not give. I ran, too ashamed and humiliated by the assault to cry out for help. I waited, silently, alone in the woods, until it was safe to come out.

Knowing when to stay silent, when to squawk, when to trumpet and when to sing is my lifelong journey.

12

WOLF
teach me

My eyes pop open into the black of a November night. I wait, knowing it will come, and within seconds it does—the low, mournful bawl of the wolf. Not since the children were babies and I lay in bed discerning their needs by the timbre of their cries have I opened my eyes at this time. Yet this has been my pattern for five nights. It's not the wolf's cry that awakens me, but something unspoken that precedes it: a subtle, internal quaking that shudders me into consciousness. A wakeup call from the cosmos.

I listen until the last waves of her sad song roll by, then notice how alive I feel in their wake. Adrenalin keeps sleep at bay, so I do what any woman would do—I think. I think about Calvin and Levi, thousands of kilometres away at university, living away from me for the first time. I think about our eldest, Max, now an intrepid young man wandering solo through Scotland and Iceland. I think about Francois, who has kept company with a succession of wolves since they began visiting six months ago, forging makeshift packs with them and our dogs during hikes or snowmobile journeys by day. Sleeping soundly beside me—oblivious to their siren calls—by night.

A wolf isolated from its companions can howl a particularly plaintive, lonesome-sounding complaint.

The wolves first appeared in May 2013, on my fifty-first birthday. Just before midnight, a haunting chorus of howls announced the arrival of three timber wolves along the melting shoreline. They faced the front of the house, standing just beyond the nascent, watery border that separated bald bedrock—rock solid since the earliest days of the planet—and the fickle, unstable spring ice shifting and dissolving, molecule by molecule. In twenty-two years, I'd seen these cautious animals only twice before. Because they're elusive, and because I'm hard-wired to seek meaning in such encounters, I took detailed note of what was happening to me during their advent. Elation. Exhilaration. The wolves are an auspicious gift, was what I was *feeling*. But close on the heels of that unfiltered gut reaction came its counterpoint—the thought that, maybe, they could be a portent.

In Druid tradition, the wolf, known as faol in Gaelic, brings a strong sense of faithfulness, intuition and learning through experience, especially about our shadow selves.

I was talking to Max about Ernest, a friendly man who was wheelchair-bound by a stroke. I'd seen him earlier that day at the hospital when I'd gone for physiotherapy for my mysteriously ailing knee. Then, Max, the twins and I had played music for him that evening as part of my volunteer efforts at the seniors' home. He'd yanked my arm forcefully to pull me close. "I can almost stand, Laurie!" he'd said, his eyes tearing. I was telling Max how I'd met Ernest's brother in an Arctic coastal community while travelling with a government commission that winter. Our mission was to hear from people across the Northwest Territories about what they'd like in addiction and mental health services. Both Ernest and his brother had attended a residential school, where the priest inside its government-funded, church-run walls sexually abused them. In a voice ragged from a lifetime of struggle, the brother told us he was getting the help he needed to live with post-traumatic stress and the demons of addiction. Every week he received an injection from the nurse—an injection of what, I didn't ask. I'd had my picture taken with him and had brought it to the nursing home in Yellowknife to show to Ernest. "I have not seen him in a long time," Ernest said, staring intently at the photo of me beside his smiling sibling, my long, skinny arm holding up a hand as I waved at the camera. "*Auggakpaluk*," he added in his language, Inuvialuqtun, as he pointed to my palm. "Big hands."

Wolves' slender front legs are "hung" close together into their narrow chests. Their knees turn in and their large, snowshoe-like front paws turn outward so that the front feet swing in and set a path which the hind feet follow exactly, an obvious advantage in deep snow, or when the going gets rough.

At that moment in the conversation, 11:45 p.m., Max interrupts and motions for me to listen. At first, we think the wailing is our dogs. Then, as the howls increase and crescendo into an unmistakeable wild call, Max declares, "Mom, that's not our dogs."

We peer out his bedroom window. Visible in the dusky light loitering late into the spring night, we detect three grey and white shapes well camouflaged against the crusty ice of the lake. Our white Husky-cross, Scott, has joined them as they cry their cryptic message. Our younger dog, Siku, accepts our invitation to come inside.

The twins, Max and I move around the house to better our vantage sight until the wolves wander off, leaving Scott behind. Francois, in a move completely out of character, says he's too tired to get out of bed to observe the animals, as if he somehow knows this isn't a one-off.

∾

While complacent is too strong a term to describe how I came to view wolf sightings during the ensuing year, it's fair to say they became our new normal, that living with wolves—sometimes literally outside our door, but more often playing with our dogs or following us on hikes or canoe trips—became routine. I didn't think they were trying to kill us or steal from us, although we had concerns they might want more from our dogs than play and companionship.

In 2002, our arthritic, thirteen-year-old Shepherd-cross, Abby, was taken by wolves. We never saw the pack or witnessed the attack, but we found the kill site—an oval bed of blood in the forest behind our house—and the tip of her tail, but no collar.

Wolves usually consume their kills to the bare bones, sometimes returning over a period of weeks to clean up the scraps.

Francois surmised Abby had been lured away by a lone wolf into the ambush of the pack. I couldn't blame the wolves for taking advantage of the situation. We've brought domestication into their wilds. I thought Abby's death nobler than what might have been her fate—a lethal injection on a stainless steel bed at the animal shelter (where I adopted her when she was eight). And, while the attack must have had initial terror for her, at least her ailing physical body didn't leave a post-cremation legacy of greenhouse gas; rather, it nourished the soil and would fuel her distant relatives in the environs where she was most comfortable.

Still, with the exception of Indigenous peoples and a few friends and neighbours, not a lot of people I know are simpatico with wolves. There are more than sixty thousand wolves in North America, mostly in Canada, and yet there have been only two known fatal attacks—an Alaskan woman in 2010 and a man in northern Saskatchewan in 2005. Their presence remains so threatening, they are often shot on sight.

Clayton Thomas, a 32-year-old father in Whitehorse, Yukon, shot and killed two wolves in 2012, after spotting wolf tracks near his doorstep, saying he was protecting his wife and two-month-old baby.

When the wolves first came to our house in May 2013, we were shooting at them, too, not real bullets, but the pyrotechnic flares known as bear bangers that are meant to frighten and disperse wildlife. Max feared for the dogs' lives, but equally for the wolves'. Given we live directly beside one of only two roads outside of Yellowknife, it was inevitable passers-by would spy the animals, and, given their bestial and dangerous reputation, want them dead.

Because of his predilection for wolves, Francois never did anything to dissuade them from hanging around, but Max and I each took a couple of turns shooting the loud, abrasive guns. I hated the noise, which would surely stress every living creature for miles around, and the message I was sending to the wolves (*I fear you, I don't trust you*), but I wanted to scare them away from this heavily peopled corridor. I wanted to prevent their death by real bullets.

One wolf, a white and grey female Francois named Sabrina, jackknifed away from my shot, her hind sidewinding so quickly it lifted her airborne before she took off down the lake, stopping once to look back at the house and howl.

But she came back. They all did. Eventually, we resigned ourselves that this must be the season of the wolf.

~

I saw my first wolf in 1991, the summer I became pregnant with Max just after we'd moved to the lake. A white form stood gazing over the water on the rocky ridge that rises from the shore. Its shaggy, moulting fur dangled like dreadlocks in the wind and its front left leg hung limp like a wet noodle. It was lame. Judging by its size, Francois said it was a male and called him Floppy Foot. We saw Floppy Foot frequently that summer and fall, delighted and amazed at his ability to carry on, to hunt—to survive. We never heard a howl, almost as though he didn't want to draw undue attention to his location, and vulnerability. Come winter, he vanished.

Four years later, another wolf made its presence known at the lake in mid-September; just days after Calvin and Levi were born. My mother was staying with us and I heard an unusual, loud moaning over the din of infant cries. A few feet from our front deck sat a large white and grey wolf, its neck stretched taut and eyes closed, in full howl.

Although wolves may howl alone and at any time, they do most of their singing in groups, often assembling for a greeting ceremony, an expression of group solidarity.

I remember urgently wanting all my family to connect with this sound, to have this call of the wild imprint directly on them. My mother was holding Calvin. I plopped Levi into the crook of her other arm, grabbed Max's hand and cradled the large balloon that was my still-stretched-but-emptied womb. We rushed outside. The wolf faced us head on and howled into the cool air once more, its breath swirling out to greet ours as we stood on the deck without coats or footwear, shivering slightly.

My mother had worked as an executive secretary in greater Toronto (a sexist title by today's standards, given she was often left in charge of the Canadian operation of the multinational company she worked for when her bosses travelled overseas). While she'd never been camping and had limited exposure to anything wild, she'd often let me push her out of her comfort zone—either too timid to protest or, more likely, genuinely excited to be thrust beyond her usual boundaries. She'd attended the birth of the twins even though she originally declined our invitation, saying that if there were complications she'd be too nervous. My doula was travelling the morning I awoke with the first crush of labour, and when I waddled up to my mother asking for her help, she didn't refuse. She gently mas-

Wolf: Teach Me

saged the small of my back throughout six hours of labour and her warm touch and gentle, encouraging voice kept me grounded. At the time of the wolf's howl, all six of us were still reeling from that birthing experience.

Wolves are highly sociable, generally living in groups of around six, mostly close relatives.

"We should go inside," my mother said quietly, when the wolf's decrescendo had faded into silence and the animal simply stood and stared at us. We continued to watch it through the living room window until it vanished into the woods.

Mom died thirteen years later. About a week after her death, I dreamt I was alone at her home, located at the base of a ski resort along Ontario's Blue Mountain escarpment. There were many dogs, all identical in appearance—mottled brown mongrels with pointy ears—swarming in such numbers they could barely turn around in their cramped spaces both inside the house and on the front yard. I stood in the living room among them staring out the window as they jostled for position. "Oh look," I said to no one in particular, pointing excitedly to a dog that looked different from the others—bigger, more majestic, with white and grey fur. "A wolf!"

Then an unfamiliar voice quietly responded, "Oh no dear, that's not a wolf, that's your mother."

∼

As much as I tell myself not to fear the wolves when they come to stay, they haunt me. We've passed three seasons together—spring, summer, and the brief yellow and orange flare of fall in the boreal forest. Winter is upon us and our lake is forming its icy, November skin, belching and booming from its depths like an angry sea monster as it expands, grinds and contracts. And still, the wolves remain.

Their mysterious night calls leave me restless and fatigued. Our house is under constant surveillance. When I open the garage to let the dogs out at daybreak, a wolf is usually waiting in the shadows to reconnect with them—or me.

One frozen morning, as I'm splitting wood, I hear whimpering noises nearby. *This is it*, I think, *a wolf has finally taken down a dog*. I run towards the noise, axe in hand, anticipating blood and gore. Instead, a tawny wolf sits in the ditch looking imploringly at me, no trace of malice on its young, eager face.

When a wolf whimpers, it always indicates a friendly, non-aggressive attitude. It could be inviting play.

These creatures confuse me. Do I shoot them with a camera, or with a flare? Are they going to eat our dogs, or mate with them? Already one hunter, convinced our dogs were under attack, had shot into a wolf pack as it chased the dogs down the highway. The pack veered into the bush, except for one, Sabrina, who had obvious affection for our dog, Scott. The hunter tells me she stood close by and watched him gather the dogs into his truck—a little startled, no doubt, to be suddenly alone.

∽

A few days afterward, I set out to skate the circumference of the lake by myself. I'm certain the ice is thick enough, but there's always apprehension when I leave the security of our bay—the depths of which I'm intimately familiar. Despite my urgings, the dogs decline the trek. Too slippery. I strap a brace to my weak, ailing knee and push off. With each stroke the ice responds with laser-like "pings," its surface vibrating like a taut drumhead. *The boys would love this*, I think. The best freeze-up in memory and none of my shinny-crazed sons are here to enjoy it with me.

Once sexually mature, most wolves leave their birth pack to search for a new territory or to join an existing pack.

Because the surface is perfect, smooth and clear enough to see plant life and the occasional whitefish rustle below my blades, I pick up speed, losing myself like a whirling dervish caught up in the freeing locomotion of my legs—until I turn attention back to myself and realize I've veered from the safety of the shoreline toward a large island in the centre, the last place ice forms. *I'm here all alone. What if something happens?* I say to myself, an unexpected sense of panic suddenly accompanying my speed.

A split second later, my skate strikes a fissure in the ice and I fly. I fly so far and so high that when my knees land on the ice, pain explodes through them like a bomb. Waves of nausea rise and fall in the aftershock. I lay heaving on the frigid surface, too scrambled to decipher how to move my limbs.

As tears well up, alongside a tremendous sense of self-pity, I hear whimpering. *Did the dogs follow me?* I lift my head towards the sound. There, among the spruce and birch of the shoreline, I see a grey and black torso winding in and out of the trees like a ribbon on a breeze. Sabrina ventures onto the ice, stops and whimpers again.

I'm prostrate and vulnerable. But, instead of fear, her appearance fills me with veneration—such raw, untamed beauty looking down on me. Shock turns to awe. A creature of the wild is, what?... concerned about me?

It is the highly developed wolf society, not human domestication, that gave dogs their social skills.

With slow, deliberate movements, I straighten up, my legs stiff and throbbing. Tentatively, I make my way home. Sabrina keeps pace, and her distance, mirroring my movements until I reach the house.

I was never alone.

∼

Solitude is challenging. As a young mother, and writer, I craved it, fearing there would never be space again for quiet introspection. How naïve, or at least impatient, I'd been, not to recognize that solitude would swamp me when the boys left home. All the energy I sank into my children propelled and fuelled them with confidence to move away, leaving me behind with a knee that mocks me with "clunks" and "pops" with every step of my aging body.

I'd hoped the solitude I would reclaim after they left would foster my writing and free up time and energy to explore a personal renaissance. Instead, I'm listless and staring down a dark well, a deep core of alone-ness into which I can toss a coin (with all its accompanying hopes and dreams) and never hear a reassuring splash.

It's scary to think about becoming infirm and alone, especially when you live independently in an extreme environment. If my knee prohib-its me from walking, how can I chop and fetch wood to heat the house? Apart from elemental necessities, how do I exercise to jar the cobwebs from my head and stimulate endorphins? As if to underscore this dilem-ma, Francois embarks on prolonged work duty travel overseas during January and February, the North's cruellest, blackest months, leaving me alone to fend for myself. I brace my knee and do the bare minimum of chores to keep the house, the dogs and myself alive during the longest stretch of minus-thirty Celsius (and colder) ever recorded here.

I can honestly say I feel close to madness. Not lunacy, not a sense of being "bushed," just an infuriatingly obstinate inability to feel whole. I wallow in my mud. I listen to every negative thought, every taunt of inferiority my shadow self can conjure against me. It's during such vulnerable times when what we perceive as an unsettled score from our past, normally simmering just below the closed-lid surface of consciousness, can rear its ugly head—my lawsuit, for instance. It had been ten years since the plaintiff's lawyer filed anything in court, so the case was awash in moral victories, but it had never received official closure (although after five years without significant action, civil courts view the case as null). I decide I need that legal rubber stamp for my own closure. Once I let the idea pick up steam, once I lift the lid on that sordid episode, what little energy I have—all those creative juices I'd hoped to unleash—leach out of me like dirty dishwater through a leaky drain. When my request to the school district to have its lawyers process the paperwork on my behalf is declined, I hire my own lawyer. I don't hear Sabrina's night calls again. I am, in many ways, dead to the world.

I yearn to hibernate like a bear until the light returns, but I need to keep warm and eat and work (I'm editing a local magazine while freelancing). I need to keep going, like Floppy Foot. Asking for help seems the obvious solution—and eventually I do—but for three months I act as if my spiral into melancholia is contagious and shouldn't be inflicted on others. The day I reach out in a joint email to my aunt Criss and my neighbour France, some of the weight begins to lift. Like Sabrina, I need companionship and protection of the pack. I need to be wolf-like.

In her pivotal bestseller, *Women Who Run With the Wolves, Myths and Stories of the Wild Woman Archetype*, Clarissa Pinkola Estés insists that being wolf-like—persevering under all circumstances—is innately part of our wild natures. No matter how sick, how cornered, how alone, afraid or weakened, the wolf will continue. She writes:

> She will lope even with a broken leg. She will go near others seeking protection of the pack. She will strenuously outwait, outwit, outrun and outlast whatever is bedevilling her. She will put her all into taking breath after breath. She will drag herself, if necessary... from place to

place till she finds a good place, a healing place, a place for thriving.

Somehow, that innate will to survive causes me to drag myself to the medicine woman's doorstep, a place of healing, to discuss what's bedevilling me. Twenty-three years previously, she'd told me I'd created the fear I was experiencing then around bears. "And you either live in love, or you live in fear," she'd said. I speak to her now of the lawsuit. She sees no merit in seeking redress from a pedantic justice system. She's onto bigger things, like universal love.

"Can you forgive this man who was suing you?" she asks. "True forgiveness from the heart is not only for the person who has hurt you, it's also equally important for you, to set yourself free. When you have lingering fear of someone you are really giving away your own power to that person and it keeps you *stuck* in different ways. Fear always diminishes us."

She goes on to say that perhaps the man suing me did so out of a place of great fear. Knowing how fear has hurt me, I might be able to see how fearful he may have been, and then have compassion. "Show peace, caring and forgiveness so you never have to feel so threatened. Doing this opens up a beautiful part of you, that is, the compassionate being."

I know from past experience she's right. True forgiveness, which can happen through a private, heartfelt declaration, feels great. It liberates the soul from debilitating negativity. It lightens the load by letting go of that proverbial baggage. It invigorates. Even if you're never again face-to-face with the one you once harboured resentment towards, I think the person will come to know, to *feel*, this forgiveness as an energetic lightness as well. Or perhaps as warmth that floods over them. That is compassion. Get enough people worldwide experiencing this, and, from the goodness of our hearts, we can uplift humanity.

I thank the medicine woman. With her as my witness, I forgive the man who was suing me and wish him well. I say goodbye to my lawyer and pay him. Then, like the wolf, I simply put one unsteady leg in front of the other, in search of a place for thriving.

~

Spirits Bay has caves along a mountain plateau overlooking a saltwater inlet that rises and falls with the South Pacific tides. The isolated tip of

New Zealand's North Island, at the end of the Aupouri Peninsula, is a sacred site for the Māori, the place where all Māori spirits are said to depart for the journey to their ancestral home. Exactly one year after my Dark Night of the Soul, we're on a trip to New Zealand as a result of my pledge to not spend another February at the lake, alone. Francois and I have chosen to camp here along the banks of the river leading into the Pacific Ocean, the mountain and its mysterious black holes looming over us.

We're wandering, without a plan, in a camper van, walking different beaches each day, hiking volcanoes, body surfing the crests of powerful waves. My knee is up for it. Through determination, exacting physiotherapy exercises, massage, supplements and an MRI that diagnosed a torn meniscus (refuting the knee surgeon's proclamation I have arthritis and must learn to live with it), it has healed.

There's gratitude now with every step. Not just for my ability to move forward, but to have been moving forward for the past twenty-five years in my marriage to Francois, who at the moment is quietly sulking because he's just learned he can't climb the mountain and explore the caves. (He'd waded through the inlet to read a small, unheralded sign stuck into its sandy bottom stating these were sacred Māori lands and no one was to climb the mountain without permission from the local *iwi*, or tribal village.)

While most travellers head to the lighthouse at nearby Cape Reinga, New Zealand's most northerly point, Francois and I typically choose the less-trodden path to Spirits Bay after reading about its cultural significance. I sense immediately after pulling off the dusty gravel road into the Department of Conservation campground that the caves are to be left alone. Sombre. Pastoral. Emerald green grasses carpet the fenced mountainside and semi-wild horses—owned but rarely cared for—zigzag narrow tracks and graze at the river's banks. This is a quiet, reflective place where darkness and shadows rest comfortably. *You should do the same*, the caves seem to whisper, behind their subtle, energetic Do Not Disturb sign.

"You're not thinking of climbing up to the caves?" I ask Francois as he lies on a mattress staring longingly at the mountain. Francois can be quite feral, especially after being cooped up in a car, an office—any place that restricts him. Upon arriving somewhere new he immediately scours the entire area with surprising speed and agility—not to mark it in wolf-like fashion as his territory (although there is often some of that), but to get a sense of its possibilities for both pleasure and peril.

"I don't see what's the harm, it's only walking," he laments.

He mopes his way to the lavatory. I take out my journal and pen to note today's events.

A few minutes later, Francois jogs back excitedly and switches his flip-flops for hiking shoes.

"I can go up," he says. "I met a guy over there who says it's alright as long as I stay to the right of the fence and don't go into the caves. Apparently people have died after going into those caves."

I look back and see a trim man with a full head of shiny white hair ambling towards us, favouring his left leg. When he reaches our camper, Francois hastily introduces him as Trevor and dashes off.

Apart from his slicked, short hair, Trevor is striking on many levels. He has effervescent, steely blue eyes that shine like beacons of light, in part because they smile in tandem with his constant broad grin and perfect white teeth. He wears a tight-fitting, black T-shirt that has "Grumpy Fuckers Club, Gold Card Member" printed inside the shape of a credit card. A pentagram on a thick, rose-gold chain (a Mason's pendant he'd found in a pawn shop, he later tells me) hangs from his sturdy neck.

This is his eleventh year camping at Spirits Bay, he begins. He's sixty-one and lives alone in West Auckland. His family lineage in New Zealand—a lively mix of Picks, Scot, Irish, English, French, Jewish and French Tahitian blood—traces back to 1840.

"I don't know why he'd want to go into those caves," he says, shaking his head. "The first time I looked at that mountain every hair stood on end. But I've always had a bit of the sixth sense you know. Actually, I have it quite strong." As proof, he explains that on his first visit he walked to the nearby cemetery where six of the original Māori landholders are buried. When he began tending their graves, a decorative whirly bird, with wings spinning like pinwheels, kept bobbing down to gently poke his shoulder, even though there wasn't the slightest breeze. He believed it was the spirits thanking him. The caves, he later learned, contain green-stone amulets and the bones of Māori who were wrapped in flax leaves and launched off Cape Reinga, their bodies drifting east to these shores.

Those who dared trespass inside the caves either died or took seriously ill. He says he was lucky his "sixth sense" told him not to go there, although it had gotten him into a "heap of trouble" as a young boy.

He goes on to tell that his abilities to tap into unseen worlds scared his mother, "who had it something fierce, too, but she resisted it," and the father who beat him as a child, who he later learned was his uncle. At sixteen, his clairvoyance prompted them to send him to a mental institution for tests. While there, he was sexually abused by some of the workers, but his parents refused to take a stand for him. Thus began a rebellious, thirty-year "party"—booze, drugs, biker gangs. He became a "toy boy," a prostitute to the rich and famous. He was brutal too, he confesses, a vicious fighter who spent years in jail. He always asked for solitary confinement, though, wanting to prove his theory that mind over muscle was the key to survival. And then there were his three suicide attempts.

"What saved me the last time was my arm was too short to hold the shotgun to my head and pull the trigger," he says merrily, his smile unwavering, his eyes still sparkling. (Furtively, I glance up the hill for Francois, but he's gone. I'm unsure whether I should fear being alone with Trevor.) He doesn't seem to mind that I've kept my journal out and am taking notes. His story and our meeting feel equal parts fantasy and fate, and I want to remember every word. He shifts the weight off his legs, which clearly are hurting, so he's now leaning against the front of the van beside me.

"That's very interesting you telling me your story, Trevor, because I'm writing a book about why it's important to speak up and protect children from such abuse, so they don't have to go through what you did." Surprisingly, there's still room for me to speak, so I add, "and it's about that sixth sense you talk about, and animals. Right now, I'm writing about wolves."

"I've had total strangers come up to me and tell me my spirit guide is the white wolf," Trevor starts up again. I look into his powerful blue eyes, my fear and apprehensions melting. "I've always admired wolves. I wanted a white wolf pup as a child and I used to get quite mad at Santa every year when I didn't get one.

"When I was young, I went to some west coast beach where it was quite rough. My mom commented that I started loping along like a wolf. You just get into a rhythm, you know, like a jogger in the zone. I can't do that now, though. I've got two ruptured discs in my back—one of my scorned lovers drove into me with her car—and my left leg here is constant pins and needles. I've learned to live with that pain, you just have to. I'm grateful I'm even feeling pain. I should've been dead so many times."

Then Trevor tells me it was his stubborn pig-headedness that kept him alive. The blind rage and rebellion that he showed as a young man, ("When I was mad I'd bare my teeth like a wolf and growl, 'I'm gonna rip your throat out and spit it back at you.'") he turned towards himself after his last suicide attempt.

"I think I just got pissed off that I failed. I got angry, and I didn't project it out for a change. That secondary emotion of anger overtook the sadness, and the anger was more far-reaching. The will to survive is stronger than people think."

Francois makes it down safely. Trevor and I exchange knowing glances when he tells us he'd heard a constant wind howling in his ears up there, even though the trees stood still.

~

I'm thinking about Trevor the next morning as I sit in the wooden long box stall that is our communal toilet. He, like so many others with wounded bodies and souls—Ernest at the seniors' centre and his brother, Floppy Foot... me—pigheadedly soldiering on.

I hear footsteps, one foot dragging along the concrete floor, and figure right away it's Trevor. At every campsite toilet along the way, I have feared someone would try to break into my stall. Sure enough, there's a rattle on the latch as the locked door is pushed from the outside.

"Open the door or I'll huff and I'll puff and I'll blow your house down," the Wolf roared at the Three Little Pigs."

Trevor makes a muffled "hrrrumph" sound and shuffles along. I laugh.

~

We leave Spirits Bay that morning. For no reason other than an anxious feeling, I'm adamant Francois and I get off the peninsula as quickly as possible, even foregoing a trip to the Cape or the famous Ninety Mile Beach.

"Oh, can we stop here?" I plead when the twisty highway opens up to a pasture where two horses, one white, one brown, lean against a fence.

We get out and I take some photos. I walk up to the white mare and stroke her muzzle, leaning my forehead onto hers, soaking up her earthy smell and reassuring heat.

"Wouldn't it be nice if we could come back to New Zealand and look after someone's farm and ride their horses while they go away on holidays?" I fantasize once we're back in the van.

The next day, we stop for lunch at a non-descript café where an older Māori man who's sitting outside watches me eat a banana crepe. As I get up to leave, my shopping bag falls off the seat.

"Don't forget your bag," he warns.

"Oh yes, thanks, it came all the way from Canada," I laugh.

"Canada?" he says. "Maybe you could help me identify some war medals that I have from all over the world, I think there may be some from Canada?"

The request seems so bizarre, I can't immediately respond.

"They're in my truck. I'll go get them," he says.

Moments later, he returns carrying a long wood and glass display case filled with war medals, a Nazi youth club knife and other paraphernalia retrieved from dead soldiers on the battlefields. He introduces himself as Eric and explains that he's a retired New Zealand veteran. He manages several of his late mother-in-law's landholdings.

"I just drive around and check on the farms now. What I really need is someone to ride the horses," he says.

I look at him in disbelief and tell him I was just expressing a desire to live here in a farm and tend to someone's horses. His eyes brighten.

At our request, he guides us to the local fish shop and then invites us to his home in Kaeo. The grounds are damp and the foliage so overgrown it's hard to see the decaying, wooden bungalow. With its peeling white paint and general rot from mould and mildew, the house is slowly returning to the soil. A large rooster and hen further blur the boundary between outside and in with apparent free range in both. When they help themselves to the cat food inside, Eric shoos them out; but signs that they've been here before linger in the air, and on the carpet. He shows us pictures of his family and answers my questions about Spirits Bay and Māori ceremonies. I pull out my notebook and tape recorder.

"When Māori people die, their spirits follow the ridgeline of how their family travelled to reach Spirits Bay, where they return to the underworld. Our hill is the Hill of the Dragon, where waves crashed so loudly that people believed the sound was a dragon's roar. It doesn't matter how they lived or died, they're all treated the same when they go. They're all afforded respect and ceremony. All of them."

His ocean-green eyes look intently into mine as he says "all of them."

I ask Eric about the Māori tradition of *hongi*, a pressing together of noses and foreheads with eyes closed, used to symbolize trust and greeting.

"We all exchange breaths. We're all part of nature. We start life on an inhale and we end life on an exhale." Just then a loud, airy *whoosh*—a giant exhale—releases right beside me. I squeal and give a frightened jump in my seat. It's the *Glade* air freshener on the table, releasing an automatic salvo in its losing battle to mask the barn-like smells invading the room.

I ask Eric if we can *hongi*, and he smiles, putting his hand on my shoulder and firmly pulling my nose and forehead towards his.

"There, now your life and my life are forever intertwined," he tells me. He feels warm and reassuring, like the white horse I connected with in a similar fashion in the pasture. He and Francois share a *hongi*. I leave Eric my card and take down his address, in case we ever return and he still needs someone to ride his horses.

~

Even while I was talking with Trevor and Eric, I knew they were providing me with an end for my musings about wolves: Trevor (the white wolf), by sharing his tales of triumph over abuse and by giving wise counsel to Francois, had communicated the need to respect another's territory. That counsel possibly saved Francois from harm, had his curiosity gotten the better of him.

Wolves mark their territory through sound and scent and do not willingly share their land with other wolves. Intruders can expect a rough reception, even death, for trespassing.

Eric had reinforced that respect for boundaries, not wanting to speak of the caves or the purported deaths there, saying they were not of his people. But he also underlined that observing boundaries doesn't mean we're not interconnected. Everything is. And while he agreed I could record his detailed description of Māori burial rites—and that part of my interview with him registered 9 MB of data—the playback display later showed 00:00. Blank. I think, like the wolf's mysterious howl, still defying interpretation despite years of study, some information is only meant to be passed on in real time, and only through oral tradition.

∿

Before we went to New Zealand, during the November when the wolves' howls kept me awake and the ice was solidifying under our feet, two members of Canada's Olympic Soccer Team came to our house on a mission to connect. Defender Carmelina Moscato and goalie Erin McLeod were travelling to remote parts of the country to learn more about the people and places they represent. In clinch moments on the pitch, they hoped to channel the positive energies of those who "had their backs." They hadn't anticipated that during their hike with us, Sabrina would howl and follow.

The women, both artists, showed great reverence for the moment, aware that the wolf's cry would now be added to the fabric of voices they were weaving into their giant security blanket. Erin told us she'd just signed an endorsement contract with the ethical clothing company, *Peau de Loup* (French for Wolfskin), and Carmelina showed us the animal medicine divination app she had on her phone. "People today don't have enough interaction, a strong enough connection, with the animal world," she commented. "Experiencing something like this changes you."

And yes, it does. I'm forever changed by the animals, birds and insects that have loped, crawled, flown, buzzed, run, and breathed fire into my life. Of all my encounters, the season of the wolves was the most intense. Each day felt precarious. Death was never far away. More than once, strangers knocked on my door—wolf hunters warning me of the pack, of Sabrina, telling me to shelter my dogs. How could I explain that Sabrina loved our dogs, that she needed their company? And, at that time, I needed hers.

We saw Sabrina occasionally in early May, then all wolf visits abruptly stopped, twelve months after they began. One hot summer's day, a friend mentioned casually he'd heard "our wolf," Sabrina, had been shot that June. A man boasted of killing her because she dared make herself visible near a campground a few kilometres past our house. We hadn't known. I didn't mourn her death because of its inevitability—she ran a human gauntlet of guns every day. She'd outlived all my expectations. Moreover, I'd come to learn that death on the physical plane doesn't mean connection and learning are lost. I carry her wolf wisdom inside me now, just as I've come to trust that my own mother's spirit is always near.

A few weeks after I learn of Sabrina's death, I'm flown to a remote fishing lodge on assignment for the *Globe and Mail*. I will spend a week there with a large group of teenage girls getting leadership training in a frank and revolutionary new sexual health program called FOXY (Fostering Open eXpression Among Youth). It focuses on teens teaching teens about self-esteem, establishing healthy relationships and preventing unwanted pregnancies and disease. FOXY also tackles the blight of sexual abuse by empowering youth with knowledge and the self-confidence to speak out and stand up for their bodies. The program is gaining the support of government and deep-pocketed donors who recognize it is a made-in-the-North vehicle for real change.

These exciting teachings are happening at the same place I married Francois twenty-five years earlier. When the floatplane lands, I walk to the spot where my family had gathered. I can practically feel my mother's presence emanating from the rocks, an overwhelming sensation that makes me sit and weep. I force an end to my tears, telling myself I don't have time for such sentimentalism now, but will come back to this spot at the end of the week and allow myself a good cry then.

When that day comes, Veronica, a strong woman of *Denésuliné* heritage, who'd led a circle of hand drum songs and smudging ceremonies each morning for the girls and their mentors, sees me crying.

"What's wrong?" she asks.

"I'm just really missing my mom," I tell her. "It's like I can feel her here."

"You need a drink of water, I'll get it for you... and when I come back, I'll smudge you again," she says.

She's gone a long time, longer than it would take to fetch a glass of water. When she finally returns, she has a glass in one hand and a folded, wet facecloth in the other.

"Here, this is to wipe your face," she says, handing me the cloth.

I laugh through my tears.

"That's so funny. My mom used to give me a damp facecloth to wipe my tears when I was little. I'd forgotten all about that until just now."

"I know," she says. "I asked her what to do for you."

I no longer seek empirical explanations for the intangible forces that shape such experiences. Is there an experiment, a lab, even a language that could attempt such a feat? They're initiations along my highly personal spiritual journey. I've received my wakeup call from the cosmos. And I can no longer walk this earth asleep.

I walk it wildly aware that by remaining open and in constant search for unity with all that lives around me—people, air, stars, birds, plants, rock, dirt, fish, sun, water, insects... animals—I'll always be guided resolutely back into my centre, that divine place where all the stabilizing resources I'll ever need await, unfailingly, at the ready.

Sources

Adler, Shelley R. *Sleep Paralysis, Night-mares, Nocebos, and the Mind-Body Connection*. New Brunswick, New Jersey, and London: Rutgers University Press. 2011.

Allen, Judy, and Griffiths, Jeanne. *The Book of the Dragon*. London: Orbis Publishing Ltd. 1979.

Amarasinghe, Mala. *Mangrove crabs: the ecosystem engineers and keystone species*. Network of Aquaculture Centres in Asia-Pacific http://www.enaca.org/ 2009.

Andrews, Ted. *Animal-Speak, The Spiritual & Magical Powers of Creatures Great & Small*. St. Paul, MN: Llewellyn Publications. 2002.

Barish, David P. and Lipton, Judith Eve. *The Myth of Monogamy: Fidelity and Infidelity in Animals and People*. New York: Henry Holt & Company. 2001.

Bastedo, Jamie. *Blue Lake and Rocky Shore, a Field Guide to Special Natural Areas in the Yellowknife Region*. Yellowknife: Artisan Press Ltd. 2000.

Bierlein, J.G. *Living Myths, How Myth Gives Meaning to Human Experience*. New York: Ballantine Wellspring. 1999.

Birds of Eden Sanctuary. *The Mute Swan, Why This Beauty is Also a Beast*. http://www.birdsofeden.co.za/index.php?comp=article&op=view&id=367

Bishop, Holly. *Robbing the Bees – A Biology of Honey, The Sweet Liquid Gold That Seduced the World*. New York: Free Press. 2005.

Bryant, Mike. *Circus of errors lands in the lake*. Yellowknife: Northern News Services. July 16, 2003.

Busch, Robert, ed. *Wolf Songs, The Classic Collection of Writing About Wolves*. Vancouver/Toronto: Greystone Books. 1994.

Butala, Sharon. *The Perfection of the Morning, an Apprenticeship in Nature*. Toronto: Harper Collins. 1994.

Buxton, Simon. *The Shamanic Way of the Bee, Ancient Wisdom and Healing Practices of the Bee Masters*. Rochester/Vermont: Destiny Books. 2006.

CBC News/North. *Whitehorse Wolf Killer Defends Actions*. http://www.cbc.ca/news/canada/north/whitehorse-wolf-killer-defends-actions-1.2441999 Nov. 27, 2013.

Campbell, Joseph. *The Power of Myth, with Bill Moyers*. New York: Doubleday. 1988.

Campbell, Joseph. *The Way of the Animal Powers, Volume 1, Historical Atlas of World Mythology*. San Francisco: Harper & Row. 1988.

Carr-Gomm, Philip and Stephanie. *The Druid Animal Oracle, Working with the Sacred Animals of the Druid Tradition*. New York: Simon & Schuster. 1994.

Cherry, John, ed. *Mythical Beasts*. London: British Museum Press. 1995.

Cluff, Dean. *First Fatal Bear Attack, Northwest Territories, Canada*. International Bear News 10, no. 3. Brookeville, MD: International Association for Bear Research and Management. August 2001.

Crozier, Lorna, ed. *Desire, in Seven Voices*. Vancouver/Toronto: Douglas & McIntyre. 1999.

DeBruyn, Tony. *Walking with Bears, One Man's Relationship with Three Generations of Wild Bear*. New York: Lyons Press. 1999.

Department of Renewable Resources, Government of the Northwest Territories. Urquhart, Doug. *People and Caribou in the Northwest Territories, "Biology."* Yellowknife: Outcrop Ltd. 1989.

Dickens, Charles. *Household Words, A Weekly Journal. Vol. X*. Buckingham, UK: Dickens Journal Online, The University of Buckingham. 1854.

Doige, Norman. *The Brain That Changes Itself, Stories of Personal Triumph from the Frontiers of Brain Science*. New York: Penguin Books. 2007.

Encyclopædia Britannica Online, s. v. "mantid", accessed July 15, 2011, http://www.britannica.com/animal/mantid

Fair, Jeff and Rogers, Lynn. *The Great American Bear*. Minoqua, Wis.: NorthWord Press, Inc. 1994.

Farmer, Steven. *Animal Spirit Guides*. Carlsbad, CA: Hay House Inc. 2006.

Fox, Matthew and Sheldrake, Rupert. *The Physics of Angels, Exploring the Realm Where Science and Spirit Meet*. San Francisco: Harper San Francisco. 1996.

Gamble, Jessa. *Ravens Among Us*. Yellowknife: Up Here Magazine. Oct-Nov 2008.

Gerber, Richard. *Vibrational Medicine, New Choices for Healing Ourselves*. Santa Fe: Bear & Company. 1996.

Hanno. *The Periplus of Hanno: A Voyage of Discovery Down the West African Coast*. Philadelphia: The Commercial Museum (from the University of Michigan Collection). 1913.

Harper's Magazine. *Findings*. Harper's Magazine Foundation. New York. April 2015

Harris, William, and Craig Freudenrich, Ph.D. *How Light Works* 10 July 2000. HowStuffWorks.com. http://science.howstuffworks.com/light.htm accessed July 15, 2015.

Heindrich, Bernd. *Mind Of The Raven: Investigations and Adventures with Wolf-Birds*. New York: Harper Collins Publishers. 2006.

Heuer, Karsten. *Being Caribou, Five Months on Foot with an Arctic Herd*. Toronto: McClelland & Stewart. 2006.

Judith, Anodea. *Eastern Body, Western Mind, Psychology and the Chakra System*. Berkeley: Celestial Arts Publishing. 1996.

Jung, Carl. *Aion, Researches into the Phenomenology of the Self, Translated by R.F.C. Hull*. Princeton: Princeton University Press. 1960.

Jung, Carl, ed. *Man and his Symbols*. New York: Doubleday & Company. 1964.

Kaplan, Michael and Ellen. *Bozo Sapiens, Why to Err is Human*. New York: Bloomsbury Press. 2010.

Kellert, Stephen, and Wilson, Edward, eds. *The Biophilia Hypothesis*. Washington: Island Press. 1993.

Korotayev, Andrey; Berezkin, Yuri; Kozmin, Artem and Arkhipova, Alexandra. *Return of the White Raven: Postdiluvial Reconnaissance Motif A2234.1.1 Reconsidered*. The Journal of American Folklore, Vol. 110, No. 472 (Spring, 2006) Stable URL: http://www.jstor.org/stable/4137924. Chicago: University of Illinois Press on behalf of American Folklore Society

Levitin, Daniel. *This is Your Brain on Music, The Science of a Human Obsession*. New York: Penguin. 2006.

Lewis, I. Murphy. *Why Ostriches Don't Fly; and Other Tales from the African Bush*. Englewood, CO: Greenwood Publishing Group. 1997.

Marshall, Thomas. *The Harmless People*. New York: Vintage Books. 1959.

Marcus, Ruth. *Surrealism's Praying Mantis and Castrating Woman*, Woman's Art Journal, Vol. 21, No. 1. Stable URL: http://www.jstor.org/stable/1358868 spring/summer 2000.

Martel, Frances L., Nerison, Claire M., Simpson, Michael J.A. & Keverne, Eric B. *Effects of opioid receptor blockade on the social behavior of rhesus monkeys living in large family groups*. Developmental Psychobiology, Vo. 28, Issue 2, March 1995, p. 71-84.

Maté, Gabor. *In the Realm of the Hungry Ghost, Close Encounters with Addiction*. Toronto: Vintage Canada. 2009.

Matthews, John and Caitlin. *The Elements Encyclopedia of Magical Creatures – The Ultimate A-Z of Fantastic Beings from Myth and Magic*. New York: Sterling Publishing Company. 2005.

McFarland, David. ed. *The Oxford Companion to Animal Behaviour*. New York: Oxford University Press. 1987.

Melzer, Werner. *Beekeeping, A Complete Owner's Manual*. Munich: Barron's Educational Series, Inc. 1986.

Mowat, Farley. *Virunga, The Passion of Dian Fossey*. Toronto: McClelland & Stewart. 1987.

Murphy Lewis, I. *Across the Divide to the Divine: With the Kalahari San's Trickster God, Mantis, an Essential Component in the Mythological Structure of an Individuated Culture. Pacifica Graduate Institute*. Carpinteria, CA: 2007

Myss, Caroline. *Anatomy of the Spirit, The Seven Stages of Power and Healing*. New York: Three Rivers Press. 1996.

National Aeronautics and Space Administration. *NASA Science/Astrophysics; Dark Energy, Dark Matter*. http://science.nasa.gov/astrophysics/focus-areas/what-is-dark-energy/

National Geographic. *Dark Matter and Dark Energy*. http://science.nationalgeographic.com/science/space/dark-matter/

Page, George. *The Singing Gorilla, Understanding Animal Intelligence*. London: Headline Book Publishing. 1999.

Perth Zoo. *Black Swan*. http://perthzoo.wa.gov.au/animals-plants/australia/australian-wetlands/black-swan

Pinkola, Clarissa Estés, Ph.D. *Woman Who Run With the Wolves, Myths and Stories of the Wild Woman Archetype*. New York: Ballantine Books. 1995.

Poe, Edgar Allan. *The Raven*. 1st published 1845. www.poetryfoundation.org. Chicago.

Primate Info Net Library and Information Services, National Primate Research Centre, University of Wisconsin, Madison. *Gorilla, Socialization Organization and Behaviour*. http://pin.primate.wisc.edu/factsheets/entry/gorilla/behav

Robbin, Martha M., Sicotte P, Stewart KJ, eds. "Variation in the social system of mountain gorillas: the male perspective" In: *Mountain gorillas: three decades of research at Karisoke.* Cambridge (England): Cambridge University Press. 2001.

Robinson, Marilynne. *Hysterical scientism, The Ecstasy of Richard Dawkins.* New York: Harper's Magazine. Nov. 2006.

Rockwell, David. *Giving Voice to Bear: North American Indian Myths, Rituals, and Images of the Bear.* Toronto: Key Porter. 1991.

Sale, Kirkpatrick. *The Conquest of Paradise, Christopher Columbus and the Columbian Legacy.* New York: Alfred A. Knopf. 1990.

Sams, Jamie. *Medicine Cards.* New York: St. Martin's Press. 1999.

Samuels, David. *Wild Things, Animal nature, human racism, and the future of zoos.* New York: Harper's Magazine. June 2012.

Savage, Candace. *Wolves.* Vancouver/Toronto: Douglas & McIntyre. 1988.

Schaller, George B. *The Year of the Gorilla.* Chicago: University of Chicago Press. 1997.

Shostak, Marjorie. *Nisa, The Life and Words of a !Kung Woman.* New York: Vintage Books. 1981.

Smith, Elliot G. *The Evolution of the Dragon.* Sacred-texts.com. 1919.

Smithsonian National Museum of Natural History. *What Does it Mean to be Human?* Genetics: The Smithsonian Institution's Human Origins Program. http://humanorigins.si.edu/evidence/genetics.

Smithsonian National Zoological Park. *Meet our Animals: Gorilla.* http://nationalzoo.si.edu/animals/primates/facts/fact-gorilla.cfm

The Gorilla Foundation. *Koko Responds to a Sad Movie* video. Youtube, Kokoflix. Koko.org. 2011.

The Wilderness Society. *Migrations of the Tundra "Whistling" Swan.* Wilderness.org. http://www.kwic.com/~pagodavista/schoolhouse/species/birds/migrate.htm

Thorpe, Natasha; Hakongak, Naikak; Eyegetok, Sandra and the Kitikmeot Elders. *"Thunder in the Tundra, Inuit Qaujimajatuaqangit of the Bathurst Caribou.* West Kitikmeot Slave Study: Tuktu and Nogat Project. Jan. 3, 2002.

Tinbergen, Nikolaas. *The Herring Gull's World: A Study of the Social Behaviour of Birds (A new Naturalist Monograph, #9).* Glasgow: Harper Collins. 1989.

Van der Post, Laurens. *A Mantis Carol.* Covelo, CA: Island Press. 1975.

Virunga National Park, official website, Democratic Republic of the Congo. https://virunga.org/projects/gorilla-protection/

Vivian, John. *Keeping Bees.* Vermont: Williamson Publishing Company. 1986.

Wikipedia. Mute Swan. https://en.wikipedia.org/wiki/Mute_swan

Wrigley, Robert E. *From Arctic Ocean to Tropical Rain Forest, Mammals in North America, Wildlife Adventure Stories and Technical Guide.* Winnipeg: Hyperion Press Ltd. in Cooperation with the Manitoba Museum of Man and Nature. 1986

Zimmer Bradley, Marion. *The Mists of Avalon.* New York: Ballantine Books. 1982.

Acknowledgments

A book that spans an entire adult life owes much to many people. Criss Hajek, who is my aunt, but who operates on a heart level as my sister, has been invaluable every step of the way, from reading ground zero drafts to providing the final copy edits. Big love. Marjorie Anderson's perceptive editing and sensitivity to the subject helped bring focus and clarity when it was needed most—a lifeline, made possible through the generous support of the NWT Arts Council. Much gratitude to both for believing in this book.

I'm deeply grateful to the Yellowknives Dene First Nation for the privilege of living in their traditional Akaitcho territory, on Chief Drygeese lands. It's opened me to so many lessons. For sharing their wisdom and guidance, I thank Anke Tuininga, Be'sha Blondin, France Benoit, Ruth Andermatt, Darlene Romanko and Ruth Mercredi. For her vast vats of integrity and compassion and for leading by example on our shared journey, I owe much to Linda Takacs.

Likewise, I'm indebted to Brent Reaney for his meticulous attention to detail and unwavering support in the final stages of my manuscript, and to Brent, Jeremy Bird and Verge Communications for publishing and marketing this book. It's been a privilege to have your talents and energy infuse this work and bring it into the world.

A special thank you to I. Murphy Lewis for answering my questions and sharing her thesis, *Across the Divide to the Divine: With the Kalahari San's Trickster God, Mantis, an Essential Component in the Mythological Structure of an Individuated Culture*, which greatly informed my Praying Mantis chapter.

I'd like to acknowledge the support I've received, moral and otherwise, from: Sharon Butala, Marni Jackson, Paul Andrew, Fred Sangris,

Doris Eggers, Graham Watt, Kate Hearn, Brian Sarkadi, Kim Shanks, the Yellowknife Public Library, Danny Beaulieu, Stephanie Irlbacher-Fox, Shannon Ward, Ann Rossouw, Wade Carpenter, Rassi Nashalik, Lynda Yonge, Rosanna Strong, Wake Up Hazel, James and Fie Terry, Sheila Street, Zoe Raemer, Bill Erasmus, Elizabeth Palmer, Shelly Palmer, Ronald Chato, Catherine Pigott, Loren McGinnis, Susan Mate, Gabriela Eggenhofer, Andrew Gamble, Judy McNicol, Tiffany Ayalik, Jillian Mazur, Sheila Bassi-Kellett, Michael Gannon, NorthWords, Judith Drinnan, Richard Van Camp, Suzanne Carriere, Bob Bromley, Harmen Meinders, Jasmine Budak, Johanna Tiemessen, Sean MacGillivray, Rosalind Mercredi, Daron Letts, Wendy Flood, Anne Forkutza and Domo Tea, Bernice Morgan, Joe and Dianne Sarkadi, Jamie Bastedo, Boris Atamanenko, and the late Deb Cooke, June Callwood, Jack Taylor and Dennis Johnson.

Writing a memoir that uses one's own family as subject matter asks a lot of them. One reader pointed out, "There isn't a lot of Calvin in there." It's true, he's the quiet one, always observing, digesting. Calvin was an early reader and my trusted go-to for editorial advice, providing, among other things, timely and astute direction on how to reorder chapters. Thank you, Calvin, for caring about this book, and me. Your still waters run deep.

All my sons, Max, Levi and Calvin, have been my greatest teachers. Together we share a grand adventure.

And to my husband, Francois Rossouw, who despite not always seeing the merit of all my unpaid sitting around time, always encouraged me to explore my creative self. There's no way I could live the rigours of our beautiful life, or write about them, without your strong back, boundless energy and dedication to family.